# DO NOT TRY
## *to* BECOME
## *a* BUDDHA

# DO NOT TRY
# *to* BECOME
# *a* BUDDHA

## Practicing Zen
## Right Where You Are

MYOZAN IAN KILROY

FOREWORD BY PIERRE TAÏGU TURLUR RŌSHI

Wisdom Publications
132 Perry Street
New York, NY 10014 USA
wisdom.org

Library of Congress Cataloging-in-Publication Data
Names: Kilroy, Myozan Ian, author.
Title: Do not try to become a Buddha: practicing Zen
    right where you are / Myozan Ian Kilroy.
Description: New York, NY, USA: Wisdom Publications, [2024]
    | Includes bibliographical references and index.
Identifiers: LCCN 2024017553 (print) | LCCN 2024017554 (ebook)
    | ISBN 9781614298946 | ISBN 9781614299073 (ebook)
Subjects: LCSH: Zen Buddhism. | Zen Buddhism—Ireland.
Classification: LCC BQ9266 .K55 2024 (print) | LCC BQ9266
    (ebook) | DDC 294.3/92709417—dc23/eng/20240805
LC record available at https://lccn.loc.gov/2024017553
LC ebook record available at https://lccn.loc.gov/2024017554

ISBN 978-1-61429-894-6        ebook ISBN 978-1-61429-907-3

29 28 27 26 25
5  4  3  2  1

Author photo by Peter Houlihan. Cover design by Marc Whitaker.
Interior design by Kristin Goble. Set in TeX Gyre Pagella 10.5/13.
Quotations from "Song of the Grass-Roof Hermitage" reprinted by
permission of Tuttle Publishing from *Cultivating the
Empty Field* pp. 72–73 ©2000 Dan Leighton.

Please visit fscus.org.

For Isabelle, Arthur, and Éamonn;
for my parents, Michael and Margaret;
for Taïgu Rōshi, my teacher;
and for my students and sangha.

It is never apart from you right where you are.
What use is there going off here and there to practice?
—Master Dōgen

# Contents

## Part One. Searching

## Part Two. Living

## Part Three. Celebrating

CONTENTS

## Part Four. Zen Here and Now

# Foreword

THE ORIGINAL PRACTICE OF the Buddha under the Bodhi Tree, the treasure of naked and unadorned sitting, was transmitted from India to China, from China to Japan, and during the past century, it has reached our Western world. This treasure is within everyone's reach, yet few understand it and live its vibrant unfolding. While it only takes our human body and our life as it is to discover it, at the same time the practice, which is an endless journey of letting go after letting go, is one of the most difficult.

In Zen sitting, or zazen, we stop everything. We let go of everything, especially any form of holiness and its stench. We forget everything about Buddhism. We remain open in openness. That's all. As Sekito Kisen points out, "the original master is present and resides neither in the South, nor in the North, nor in the East, nor in the West." There is no place to stay, no host to entertain; the light naturally returns to its source and reflects everywhere. We don't even worry about it: we simply let the light turn around and reflect, as has been expressed by all the ancients since the Buddha. Letting body and mind return to the great treasure of light and abandoning all concerns there, as Ejo expressed it, is in itself the art of sitting Zen, the path of silent illumination. The hook of questions is no longer cast toward the world but in the direction of the source from which it arises. The answer that we truly are illuminates itself. And we no longer give in to escape or search; everything is welcomed with a heart of equanimity. We do not seek to be the raindrop trickling down the window, the engine rattling, the shouts of children playing, the barking of a dog, light and shadow around us, colors and shapes, smells and tastes; inside, outside, and in between all collapse, and we have nothing to do with it. We realize that we are sitting far beyond this skin bag, and sometimes the body straightens and relaxes on its own, without our decision. Everything is welcomed here, without judgment or preference, and without cultivating or holding on to anything. We grasp nothing, we reject nothing. It is because we abandon all ideas about sitting Zen that it accomplishes itself.

It is important to cultivate a mind that does not dwell. A thousand thoughts whirl around; a serene and calm sky extends endlessly: it's all the same. Sometimes thoughts get lost and dissolve like birds leaving no trace. Sometimes, like clouds, we observe thoughts and let them free themselves and dissolve on their own. We always wake up from a waking dream and simply return. Again and again, we return. Sometimes attention rests in the palm of the left hand, sometimes it follows the breath in the abdomen, or it dwells nowhere, but is simply attentive to the sitting body as it is. Sometimes the half-closed eyes in front of us contemplate distant mountains without fixing or grasping; sometimes the eyes close, and it's the sound of things and the song of beings that the ears contemplate. Zazen, which is the universe manifested as it is, zazen that fills the universe, cannot be manufactured; in the renunciation of doing, true action arises. The full moon of sitting has no concerns or particular thoughts to cultivate; it appears on its own: it is zazen that sits us. As it is said: Collect a little water in the hollow of your palms, and the moon is in your hands; play with the flower, and its fragrance will scent your clothes.

It is increasingly evident to me that when we simply let ourselves be lived by the universe and its dynamic unfolding, without controlling, grasping, or manipulating it, life becomes much easier. We end up living what is, suchness and only that, abandoning the chimeras forged by yesterday's dreams and nightmares, free from any hope or judgment. At least, that is my experience, or rather, what passes through me in a wonder filled with humor, gentleness, extravagance, and energy as well. The matrix of this is the zazen of the buddhas and patriarchs, free from any trace, any form of judgment, the play of identifications, and especially so clear when it reveals the extent of our own self-delusion. The essential is always not to take oneself too seriously. I am merely a mirage and will soon disappear. What carries and animates me, and animates each of you, is ineffable. It does not belong to me or you, nor to space or time, yet it bears the ten thousand faces of both. The reality of Indra's net unfolds the fabric of interactions and the still dance. Here, it is before any thought or belief.

I met the one I would give the name Myozan—the wonderful mountain, the mountain of zazen—online, some twenty years ago. I was already living in Japan at that time. As often happens, the one who knocked at my door had been announced, and meeting him felt like an inevitability: I immediately recognized him as a brother, a son, and much more. We then began a Dharma relationship of several years, during which we met on several *sesshins* in Belgium and the United States, and had frequent exchanges during *dokusan*, where the key moments of the lineage transmission were pondered. Two happy cows in a vast green meadow—until the time came to transmit what cannot be transmitted. Myozan received Dharma transmission from my empty hands and became my successor. Indeed, there is no master, because no one arrives or reaches anywhere; those who adorn themselves with titles and hats have lost the plot. There is no greater power than abandoning all power, no truer authority than infinitely surrendering to things as they are, stripping away everything, again and again. This is the heart of the practice of zazen, letting go of body and mind.

May you find in these pages the inspiration that leads you to the cushion and to your true face.

After many years of teaching in France and England, **Pierre Taïgu Turlur Rōshi** moved to Japan in 2006. Originally a student of literature and philsophy, Taïgu has been practicing Sōtō Zen for nearly fifty years, and he received Dharma transmission in 2002 in the lineage of Niwa Zenji. His students and heirs teach in Europe, the United States, and Asia, and he has published numerous books in French on Buddhism and its Zen expression.

# Preface

THIS BOOK HAS GROWN out of almost thirty years of Zen practice. Unknown to myself, I have been following the advice of
Uchiyama Kōshō Rōshi: "Sit silently for at least ten years. Then,
after ten years, sit for another ten years. And then, after twenty
years, sit anew for another ten years."[1] If you are lucky to live
long enough, you should go back to the start of Uchiyama Rōshi's
advice and begin again. There is no end to this joyous practice.

But to keep going—or even to start—we need some inspiration. I hope some of the meditations in this book will prove that
inspiration for you. Although the book can be read in any order,
the work is divided into a series of four sections. Starting out by
looking at zazen itself, it moves on to look at the ethical life and
the role of ritual in Zen, before considering my own practice in
its unique time and place. Each short chapter has its main point
highlighted at the start, as a kind of meditation in its own right.

The beating heart of Zen is silent sitting. But practice is realized away from the meditation cushion through ethical action and
through the lived wisdom that all things are interconnected. This
wisdom is based on a larger understanding of what constitutes the
self. As our days become weeks and months, the liturgical unfolding of each year offers a vessel for our practice that sustains and
inspires it. Zazen itself is the purest of all rituals. And all around
it, in a supporting role, are the rituals of birth and death, renewal
and dissolution. These rites and practices come up from the very
soil we stand on. The rhythm of the place where we find ourselves
is the true rhythm of our practice.

So, my Zen flowers in the time in which I live and in the place where I am. It was no different for the great ancestors of the Zen tradition. And it is no different for you. Where else can you begin your journey other than where you are now? What other life can you live, other than this life that is yours? I hope some of the teachings in this book help to clarify these ancient truths for you; that they help you orient yourself in the swirling, turning of your days and to see anew that everything you need is already with you. If you sit down and come home to yourself, your Dharma eye will inevitably open. The whole world will be transformed into what it always was to begin with.

Apart from those important people this book is dedicated to, I would also like to express my gratitude to the *tanto* at Dublin Zen Centre, Hōdo Gomoku, and the *shuso*, Kōzan Kokai. Without their constant hard work, our center would never have opened in the first place, or continued on for very long. They will both make fine Zen teachers in the years ahead. Monk Koryu Shinso and the *jisha*, Sansa Nanso, also deserve mention for their unflagging dedication and service to the sangha; as do our wider sangha membership, many of whom support Zen Buddhism Ireland and Dublin Zen Centre in many ways, both seen and unseen.

Special thanks are due to Mick óg McGee and Annraoi Mac Aoidh for their consultation on the Gaelic language references in the book, as well as a massive and heartfelt thanks to my editor at Wisdom, Ben Gleason, for his always helpful suggestions and his thoughtful and sensitive editing, informed by his own Buddhist practice.

Thanks are due to my partner, Isabelle, for her careful reading of late drafts of the book, as well as to our wider "Order of Mountains and Clouds" sangha—in France, Wales, Spain, the United States, Iceland, Germany, Japan, and many other places. My teacher's heirs are flowering everywhere that they have put down roots.

Finally, Taïgu Rōshi, thank you for your teachings. Thank you for trusting me. May your powerful *katsu* resonate in all places and for all time.

*Sanpai.*

PART ONE

# Searching

# Seeking Peace

*There is some miracle at work here, but it is not*
*the kind of miracle that we conventionally conceive*
*as miraculous. This is the miracle of the habitual*
*and ordinary. Only when we can see the endless*
*wild forest in the grass that grows underneath*
*our feet will we be able to see this miracle.*

ZEN HAS SOMETHING TO teach you. What you have been search-ing for is within reach. Indeed, it has never been closer—indeed, it has never been far away. Your whole life, it has been with you, and you have spent a lifetime looking for it. You may even have come to a point of anxious exhaustion, feeling as if the search has worn you out. If I ask you, "What is it that you are look-ing for?" how will you answer? Maybe you cannot answer. Maybe you will offer an abstract word, like *happiness* or *peace*. What do these words mean to you? Where can they be found?

When I was a child, growing up by the coast of the North Atlantic on the west coast of Ireland, sometimes my mother would be searching for something she had lost in the house. It might be something as simple as a set of keys or her purse. As a devout Catholic Irish woman, if she could not find it, she would go to the local church and make an offering to Saint Anthony of Padua, the saint of lost things. In a dark corner of the chapel, she'd light a can-dle, which suddenly illuminated the darkness, making the statue of the Portuguese friar clearly visible in his brown habit, holding the infant Christ in his arms. Then, within a few days, having forgotten about the thing she had lost entirely, it would miraculously show up. The keys would have been under a cushion, or the purse under a seat in the car—the kind of lost and hidden corners where Saint Anthony does his work. By giving over the search to faith, and by stopping the search herself, things righted themselves, all by themselves. How much Saint Anthony had to do with it is a matter for you to decide. But to me it seems that he played his role quite well.

During my mother's search, did the keys get magically moved by a hidden hand? Or rather, did they stay where they always had been?

In the Lotus Sutra, an important Buddhist scripture composed in the first century or thereabouts, there is the story known popularly as "The Parable of the Hidden Jewel." In it, a poor man who is to go traveling visits the home of a rich friend, where he spends the night in great revelry and falls asleep, having drunk far too much. His wealthy friend, having to depart on business before his poor friend wakes, sews a precious jewel into his friend's clothes, securely hidden in a place to be found later, when his friend is most in need of it. The poor man wakes up after his drunken night and sets forth on his travels, facing poverty and deprivation after a time, enduring many hard times of want, not knowing about the jewel he has had with him all along, stitched deep into his clothes. One day he meets his rich friend again and tells him of his many hard experiences. His friend throws his hands up in the air and scolds his poor friend—did he not know he carried a precious jewel with him the whole time?

The Zen tradition has many stories and parables like this. And still, I meet Zen students searching to find the answer in far distant lands, rather than in the green grass that grows beneath their feet. Maybe if they could find a Tibetan monastery in the high Himalayas then they would find peace? Sitting meditation in a cave in Thailand might reveal to them the secrets of life. Even after a time in an Indian ashram, there is still another, better ashram that eludes them, overseen by a better and wiser teacher, someone holier than any other they have encountered before. Maybe it is a strict Zen training monastery that they need? A place buried deep in the snowy mountains of Japan, where you rise at 3:30 a.m. and live on thin rice gruel in freezing conditions. Maybe only the Shaolin monastery itself will do, where the great Zen teacher Bodhidharma spent nine years facing a wall in deep meditation before realizing the great truth.

Master Dōgen, the founder of my Zen school, was himself a searcher. As a young man in his twenties, back in 1223, he left his native Japan along with his teacher Myōzen to make the dangerous crossing to China. There he studied Zen for a number of years before returning home and founding the Japanese Sōtō Zen school, which still exists today. In China, he felt that he had resolved the great matter of his life, and he wrote down his teachings on his return home: "The truth originally is all around" and "We do not stray from the right state."[2] These were the truths that he had discovered. When asked what he had learned in China, he said "nose vertical, eyes horizontal." It was as evident and open to be seen as the nose on his face. As we say, it was under his nose all along. Dōgen was adamant that the truth was there for all to see, no matter what time they lived in, no matter what age they were, whether they were a man or a woman, an adult or a child, whether they lived in a remote backwater—as was the Japan of his day—or in a great metropolitan and cultural center, as parts of China were back then.

So, why could this truth not be seen from the start? Why was the search needed to begin with? Why did Dōgen have to go to China to see clearly what had always been there to be seen? To put it another way, with what divine intervention did Saint Anthony conjure up the lost keys? There is some miracle at work here, but it is not the kind of miracle that we conventionally conceive as miraculous. This is the miracle of the habitual and ordinary. Only when we can see the endless wild forest in the grass that grows underneath our feet will we be able to see this miracle. But it is the miracle that will heal our lives.

# Why We Search

*What is your reason for seeking, then? What has set you out on this journey? It is worth looking closely at this question. Allow it to reveal itself to you over time. Just look at it; without judgment. Eventually it will show itself.*

W HY DO WE SEARCH and yearn in the first place? What is it that drives us in the endless quest? Is it some lack? Some feeling that there is something missing from our lives? Some deep dissatisfaction or profound disillusionment with things as they are?

The historical Buddha taught that *dukkha*, or the unsatisfactoriness of life, was a fundamental reality of human existence. We all feel this keenly. We cannot escape it. We don't have the things we want. Things and the people we love are destroyed and pass away. We see unethical people prosper and lies celebrated as the truth. Even our most precious moments of bliss and happiness, although wonderful and vital, are temporary—they come and go. What are we to do in the face of this? How should we respond? The search to answer this question leads us to set out on this quest.

When I was studying for a master's degree in English at university in Galway, I had no choice but to face these questions myself. I was in my twenties, a single man living at home with my parents, and desperately trying to find my place in the world. I was no longer a teenager or young student, and was at that place of transition in life where we stop being one thing and become another. It is the type of life boundary where we are vulnerable and delicate. Anything can happen. The random chance of life can lead us in any direction. And so, we feel disoriented and threatened by the uncertainty of things.

For me, this disorientation manifested in terrible panic attacks. I'd be walking down the street or in a social situation, then this terrible fear would come over me. My heart would pound, and I'd fear I was having a heart attack. As the experience grew more intense, I felt that I had to escape. What made the experience more difficult was that I felt I had to hide it from those around me. As well as the physical experiences, there was the psychological dread that came with these attacks: an irrational fear that I would harm myself or others. Sometimes I felt that I was losing my sanity. I know now that it was the fight-or-flight response of a panic attack, and that I needed to learn how to ride the intensity of each wave of panic when it came, to be with it and allow it to pass of its own accord. Central to all this were the fears and anxieties of growing up and becoming a new person. What would I do with my life? Would I meet someone to spend my life with? How would I ever finish this dreadful dissertation I had taken on board as a master's student? Was I even good enough for the life I was living?

For different people, different things bring them to Zen practice. For me, it was these panic attacks. And so, as a college student, I renewed an interest in Zen meditation, which I had explored when I was a teenager by reading books on Zen Buddhism, texts that were just filtering through to Ireland in the 1980s for the first time. I didn't have any money, so I read Suzuki Rōshi and the Diamond Sutra on numerous visits to O'Gorman's Bookshop on Shop Street, standing in the corner, pretending that I was considering a purchase. Then, in my bedroom, I'd try and sit meditation myself, surmising (incorrectly from these texts I'd read) how it should be done. I didn't realize that a proper meditation teacher was required. And yet these childhood experiences of "Zen" came back to me years later when I was having these awful attacks. I remembered the calm composure and stillness of sitting meditation, of how any turbulence seems unable to disturb the steadfastness of just sitting in the meditation posture. Just to remain in the posture was enough. Anything that disturbed my mind seemed to gradually lose all power as this stillness established itself. And, over time, I returned to the practice of just sitting like this, and the panic attacks slowly began to fade away. They never disappeared fully. But now I see them for what they are. They have lost all power. When they show themselves again, I acknowledge them: "I know you very well; don't think I don't." And they dissolve again. Now I know that they were a precious gift, because they brought me to Zen practice. And Zen practice is one of the most important things you can do with your life.

What is your reason for seeking, then? What has set you out on this journey? It is worth looking closely at this question. Allow it to reveal itself to you over time. Just look at it; without judgment. Eventually it will show itself. It seems to me now that this *dukkha*, this dissatisfaction, is itself the gift of practice.

One evening recently, I asked my Zen community what wounds in their lives had brought them to practice Zen. For one woman, her daughter was killed tragically in a road accident—something she couldn't stop, even though she had had a premonition of the terrible event. For one man, it was the trauma of growing up in a household where both parents were alcoholics, and where terrible things had happened. That evening, many said some personal loss had brought them to Zen, such as the loss of a brother or parent. One woman spoke of how her mother committed suicide when she was just a little girl and needed her mother so badly. Everyone seems to have had something in their lives that set them searching—although this something may not be acknowledged until many years later, or sometimes not at all.

The meeting that evening of the sangha, or community, was an amazing moment of release, when all this hidden pain was acknowledged. It was a revelation. One woman said it felt like we were living out the parable of Kisa Gotami. This is the story of a woman in the ancient Indian city of Savatthi whose only child has died. Distraught, she goes from house to house, asking who can bring her child back to life. Someone directs her to the Buddha, who was teaching in the area at the time. He tells Kisa Gotami he can help her if she brings him a mustard seed from a house never visited by death. Frantically, she goes from house to house, with her dead, cold child in her arms. But she cannot find a house never visited by death. Realizing what the Buddha was teaching her, she was able to grieve for her child and have a funeral conducted. Afterward, she went to the Buddha and became his disciple. She had learned from the terrible and inevitable truth of *dukkha*, the teaching of suffering. She had learned, too, the teaching of *anicca*, the Buddha's teaching that all is impermanent. Her liberation had begun.

# Identity and
# Intoxication

*We encounter suffering only when clinging
to our identities. If we do not cling and are
that bit freer, we can live with change. We
can learn that we are something other than
the stories we construct about ourselves.*

O N OUR GREAT JOURNEY, we are looking for nothing less than
our self. Who are we? What is our true and authentic self?
Many of us spend our entire lives in pursuit of this question. So,
the search involves the search for the self. And in this process,
there is a tendency to try on different versions of the self, to see
which one fits. We are caught up in the taxing and energetic process of constructing a self. It can take up all our energy.

One of my friends growing up went through this process
many times. He joined one religious community, then another. He
grew his hair long, then cut it all off. The way he dressed and
his entire image changed every few years. He was like a chame-
leon, changing colors—not to hide himself, but rather to stand
out and make a statement. He was engaged in an earnest search
for a self that he could be comfortable with. Having domineering
parents who criticized him all the time, he did not hold himself
in high regard. He wanted to find a version of selfhood that he
could accept. Still his journey seems endless, dogged by bouts of

depression and self-doubt. But as he ages, he seems to finally be settling on a self that he can love and accept. Maybe that karma that has followed him all these years is now finally being spent and burned off. Maybe he has found a self that he can accept.

This search for the self, this construction of an identity, is a vital process. It is something we must do to make our way in the world. When we are confronted, we need to have a story—like children raiding an apple orchard who have a cover story if caught: "We climbed in to retrieve our kite."

When asked "Who are you?" we have a narrative we can reach for: I'm a Zen priest. I'm a college professor. I'm a journalist. Or mother or teacher or whatever. For many of us, our work is the central part of this narrative. It offers us an identity in the world. When we have no work, we may become despondent and aimless. When we retire, we can struggle to find meaning in our lives again.

Whatever identity we settle on is always provisional. At some point it is challenged by inevitable change. We define ourselves as a mother or father, and then our children grow up and leave home. We define ourselves as a baker, and then we lose our job. We hold dear that we are young and athletic, and then our body fails us. These are manifestations of *dukkha*, or suffering. But we encounter suffering only when clinging to our identities. If we do not cling and are that bit freer, we can live with change. We can learn that we are something other than the stories we construct about ourselves.

There is a lovely story from the Vimalakirti Sutra that touches on the provisionality of identity. In this Buddhist text from almost two thousand years ago, we see one of the Buddha's principal and original disciples, Shariputra, claim that a goddess in his company cannot possibly achieve enlightenment because she is a woman. At the click of her fingers, she exchanges bodies with Shariputra, who must now confront his newfound female state. In response, the Buddha—who is present and has been listening to their conversation—says, "In all things, there is neither male nor female." While men and women remain, of course, there is something deeper and less provisional beneath. The goddess has taught Shariputra an important lesson. She also teaches us. We may find pleasure and meaning in our identities in the world, but we are much more than these provisional identities. When we learn this, we can retain our equilibrium when these identities begin to crumble or change—or when we cannot settle on an acceptable identity in the first place.

For many of us, however, it is not finding a personal identity that is the problem. Rather it is that we do not like the self we have found ourselves in. Indeed, this may be at the root of the ongoing search for a new identity. It may also be at the root of some addictions. Wanting to escape from the self we are lumped with, we find ways to get out of our selves, even if only temporarily. When we cannot take the search any longer, we dull our senses. This may even help in the short term, offering a kind of relief, an enchanted city in which to rest before continuing the journey. But there is the great danger that it will only imprison us, that it will become an end in itself, which we can no longer escape. When the search becomes unbearable, we can lose our way like this.

But there are no hard and fast rules that apply to all. I remember an old man that used to drink pints in a pub in Galway. Most days he'd be in the pub for a while, chatting to people and having a few beers. He was a fixture at the bar, particularly during the winter, when the days are short and the Atlantic rain sweeps over the streets of Galway for days on end. He looked like something from the last century. In his shirt and tie and tweed cap, he appeared genial and happy, and never drank to the point of heavy intoxication. He was there for the chat and the company as much as the beer. I rarely paid any attention to him. He was a fixture, like the furniture you paid no attention to. One day I did chat to him, however, when ordering a drink at the bar. Somehow my Zen practice came up in the brief conversation. He was all in favor of the idea. Then he held up his pint of Guinness for my consideration. "See this," he said. "This is my Zen." He smiled at this. Maybe he was right.

# Stopping

*Zen is a radical counterpoint to all the usual activity
that we have engaged in for many years, and that
has not managed in any way to solve our problems.
We sit in zazen and leave all this behind. We are
always doing, but in zazen we are not doing. We allow
ourselves and the entire universe to come to rest.*

WE PERFORM OUR SELF in the world. When we stop performing, our true self appears. But as many of us have such
discomfort in seeing ourselves truly, we distract ourselves with
busyness. We watch TV and go out all the time; we work or keep
ourselves frantically occupied with the myriad responsibilities of
life. We go on holidays and have a full schedule with all the sights
we want to see. Rarely do we stop and do nothing at all. When we
stop like this, all the distraction falls away and the contents of our
body and mind reveal themselves. This can be quite difficult to
experience in the beginning.

Essentially, meditation is stopping our activities and returning to a still state of being. It is taking a genuine holiday from our
responsibilities and all our engrossing commitments—every day,
without going anywhere, right where we are.

Like a hunter, remaining still for a long time beside a forest
clearing, waiting for a deer to appear, we still ourselves and remain
relaxed and motionless, observing whatever it is that shows itself.
We may come to this still state by bringing our attention to the

natural rhythm of our breath. We may center ourselves by counting our inhalations or exhalations, from one to ten. But to just sit, we can let the focused attention on the breath fall away, too; once it has centered and calmed us, we can let the effort of paying attention to each breath fade away, and then just see what happens. Who knows? Maybe a deer will enter the forest clearing. Maybe a fox or bird will pass through the space. Maybe just the wind will blow through the forest trees and very little will happen at all.

With time, inevitably the contents of ourselves will show themselves, and the stories we create will play out before us. Our recurring obsessions and fantasies, our painful past, our anxieties about the present and future—all these will come forward for our attention. But we have not come to this still state to work through all of this. We have not come to meditation to consciously devise strategies to solve our problems and come to terms with our past and present—reasoning with our situation, trying to find some rational explanation for what has happened and what we should do. To spend our meditation time doing this would be a waste of time. It would just be replicating what we do when not meditating, except with greater focus and without the distractions of our usual responsibilities. No. Meditation, or zazen as it's referred to in Zen, is a radical counterpoint to all the usual activity that we have engaged in for many years, and that has not managed in any way to solve our problems. We sit in zazen and leave all this behind. We are always doing, but in zazen we are not doing. We allow ourselves and the entire universe to come to rest. We are not even trying to meditate well, creating another burdensome, competitive goal that we have to live up to and by which we can evaluate our level of success and attainment. This is not another race to be the best. Zazen leaves all that behind. It is a genuine space of freedom. It is that space in your life that is unshackled and liberated. It is not another instance of having to perform or be great. It is that place you return to every day to put all things back into balance. You ask nothing of it and make no demands of it. You just return to be there. It is a vast landscape that you cannot control, and so you must give up trying to control it. Like being in the mountains in spring, or beside a still lake on a winter's morning, you ask nothing of it other than that it just be there as itself. It is natural and not consciously constructed. It just is as it is. No more than that.

Zazen is an ancient, tried, and tested practice—for thousands of years—since the time of the Buddha and long before. It is a natural state of being, which generations of human beings have discovered for themselves, again and again. It has been passed on, from teacher to student, for almost one hundred generations, since the historical Buddha first discovered its precious secrets, which he says were in plain sight all along. Indeed, even as a child he had experienced this still state of liberation and happiness. While hiding in a rose bush as a young boy, he remained still for some time and was spontaneously overtaken by a sense of profound peace and joy. Later, when he experienced his great enlightenment, he remembered this childhood experience and realized that he had discovered something then: a taste of the truth, a sense of the authentic way to live as a human being. He realized, too, that this truth was available to everyone and anyone. That no matter who you are, by simple virtue of being a human being you are capable of experiencing and living in this state of liberation, wisdom, compassion, and joy. It is your birthright. It is there for you and always has been. Like a beautiful city or a great mountain range, it is always there, even before you enter and experience it for yourself. And when you enter it, how can you sum it up in words? That would be to ask the impossible. Having been to the Alps or the Rocky Mountains, how can you sum them up and describe them? They are far too vast for that. Some things are beyond us— and that is the point. This is something the great eighth-century Chinese Zen master Shitou Xiqian knew well.

Just sitting with head covered, all things are at rest.
Thus, this mountain monk doesn't understand at all.
Living here he no longer works to get free.[3]

Not everything can be understood and figured out. Life is far too rich for that. There are times we need to stop mapping and measuring the mountains, and just sit down and appreciate them for what they are.

# Capturing Fireflies

*Zen is experiential. It is a taste and a smell, rather than a description of what something tastes or smells like. In other words, Zen has something important to teach in an academic setting—but it is something the purely academic perspective is often blind to, unable to see the limitations of reason, to which it has sworn its undivided allegiance.*

ONCE I WAS INVITED by the Trinity College Philosophical Society to talk about Zen to the students. I was happy to accept the invitation and offer any insights I could into Zen Buddhism for the young philosophers that would attend the evening's meeting. It was a great pleasure to walk through the atmospheric archway that marks the entrance to Trinity College again. It is so beautiful, an island of calm in the center of Dublin. Its old stone walls, cobblestones underfoot, and carefully manicured lawns proclaimed it as a secular temple of learning—probably the last place a Zen priest should venture.

That evening, I shared the billing with a Hindu swami and a Hare Krishna devotee, both of whom spoke before me. I was struck at how Buddhism differs so considerably from these two other paths. For both speakers, the material realm, the realm of the body, constituted a lower order of being, something to be cast aside in favor of the immaterial soul. For them, it seemed to me, the spiritual side of reality was something higher and purer than this "fallen world." Both speakers had a clear philosophy to impart, which could be communicated as ideas about the human condition, essentially a coherent set of propositions about reality.

I was nominated to speak last, and was dreading it. Zen is nothing like those ideas put forward by the other speakers. I could talk about Buddhist philosophy, sure. But that is not what Zen is concerned with. Zen is experiential. It is a taste and a smell, rather than a description of what something tastes or smells like. In other words, Zen has something important to teach in an academic setting—but it is something the purely academic perspective is often blind to, unable to see the limitations of reason, to which it has sworn its undivided allegiance.

As I spoke, I could feel the skepticism in the room. I was expected to trot out some dogma or other—after all, I was dressed in religious robes. As a religious person, surely I had some theology to convince others of. But instead, I spoke about the limitations of both dogma and philosophy. How the vital experience of encountering reality in the moment was beyond the pale of such considerations. They were not having it, and I was questioned from the floor on the Buddhist teaching of emptiness. This is the reality that nothing is fixed and permanent, and all reality is a constant stream of change, meaning all things are without an independent, permanent, and fixed identity—a teaching often expressed alongside the Buddhist concept of no-self. Emptiness is a difficult concept for those new to Buddhism, and even when one understands it intellectually, it can take a lifetime of practice to fully appreciate what this profound truth really means in our lives and our world.

"If there is no self," said the self-confident student from the floor, his feet propped up casually on the chair in front of him, "then why don't you hand me over your wallet now. There is no 'you' that needs it." His delivery felt like a pre-prepared line, something to catch the Buddhist out with. To give him his due, it was witty, in an undergraduate sort of way.

"It is not that there is no self," I responded. "Rather, it's that there is no permanent and enduring self—and my own self will endure long enough to need my wallet to pay for the train fare home."

Touché! Each of us had scored a point. But communication had hardly happened. He was seeing the world from another paradigm. For him, and some of the other students, all three religious people before them were merely examples of people lacking reason: individuals hopelessly drowning in faith. Here Hamlet's line might have been of use: "There are more things in heaven and Earth, Horatio, / Than are dreamt of in your philosophy."

But it is not only young philosophers that fall into this trap. Zen students do too. So many times in the *dokusan* room, where the teacher and student engage in a profound "Dharma encounter," I've met students trying to grasp the meaning of some Zen teaching or other. It might be a teaching story or koan under discussion, and the student feels that if they can just rationally come to terms with it, intellectually understand and grasp it, then a breakthrough will occur.

But Zen cannot be understood in this way. The mountains cannot be held in your mind as a total reality. They are far too vast for that. Indeed, any conception we have of a mountain range, or even of a single peak—like Ireland's holy mountain, Croagh Patrick— even just one mountain such as this can be only a shadow in your mind of its actual reality. We can understand facts about such a mountain: it is in County Mayo, on the west coast of Ireland; it is associated with Saint Patrick; it was a pagan holy site long before Christianity came to Ireland. But each of the millions of rocks that rest on its slopes makes up the totality of the inconceivable mountain as a whole. And each day, rocks are dislodged and change position; the mountain is eroded by rain and wind; some new person climbs it and becomes part of the mountain's ever-flowing story. Even the mountain in its totality cannot be held static for an instant. Even if it were possible to understand it, an instant later it has changed. Croagh Patrick is a truly wondrous mountain; a majestic beacon on the west coast, overlooking the massive Atlantic. Its endless wonder is dwarfed in any conception we have of it.

Once, my family spent a summer in Westport, Connecticut—my wife and kids and I—and we saw fireflies for the first time. In the heat of a summer evening, in the garden of the house where we were staying, fireflies would appear at twilight, when the sun had gone down and the heat of the day had eased. It was so hot that my kids wore only their underwear, running here and there in the garden, trying to capture the fireflies in a jar—just as my Zen students try to capture the meaning of a Zen teaching in one coherent thought. The only thing was, when they managed to capture a firefly, its light suddenly dimmed. The whole joy of it was in their not being captured and contained. The free-flowing reality that they were was the whole point. A poem came from that evening that I added to my collection, *Three Rock Sonnets*:

*Sonnet LXXXII*
Halfway through this life to see anew.
To see fireflies for the first time,
Their green-yellow flares light up
The darkness of a Connecticut night,
Where bats flit among imposing trees,
And the unfamiliar is hidden at dusk.
No knowledge to shine its obscuring light,
But fireflies opening the eye of wonder.
The children half naked in the heat,
Trying vainly to catch the light, laughing,
Running from fly to eluding fly,
The game needing no victory for its joy.
Until they net one to ponder closely,
Only to find its captive light's put out.

The deepest, most precious meaning of life is life itself. It is something that can never be caught and held motionless so that we can inspect it. It is wonder, uncontainable. Philosophy cannot stretch to accommodate something like this.

# A Healing Practice

*That moment when we taste freedom is hard-won.*
*It is available at every instant and comes all of a*
*sudden, when the obstructions we have set up for*
*ourselves are finally dropped and we allow the practice*
*to heal us, to make us new and "innocent" again.*

SIT QUIETLY FOR LONG enough, and the things that you've buried in your life will come to the surface. The things that you have been avoiding will have to be faced, because when all our strategies for covering things up fall away, we have no choice but to look at ourselves directly. This is not always easy, and not everyone is ready for this. It involves stopping all our activity: our busyness, our dreaming and fantasies, our addictions, and the myriad ways we distract and intoxicate ourselves. Then often what we see is what we have been avoiding looking at, sometimes for years. This can be very difficult. This kind of spiritual practice is for those who are ready. It is for those who are ready to look directly at themselves, who have reached a point where they no longer have any choice.

For these reasons, it is important to practice in a community under the guidance of an experienced teacher. The community, or sangha, support one another on the journey of practice, sharing their experiences with one another. The teacher is there to offer support and advice, and to point out what we are not seeing—to correct and console, to scold and praise, as is required. If we practice alone, we are in danger of falling into the many traps and misguided convictions that can result from practice. We can also damage ourselves, in that we may not be ready to face what comes up in practice without support. That is why it is not advisable to follow this path without the structures and conventions that the Zen tradition has developed over millennia to deal with the pitfalls that can come with practice. Unless you are ready to go on an intensive retreat by yourself, practicing in isolation can be problematic. You may be left to deal with anxiety and panic, having to face on your own what has come up for you during your days of meditation. That is why the support and structure of a community and teacher are vital. It is ill-advised to perform deep psychological surgery on your own, without other people looking out for you.

In Zen, regular intensive group retreats are very important. Called *sesshin*, they often last from between two and seven days and involve many hours of meditation every day. *Sesshin* means "touching the heart and mind" deeply, and *sesshin* involves days spent in total silence, rising early in the morning to sit zazen, with the whole focus of the day placed on long periods of seated meditation. We even face the wall when sitting in zazen, which takes out all visual distractions and places the focus solely on our own experience, rather than on the experience of others. This prevents a kind of "Zen Olympics," where people are looking at how others are getting on sitting, and comparing themselves, either favorably or unfavorably, with how they are doing. We want to prevent making Zen into just another competitive sport—that's the last thing we need. During *sesshin*, you go much, much deeper into the practice. It is a difficult yet rewarding experience. Often on such retreats, people experience great breakthroughs in their practice, even getting a glimpse of the great awakening experienced by the Buddha all those years ago in Bodh Gaya, in northeastern India.

Often, too, *sesshin* is an experience of great healing. It has been a privilege to sit in the teacher's chair over the years, watching these healing experiences unfold for people. Often it all comes to a head in *dokusan*, the private meeting between the teacher and student, a kind of openhearted meeting, where all sorts of things come up and the student's practice is reviewed. I remember an elderly man on retreat once who had been very quiet and turned in on himself for the entire *sesshin*. Then when he came to *dokusan* he spoke quietly and intimately about how he and his partner had terminated a pregnancy many decades before, when they were not ready to be parents. The pain associated with that had been buried deep within him for a long time but had come to the surface during the many long hours of meditation. He said he was finally acknowledging and releasing this pain, and he broke down in tears. The *sesshin* had been a great experience of healing and release for him. But I never saw him again after that.

Other people have spoken in *dokusan* about feelings of inadequacy, about broken familial relationships, about experiences of homelessness. People have sometimes left, finally willing to face up to their addiction or anger. The *dokusan* room is often full of tears and laughter, as people face up to the profound truths of their lives and find some kind of healing and peace. This is something I witness as a teacher, rather than something I initiate or bring about. It is the practice itself that heals them. I am not a psychotherapist or counselor. These professionals might be sought out as a result of Zen practice, or in conjunction with it. And Zen practice is not a substitute for seeking this type of help. Yet Zen can be profoundly healing for those who open themselves up to the practice. Many years of denial can be dropped in the still state. Again, the teaching of old master Shitou Xiqian comes to mind.

> Let go of hundreds of years and relax completely.
> Open your hands and walk, innocent.
> Thousands of words, myriad interpretations,
> Are only to free you from obstructions.[4]

That moment when we taste freedom is hard-won. It is available at every instant and comes all of a sudden, when the obstructions we have set up for ourselves are finally dropped and we allow the practice to heal us, to make us new and "innocent" again.

# Returning Home
# to the Body

*It is important to understand that meditation
is not another cerebral activity, where we sit
motionless in denial of the body, analyzing the
content of our consciousness. This is not it at all.
Meditation is a profoundly physical activity.*

I GREW UP IN A culture ashamed of the body. When I was a child,
when there was sexual intimacy on television, it was immediately switched off. It was "filth" and "dirt." This was not just
my parents—it was the culture in Ireland at the time. We were
outwardly devout and pious, but privately a whole misogynistic
value system was imprisoning unmarried mothers in so-called
Magdalene Laundries, using them as virtual slave labor and taking away their children for adoption. There was widespread but
hidden abuse of children, by both church and state, and an active
cover-up and shielding of the perpetrators by the Catholic Church
hierarchy. As sex and the body were shunned publicly, a sick
relationship with the body festered in a private and suppressed
space. The place I grew up in was a place with no acknowledged
homosexuality, no available contraception, no divorce (no matter
what the marital circumstances), and no abortion (no matter how
the pregnancy came about and no matter if the pregnancy was a
threat to the mother's life). The human suffering that resulted from
this hatred of the body is incalculable.

What is true of my Irish Catholic upbringing is true for many others—Christian and otherwise. In a theology where the world is a "dirty" or "fallen" place, the body will inevitably be viewed as undesirable and a barrier to spiritual growth. The price of this theology is a whole spectrum of psychological problems. It manifests as an unhealthy attitude toward sex and the material world in general. It is a theology that made its way into our universities and education system, which emphasize cerebral and academic pursuits, with little to no emphasis on our physical health. In school, I could spend many hours in sedentary learning, but little to no time in physical activity. The mind and the spirit were valued much higher than the human body. For this reason, many of us are alienated from our bodies. We neglect them by rarely exercising and by eating and drinking too much. Many of our anxieties and problems result from not finding a balance in life, where we take care of, nurture, and value our bodies. If we listen to our body, we will see that it is a great teacher.

When a student is new to meditation, a great exercise is to scan the physical body, simply bringing the attention to each part of the body in turn, seeing what kind of sensations are to be found there. This is a grounding and centering exercise. It is important to understand that meditation is not another cerebral activity, where we sit motionless in denial of the body, analyzing the content of our consciousness. This is not it at all. Meditation is a profoundly physical activity. As we witness the ever-changing contents of our heart and mind, we also witness the shifting and changing feelings and sensations of the body while in the meditation posture. To be attentive to the posture is the foundation of practice. Regardless of whether we are sitting in one of the cross-legged positions or sitting in a chair, we take on the posture of Buddha and seat ourselves on "the diamond throne of awakening."

We may start by scanning the body, then maybe we can bring our attention to the natural rhythm of our breath. This focused attention, or mindfulness, was taught over two-and-a-half thousand years ago by the historical Buddha in the Anapanasati Sutta (MN 118), as well as in other teachings. It establishes *samatha*, or calmness in the mind, which is where all meditative practice must begin. It is a practice based on the reality of our physicality as beings. When we breathe, our whole body expands and contracts with each inhalation and exhalation. If you look at someone close to you breathing, you will see their shoulders rise, their chest and stomach rise and fall; you will see the exact rhythm of life flowing through them. As oxygen enters and leaves their body, they are breathing into themselves what the external world has to offer. The oxygen made by distant trees and plants sustains them. The wind that blows across oceans keeps their body vital and alive. It is miraculous, this human body, this breath that we take for granted. If we look at it again with the awakened eye of Buddha, we will see the miracle that it is.

In the Buddhist tradition also, too often the body has been seen as something undesirable and dirty. So often in the Buddhist scriptures the transiency of life is emphasized to such a degree that the body is rejected or shunned. In some Buddhist traditions, there is the practice of visualizing the body as something unsavory and prone to decay. There is the practice of meditating in charnel grounds, where bodies are left above ground to putrefy and decompose. While these meditative exercises have a deep value in some traditional approaches to Buddhist training, they may also lead to a morbid negativity regarding the physical body if overemphasized or indulged in too much. It is important to remember that the body is also beautiful and precious, as well as subject to transiency and decay—maybe even *because* it is subject to transiency and decay.

Shakespeare's Hamlet saw the world and humanity as nothing but dust. He was a man disenchanted with the world, sick in his mind. And yet he observed, "What a piece of work is a man! How noble in reason, how infinite in faculty! In form and moving how express and admirable! In action how like an angel, in apprehension how like a god! The beauty of the world." But despite this beauty, all Hamlet could see in this play was the death mask behind the soft loveliness of the human face—culminating in the death and destruction that ultimately leads to the play's tragic end.

It is the same hatred of beauty that sees misguided religion turn its back on the bounty of this beautiful world. In love with death, or the world hereafter, such corruption of religion hates life and everything to do with life. Women and children have most often been the victims of this life-loathing view. It is a view of the world that most often masquerades as piety. But, in truth, it offends against all that's good in the world.

There is a great and instructive Zen teaching story that is apt here. It was first written down in 1283 by the Japanese monk Mujū Dōkyō, in his book of Zen parables, the *Shasekishū* (Collection of Stone and Sand).

Once, two monks were traveling the countryside on foot. One monk was young and fanatical; the other monk was old and experienced. On their journey, they came to a rushing river that they needed to cross to continue on to their destination. As they were about to wade across, they noticed a young woman was hesitantly considering crossing the river as well. However, she was slight in build and the danger of crossing the river was more considerable for her. She noticed the monks were looking her way. "Can either of you venerable monks help me across the river?" she asked. The monks looked at each other. They were in a bit of a fix, as they had both taken monastic vows never to touch a woman. Then, suddenly, with no further hesitation, the older monk offered to take the woman across the river on his back. She agreed, and he carried her across. Then the two monks, having crossed the river themselves, continued on their journey.

For a good hour after this incident there was silence between the monks. The young monk was bothered by the whole episode. Eventually he challenged the older monk. "We have taken monastic vows not to touch women, and yet you carried that woman across the river on your back," he said disapprovingly. The old monk was unconcerned with his disapproval. He responded, "I carried that woman for less than a minute; but an hour later, you are still carrying her." The young monk made no response.

# The Sacred Scripture
## of the World

*I think what Zen is teaching is much bigger than
what Zen can possibly teach. That is its teaching.
While it values the scriptures and holy sutras, it
knows that they only set us out on the path of truth.
The path itself is another matter entirely. Our lives
and the world all around us are the real and living
sutra. This is where the truth is to be found.*

WHEN I WAS NEW to Zen, as a sixteen-year-old teenager, one
of my first questions was "What books should I read?" I
trawled the bookshops of Galway after school and on weekends. I
had read the Diamond Sutra and not understood it. Then I found
various books over a few months: *Zen for Beginners*; *Zen: Direct
Pointing to Reality*; and *Zen Mind, Beginner's Mind*. I still have these
books on my shelf almost forty years later. They were very important books in my life, and they started me out on the path.

But these books really did not give me any insight into what
Zen truly is. Only through sitting zazen daily over the intervening
years can I look back at these books and come close to understanding what they were teaching. What was in these books only makes
sense in light of experience.

Now that I'm a Zen teacher, I see many people in the same
position I was in at sixteen. Sometimes they are not that interested

in sitting Zen. Much more exciting to them is to try and gain some understanding of Zen through their reading. But this is a bit like reading a manual on how to ride a bicycle, and then getting on a bicycle for the first time. The manual might be of some help in that it leads you to actually try out the bicycle, but that's where its usefulness ends. Through the experience of riding the bike itself is how we learn. Zen is like this. Zen is a practice. Zen is medicine you take to clear your sickness. This will not happen if you only read the prescription that the doctor gives you. You must actually take the medicine for it to have an effect.

The founder of Zen in China was Bodhidharma. He brought Zen to China around the fifth century, from its origins in India a thousand years before he was born. To find Buddha, he taught, you have to look into your self and your own experience; look into your mind. This is not something you can find in a book. Famously, this Zen is a teaching "outside the scriptures." It is a "direct pointing at reality" and is "not dependent on words and letters." This spirit of emphasizing the experiential runs through-out the Zen tradition. In seventh-century China, six generations after Bodhidharma, you see this same spirit with the famous Zen master Huineng. A poor, illiterate country boy, Huineng became one of the greatest Zen masters in the whole tradition. There is a well-known thirteenth-century ink drawing of Huineng tearing up the sacred Buddhist scriptures to drive home the teaching that book learning is not the point. Whether Huineng really did this or not, the meaning of it for Zen practice is clear: What you are look-ing for you will never find within the pages of a book. Not this book, not any book.

Maybe this is something you already know. How many books have you bought and read in order to change your life? Maybe they are all stacked up in your bedroom, beside your bed. Maybe some even remain unread. This book in your hands right now—it, too, cannot change your life. Only you can change your life. Books can only point out the way. Books are a wonderful thing and are very precious. Scholarly work is vitally important and should be respected. Books are a map, but they are not the territory itself. If we confuse the map for the territory, as we so often do, many problems can result. We expect life to measure up to our theories about it, not the other way round. And so, we are confounded when reality does not conform to our thoughts and wishes of it.

I remember once, many years ago, when I was out hiking on Cnoc Mór na nGaibhlte, or Galtymore Mountain, on the border of Limerick and Tipperary. I drove up from the city of Cork, where I was living at the time, on a quiet midweek day, to take a hike on my own. I had planned my route on the map over breakfast, and it looked straightforward enough. And most of the climb itself was magnificent, with breathtaking views of the patchwork of green fields far below, which became intermittently visible, as thick fog drifted in. As the fog settled and thickened, what began as a pleasurable hike became more difficult and dangerous. It became difficult to find my bearings. Suddenly I realized that the slope I was on was much steeper and more dangerous than it had looked on the map at my breakfast table that morning. The reality of the mountain now appeared much larger to me than my idea of it. Veiled in fog, the mysteries of the mountain were hidden from me. Theory and reality had met, and reality had trumped theory on the side of this mountain. Some years later, I remembered parts of that hiking experience in a poem—an amalgam, really, of the many mountains I've climbed in Ireland over the years.

From my collection, *Three Rock Sonnets*:

*Sonnet XXXIV*
This mountain is unknowable. Infinite paths lead to it,
Every view is partial, with as many moods
As Montagne Sainte-Victoire. Its streams issue
From a place untraceable, every rivulet and drop
Of water on it moves, down stems, dripping
Off its forest branches. Pebbles even never rest,
Are nightly disturbed by badgers from their setts,
Are washed down rock in winter storm and hail.

Its contours, static in the hiking map, ebb and flow,
Are frighteningly fluid on the ground—
The solid rock itself flows like liquid, age to age,
You'd stalk these slopes a lifetime, with bent back,
Staff, rough beard: a wild-man mountain sage,
But only grow more ignorant and enraged.

I think what Zen is teaching is much bigger than what Zen can possibly teach. That is its teaching. While it values the scriptures and holy sutras, it knows that they only set us out on the path of truth. The path itself is another matter entirely. Our lives and the world all around us are the real and living sutra. This is where the truth is to be found: here, in the sacred scripture of the world—in the fields and cityscapes and situations of our lives. As Zen Master Dōgen writes, "The mountains and rivers of this present moment are the realization of the words of eternal Buddhas." It is like "the word of God" is the rain and the lapping waves and the sound of the traffic passing. When we sit quietly in zazen, we can begin to hear these words. We just need to stop and listen.

# An Ocean of Joy

*At a more profound level, you were never born and will never die. Deeply connected to all things in the universe, you are part of that ever-flowing stream of reality. In Zen, it is often illustrated as being like waves on the ocean. You and all phenomena are like individual waves on the great ocean. They rise and fall but have never really disappeared.*

ONE THING THAT HAPPENS when we stop and remain still is that we clearly see that everything about us is constantly in a state of change, including ourselves. From "the diamond throne" of zazen, we get a unique perspective of reality. We see that our thoughts and emotions come and go, in a constant stream of transformation. We may start our session of meditation short tempered and irritable, but as we sit, we can observe that transform into a settled balance, a more peaceful state of mind. Hundreds of thoughts may arise as we sit, but they just rise up and return to where they came from. When we sit early in the morning, it might be dark when we offer incense at the altar at the start of our sit, but after a time, the orange and rose of dawn creeps through the light of the room and the day begins. As the poet Seamus Heaney writes, a "pure change" has happened. One moment has inevitably moved into the next. By the end of a sitting, we are literally a different person.

The thing about change is that we love it when we are suffering, because we know our suffering will end, but we hate it when we are happy, because it takes our happiness away. When I get an injection at the doctor's, for example—and I hate getting injections—I grit my teeth and bear it, as I know the pain will last for only a few moments. But when I'm reading a really good book, I just don't want the book to end—but the story must come to an end, otherwise it would not be a story.

In the Zen tradition, this reality of impermanence is called *mujō*. It is an inescapable truth of existence. The question is, what attitude do we cultivate toward this truth? In Japanese culture, there is the phenomenon of *mono no aware*, which is a sensitivity and gentle empathy toward ephemera. This is a beautiful relationship to the transience of life. It is deeply rooted in Japanese culture. So, each spring, the cherry blossoms flower and are treasured as precious, precisely because they are so short-lived and beautiful. It is a wistful and gentle sensibility, a strange mixture of joy and sadness. It is the way we feel sometimes when someone we truly loved passes from this world. We are so grateful that we have known them but are so sad that they have gone. We ask ourselves, "Why did they have to die?" We may even wonder, "Where have they gone?"

In Zen Buddhism, we have quite a different take on death. Accepting that everything is constantly changing, we see that nothing has a fixed and permanent self. Where were you before you were born? Where will you go after you die? Like spring, summer, autumn, or winter, you are here now, and then you will not be here.

But at a more profound level, you were never born and will never die. Deeply connected to all things in the universe, you are part of that ever-flowing stream of reality. In Zen, it is often illustrated as being like waves on the ocean. You and all phenomena are like individual waves on the great ocean. They rise and fall but have never really disappeared. Each wave is part of a much bigger truth, an oceanic reality that we can hardly imagine. We rise and fall but are never really born or die. We endure and remain as part of the great ocean. Indeed, we have never left it. We do not need to believe in anything supernatural to see this is true. But the supernatural or unknown is not denied either. The vast ocean contains everything we can imagine, and even things we cannot imagine.

Growing up by the ocean, I often used to contemplate the water as it lapped up on the beaches of Galway and Connemara. Sometimes the ocean was still and calm, like a flat, motionless mirror reflecting the sky. Sometimes it was turbulent and rough, with waves crashing in over the rocks and with sea spray and seaweed thrown up into the air. I was always amazed that these waves had crossed the surface of the entire Atlantic Ocean to where I stood on the beach. They had come from far distant waters, many thousands of miles away. They may even have crossed from Newfoundland, the Caribbean, or somewhere on the eastern coast of North America. Then, after this long journey, the wave broke where I stood and was no more. It was an incredible privilege to witness this wave. It made me feel close to distant places and realize how all those faraway places were also, in a sense, here with me, in the very place where I stood.

In this endless web of interconnection that is our life, all things are with us, right where we are. There is nothing that is faraway and absent. This is the boundlessness of the world; it is its liberated nature. Even the past and the future are present with us when we see reality in this way. For Zen Master Dōgen, the image he used to convey this reality was standing on a mountain and viewing innumerable peaks at once. For him, other times and places were like those other mountains that he could view from where he stood. Times and places faraway had a real and immediate reality that he could see. Now he stands on this peak here, but earlier he stood on that peak over there, which still endures and exists, and which he can see from where he is now. It's a beautiful image of the way things really are.

For me, it is the image of the ocean that teaches this truth. I stand beside the ocean now. Its waves break at my feet on the sandy shore. It is an ocean full of fish and whales and dolphins, the ocean off the western seaboard.

These words I write are like a message in a bottle. I place them in the ocean of time and space, and they are carried away on their journey. As chance would have it, the great heaving ocean has carried these words to where you are right now. Look closely. A wave is breaking at your feet.

# Taking Control
## of Your Life

*We gain incredible mental strength through this
practice, especially the strength to accept that we
cannot control things. This is a great irony. In taking
back control of our lives, we see that we cannot
control many things. However, in the zazen posture,
seated in the form of Buddha, we have the strength
to accept that we cannot control everything.*

ZEN IS A VERY disciplined path. If you are lacking self-discipline, Zen is the perfect medicine for you. I lack discipline myself. That is one reason I have so much to learn from Zen practice. I sit zazen at seven most mornings, and I hate getting up in the morning. As a teenager, I had to be hounded out of bed every morning. My mother would come into the room and open the curtains. I was like a vampire hiding from the light. At that time in my life, I could never have imagined rising at 3:30 a.m. on retreat to sit zazen sometimes for fifteen hours a day. Still on retreat, when the morning bell is sounded, I just want to roll over and fall back to sleep. But I don't. Outside it's the darkest part of the night, and the bell ringer runs up and down the halls of the retreat center, clanging out the loud din that wakes everyone up. Then there is frantic changing and teeth brushing in silence. One or two people squeeze in a quick shower, if they can manage it.

Then the loud wooden *han*—an instrument made up of a wooden board struck with a mallet—starts to sound as the time for zazen approaches. Soon everyone is sitting in the meditation hall, and the morning incense is carried around the hall before it is offered at the altar. The big bell sounds that zazen has started, and nobody moves. The birds have not yet woken up, and a profound silence covers the whole world. Nothing is stirring, and the Zen hall is deeply still, despite all the people sitting in it. It is moving and beautiful—and to think, all this would have been missed if I had rolled over and fallen back to sleep!

The discipline of Zen is something that people find very hard. Just being on time doesn't seem to come naturally to us, especially in Ireland, where people are always late. It's part of the culture. So, when people show up late for zazen and find that the door has been closed already, they are a little taken aback. Because the Zen hall is a sacred womb of silence, we must guard that silence. To protect it, we close the door when the meditation session begins, out of respect for those who have arrived on time and are already sitting in absorbed meditation. So, latecomers are not admitted. Because of this, the latecomers are sometimes outraged. They do not see the situation from any perspective other than their own. They do not see that this is individual and group practice at the same time, and that there is a responsibility to everyone else to be on time. This type of practice is a good antidote to the obsessive individualism of our culture. We are often encouraged to forget that we have responsibilities to others—and Zen practice corrects that.

Essentially, Zen offers the training to take back control of our lives. It is a disciplined practice in a world without discipline. It requires rigor, effort, and punctuality. It is full of formal rules around how one deports and conducts oneself in the Zen hall. Many newcomers find the rules and discipline off-putting at first. They want to eat at the time that suits them, or speak when they feel like it. But these training rules should not be neglected, as they have something valuable to teach us. They teach us to tame ourselves—as the Dhammapada says, "a tamed mind brings happiness." In early Chinese Buddhist writings, the unruly mind is often described as an animal being brought under control and mastered. The animal—sometimes a monkey, sometimes a horse—is a metaphor for our mind, which is chaotic and disorganized, jumping from one thing to another. We notice how unruly the mind can be when we sit still for long enough.

When I was a child, I used to spend some of the summer in Caltra, in east County Galway. On my uncle's farm, sometimes my uncle would take out his bull, so that the bull could inseminate the cows that other farmers had brought for this service. The fee for this and the other details were entered into the large "Bull Book" that my uncle kept. Then the bull would be taken out to do his job. My brother and I often sat on a nearby wall watching, not knowing really what to make of it. But what always struck me was the power and demeanor of the bull. His muscular torso was full and heavy, and he resisted the control my uncle exercised over him. It took some effort to get the bull to do as my uncle wished. What I was witnessing was just an ancient dance, something that you could have witnessed thousands of years ago, something the Buddha himself may have seen.

In the Pali Canon—Buddhism's earliest scriptures—the bull symbolizes the effort needed to control and tame the mind. In the twelfth century, the Chinese Zen master Guoan Shiyuan used the symbol in his famous series of poems and drawings, the Ten Ox-Herding Pictures, to teach the stages traveled toward enlightenment. My own teacher, Taïgu Rōshi, sees this stage of trying to control the animal as still "immersed in the world of duality."[5] The original and ever-present radiance of awakening is always there, no matter what "stage" of the journey you are on.

Yet to reject fully the traditional reading of the Ten Ox-Herding Pictures as involving discipline and progression would itself be dualistic. From the relative perspective only, the wildness of the bull must be tamed and mastered before he is freed again. It is this great effort of taming that people so often resist in Zen training.

What they want is the freedom part only. But that is not how it works. To arrive at the cushion on time and to sit motionless until the bell sounds to end the session—this practice offers the conditions for us to achieve the freedom we seek. By gathering ourselves in and disciplining ourselves, we become masters of our own lives again. We gain incredible mental strength through this practice, especially the strength to accept that we cannot control things. This is a great irony. In taking back control of our lives, we see that we cannot control many things. However, in the zazen posture, seated in the form of Buddha, we have the strength to accept that we cannot control everything.

As we sit in zazen, we want to move; we want to scratch our face; we want to stretch or give up. The point of this practice of sitting zazen is to get beyond these wants and desires. This is vital training. We need not be at the mercy of their own whims and short-term wants. We have a choice in how we react. When someone shouts at us, we do not have to shout back. When we have promised to do something, we can be disciplined enough to live up to that promise. This way of behaving may not be our natural disposition, but by training ourselves, little by little, we can live like this. And that is empowering. It makes us feel we are in control of our own lives again. It even allows us to accept the many ways we are not in control.

# The Whole Mountain

*In meditation practice, we feel the sun on our face. But we also face these existential moments where we are vulnerable and lost. It is at these moments that we most need a guide—someone who has walked these paths before us.*

ZAZEN IS THE WHOLE mountain. It is the peaks and valleys. It is the boring flatlands and the exhilaration of the heights. It is not one or the other. It is all. Sometimes it is the warm glow of bliss and the flush of joy. Other times it is endlessly tiresome. Then there are the days it is dark and treacherous, with dark pits and chasms in which it is possible to fall—deep troughs where you feel it is possible to lose yourself. Stay committed, and you will see that each part of this journey is the whole journey. There is no journey without each part.

In County Kerry, there is a sacred mountain called Cnoc Bréanainn, or Mount Brandon. It is named after the fifth-century monk, Saint Brendan the Navigator, whose journey to the west is detailed in an *immram*, a type of Irish story concerned with sea voyages. Titled *Navigatio Sancti Brendani Abbatis* (Voyage of Saint Brendan the Abbot), it is a kind of allegory for the spiritual quest. Some believe he made it as far as North America. Certainly, he is known in Icelandic and other early European records. But in Kerry, his legacy is remembered in the sandstone of Brandon's Peak, which, because of its extreme western location, had been a site of pilgrimage even before the arrival of Christianity. It was the last land at the edge of the known world, overlooking the endless ocean where the sun set in the far west. On this mountain, Brendan went on a solitary retreat before his voyage, and is said to have been visited by an angel and shown a vision of the mythical lands to the west. These mythical lands are really another expression of the Pure Land of Amitabha Buddha, the celestial buddha of infinite light.

Once, climbing this sacred mountain, I learned how different the various parts of the journey can be. It was a beautiful spring day in February. On the lower slopes, sheep grazed among clumps of yellow daffodils. There was birdsong and warm sunlight. A light breeze blew. It was cold when the sun was not on your face, but it was perfect weather to take on the mountain.

As I ascended, the temperature dropped considerably and the wind picked up. The peak was above the clouds, and as I entered the clouds the stone became slippery and icy underfoot. If it was a pleasant spring day below, it was a harsh and cruel winter up above. I was glad of my extra jacket and warm, waterproof trousers. My flask of hot tea, which had been an afterthought below, became suddenly precious and important. Visibility became poor, and soon it was hard to see anything, even just a few yards away. There was snow underfoot, and more snow swirling down from above. Luckily the path was clear to follow. But that soon changed.

As I neared the peak, it became harder to judge directions. Mountain and sky merged in a swirl of white snow. My friend, who had gone on ahead of me, was an experienced mountaineer, and I met him coming down. He said it was treacherous above and easy to lose one's way. He handed me his compass and told me the bearing to the peak from the end of the path where we stood. Then he left me as I followed the compass arrow into the blinding whiteness.

After a few minutes, I found myself at the stout concrete pyramid, or triangulation station, that marks the top of the mountain. It appeared to me out of the thick mist, and I put the compass in my pocket to have a brief look around. It was harsh and cold in the wind, and I wasn't going to stay long. Then I realized that I simply did not know from which direction I had come. I was totally disoriented in the whiteout. I knew if I walked in the wrong direction, there were some potentially fatal falls. I needed to know the way that would lead me back to the path.

We all need a guide, and mine had given me the compass some minutes before. I needed it now. But for some reason the bearing had gone totally out of my mind. What was it again? Then it came to me, and I followed the line 180 degrees back from its directional arrow, along the line I think I had come from. I judged that after about 150 paces I'd be at the start of the path down. So I counted my paces along that bearing but could see nothing. It was an awful feeling. Then I noticed a familiar looking rock a little way to my right. I had wandered a bit off the straight line as I paced. That was the top of the path down. I was so relieved. And within forty minutes I was down again where I could feel the sun on my face and see the clumps of daffodils growing in the spring grass.

In meditation practice, we feel the sun on our face. But we also face these existential moments where we are vulnerable and lost. It is at these moments that we most need a guide—someone who has walked these paths before us. The relationship between the teacher and the student is so important in Zen, as is the tradition that instructs us both. We both listen to the voices of the many masters before us, people who have learned from their experiences and mistakes, generation after generation, all the way back to the historical Buddha, our original teacher.

Before setting off, it is important to realize that the mountain is made up of dangers as well as joys. It would be dishonest to say it is not so. We do not get to select only the bits of the mountain that we like. To reach the peak, we must walk the flatlands and navigate the slopes. Some days this is easy; some days this is hard. But all days taken together are what the journey is about.

# Rituals around Practice

*Some days you will want to sit, while others*
*it'll be the last thing you want to do. Therefore,*
*sitting in meditation must become something that*
*is above and beyond your wants and whims. It*
*must be something that you do regardless of how*
*you feel. It belongs to that part of your life that is*
*beyond considerations such as likes and dislikes.*

O N THIS PATH, WE sit zazen every day. This is very important.
We need to create a space in our lives where we come every single day to center ourselves and return to who we really are. By sitting every day, the practice perfumes our whole life. It becomes part of who we are. And when zazen becomes part of who we are, then it is with us as a benign influence, no matter what situation we find ourselves in.

When I was a child, I was taught that I had a guardian angel. At all times, day and night, I was being watched by this angel. That's what I was told. Maybe this was meant to be a kind of comforting idea, but I found it somewhat disturbing. I felt as though I was under surveillance at all times. The angel stood at the end of my bed. It watched me as I went to the toilet and washed. I was being watched, rather than being accompanied with protection and care. There was a controlling and oppressive character to the religious faith I was brought up in. I know now that it didn't have to be like this, and that what I experienced was a particular manifestation of the Christian faith that is toxic, patriarchal, and obsessed with power. In this version of the Christian religion, even the guardian angel had been turned into a mechanism of control.

Zazen can be a much more positive kind of guardian angel. When you carry this practice with you, the control being exercised is self-control. You are your own guardian angel. The spirit that accompanies you in every situation is the spirit of wisdom and compassion. It is the spirit that you cultivate through your Zen practice. It is a much more realistic and forgiving kind of guardian angel. But if your practice is sporadic and intermittent, it will not enter your bones. So, how do you make Zen part of your life?

Some days you will want to sit, while others it'll be the last thing you want to do. Therefore, sitting in meditation must become something that is above and beyond your wants and whims. It must be something that you do regardless of how you feel. It belongs to that part of your life that is beyond considerations such as likes and dislikes. Zazen accepts all and is beyond the bounds of such distinctions. It is a field in which all is reconciled—your joys and pains, happiness and sadness, likes and dislikes. It is a practice beyond such dualities. It is the unconditioned state where our innate Buddha nature plays, where our enlightenment is realized. And yet there will be days when it does not feel much like enlightenment, when it feels boring—or even a waste of time—to sit. How do we overcome these hindrances that stop us from coming each day to this still and balanced state?

Here, habit and ritual have a role to play. Zazen needs to become something that you do every morning, habitually. You rise, you wash your face, take a drink of water, and then you offer incense and sit. That is all. It is your daily activity. It is ordinary. Then, after a while, if you do not do it, you feel that something is missing. Like teaching a child to brush their teeth every morning, you have taught yourself to sit zazen. It is just something you do. You do not think or analyze it. It is a ritual in your life.

This is the great wisdom of ritual. It is a value or principle embodied in an action or a choreography of actions. It is in the realm of body memory and body wisdom. Knowing the shortcomings of the rational and conscious mind, you have handed yourself over to the wisdom of the body, which is realized in habit. This allows your practice to enter your life at a deep level. Maybe you have set up a special corner of your room where there is a Buddha statue and meditation cushion. You might sound a bell to start your sitting, and there might be incense, flowers, and a lit candle where you practice—the traditional offerings at a Buddhist altar. Because this is part of the furniture of your house, it will remind you to practice. It is a physical signal to you that you should sit zazen each day. It is your place of refuge, a space of freedom within your house, where you leave aside all your other commitments and worries for a period each day and enter the still state.

To keep going with this practice, it is necessary to make a vow of practice. This is a solemn promise to do something, even if at one point it is no longer something you feel like doing. A vow is a promise made outside time. In the future, conditions might change, but because you have made a vow you keep on going. "In sickness and in health." A vow takes things up to a level beyond the fickle changeability of our lives. It resides in a space that is not conditioned by circumstances. We fulfil the vow, no matter what. This is the amazing power of a vow.

But if it is left to us alone, we may break that vow. This is why we need the support of sangha, or the Buddhist community. In sangha, we hold each other up. We support each other. Sangha is one of the three treasures of Buddhism, also known as the triple gem: Buddha (the historical teacher and founder of Buddhism), Dharma (the Buddhist teachings), and Sangha (the Buddhist community). In sangha, we are not alone. Our energy and positivity lift others, and our character flaws and failings are moderated inevitably by our interactions with other people. One pillar cannot hold up the temple roof, but many pillars standing together can. So, following the Way in the context of sangha is vitally important to maintain this journey in the long run. In the Zen tradition, taking the vow to practice has become formalized in a specific ritual called *zaike tokudo,* or *jukai.*

In the *jukai* ceremony, we formally enter the Zen Way as a layperson. It is like a kind of baptism for adults. In addition to studying and practicing, we prepare for *jukai* by sewing a small ceremonial garment. We wear this bib-like garment, or *rakusu,* around our necks during Zen practice, and it symbolizes the larger robes worn by Buddhist monks. It is the robe of Buddha and is given to lay practitioners as part of the *jukai* ceremony. In this ritual, the lay follower makes a public commitment to follow the Buddhist way of life and to live by the ethical precepts of Zen Buddhism. By taking these vows publicly, we take refuge in the Buddhist community and in the Buddha. Knowing full well that we need this support, we acknowledge our own limitations and allow ourselves to be buoyed up by others. It is a vital initiation and a meaningful ritual that supports us on the path we have chosen. Without sangha, plus the strength that our commitment draws from the vows we take at *jukai,* we may with time lose heart and slowly fall away from our dedication to renew and heal ourselves through this practice. This ancient path is wise in its realization of what we need to awaken and find peace and self-acceptance. Like the rituals we engage in to look after our own health, the rituals of Zen practice take care of things with a deep wisdom. It is a wisdom we should not leave at the mercy of our ever-changing moods and varying levels of commitment. There is a choreography of practice that we can learn from others and from the ancestors who came before us. It does not have to weigh heavily on our shoulders alone.

# Fear of Losing Oneself

*In realization, or even in passing through the dark
night, one is not lost. In many respects, you remain
the same old person you always were. Something has
changed and, in a sense, nothing at all has changed. The
water is not disturbed by the reflection of the moon.*

WHEN OUR NEW LIFE begins, we are gripped by fear of the
death of our old self. We want to change, but at the same
time we do *not* want to change at all. We are stuck, and something
must force the situation. We can remain stuck for years. We know
what we are losing but we do not yet know the liberation of what
is to come. An act of faith is required. A great leap is necessary.
For awakening or spiritual growth to occur, first we must pass
through a "great death."

This sounds scary and darkly existential, but in fact, it is quite
ordinary. You have already experienced more modest versions
of the great death in your life. This might have been your wedding day, when you were gripped by fear before the ceremony. It
might have been the news that you were pregnant or when you
ended years of happy education and were handed your diploma at
graduation. Apart from these voluntary changes in life, it may also
have been change that you did not choose. Maybe the death of a
loved one, or the end of a relationship you did not want to end. In
so many of our life-transition experiences, we feel vulnerable and
exposed. We know how reassuring the familiar past is, but as we

set out into the unknown, we are gripped by a deep-seated fear. What if what we are moving toward is a huge mistake? What if what we had is better than what we will receive? What if we lose the person we were by taking that new job or saying "I do" in that wedding ceremony?

On the path of awakening, we experience the great death in a deep and intimate way. It can even manifest as a visceral, unsettling experience in our meditation.

In my own practice, I clearly remember this "dark night," as Saint John of the Cross described it. I had been meditating already for many years and found it a journey that settled me and offered psychological equilibrium. I had tasted calm abiding in my practice and it felt familiar and reassuring. It was like a comfortable house that I had built for myself in meditation. Doubtlessly, I needed that comfortable house, having gone through the anxiety and panic that I talked about earlier. This zazen was warm and safe. It was the bright side of the moon, lighting up the sky and the road ahead as I traveled. I was unaware that there was a dark side of the moon also.

One day, in the words of Saint John of the Cross, "my house being now all stilled"[6] in meditation, I felt the core of my self dissolving into a blank darkness. It really is impossible to describe in words. "No one saw me," and myself as a witness to this was also slipping away. "I abandoned and forgot myself," says Saint John. And this was exactly it. It was the falling away of self and all things. I felt surrounded by an endless and impenetrable night—even as I sat zazen in full daylight, in my room, before a massive bedroom mirror. Even with my eyes open and seeing my reflection, this night was my sense of things. I felt an infinite chasm opening up under me, and I feared that if I fell, I would fall forever. I had not yet made that choice of abandonment that Saint John describes. I was like a groom having second thoughts, vacillating as to whether to enter the church and be married. I was afraid of losing myself.

Then, in one instant, I decided to allow myself to fall. I felt as though I were falling into that infinite darkness. I had abandoned myself to it, or as Saint John says, "all things ceased; I went out from myself." And so I fell and broke through something like a false floor below me. I had fallen with faith and was delivered through to a sense of infinite and powerful light. Everything was suddenly illuminated. It was not a presence, but it was the truth of all things. It was an exhilarating experience—in no way easy. And although there have been many other experiences, this only happened once. It was a moment of pure change.

There is a great story about this kind of change in the *Blue Cliff Record*, a collection of Zen koans compiled in China in 1125. In case 4 of the collection, the sutra scholar Tokuzan Sengan (782–865) has come to study with a Zen teacher, Ryūtan Sōshin. Sengan is full of doubt. He ascends the mountain and begins his training with the master. Sengan is an academically minded person, someone who likes to know. He must have found the not-knowing of Zen training very challenging. Indeed, as a sutra scholar, he may even have seen it first as a kind of heresy, as Zen relies on direct experience rather than "book learning."

One dark night, Sengan stepped out of the mountain hermitage, probably to take some air. Outside the warm hermitage building, the mountain night was deep and impenetrable. He went back to the hermitage door and told his teacher it was far too dark outside to see. And so his teacher lit a lamp for him, and Sengan reached out to take it. Just as he was about to take the lamp, Ryūtan blew it out suddenly, leaving Sengan in total darkness. At that moment, Sengan experienced a great awakening.

Sengan had seen his blindness. All around him was the unknowable mystery of things. He needed the mountain darkness to have this truth lit up for him so clearly that it dazzled him with its brightness. Having been thrown into darkness, he discovered something like faith. He realized that he did not lose himself in the darkness. He realized that there was no need to be afraid. He passed through the "great death" and remained intact. His fear had lost its power, and he was awake and new. He did not need to know everything anymore. Indeed, he realized that his attempt to know everything was doomed from the start. The openness of not knowing dawned on him.

As a great meditation teacher, Master Dōgen was fully aware of this fear of losing the self that one can encounter in zazen. He, too, understood that this fear was a kind of illusion, something that needed to be passed through, a blockage on the path. In his teaching "Genjōkōan," he used the classical image of Zen enlightenment—the brightness of the full moon—to talk about the realization that breaks through the darkness.

> When a person attains realization, it is like the moon's reflection in water. The moon never becomes wet; the water is never disturbed. Although the moon is a vast and great light, it is reflected in a drop of water. The whole moon and even the whole sky are reflected in a drop of dew on a blade of grass. Realization does not destroy the person, as the moon does not make a hole in the water.[7]

In realization, or even in passing through the dark night, one is not lost. In many respects, you remain the same old person you always were. Something has changed and, in a sense, nothing at all has changed. The water is not disturbed by the reflection of the moon.

However, it is important to remember that all transformation and birth is fraught with danger. This is why meditation is best practiced in the context of a wisdom tradition, rather than in the commercial setting of a class. If a student has a tendency toward psychosis or feelings of depersonalization, maybe they need to go gently with zazen, or find another practice altogether. Zen is not a replacement for professional psychological help and support. If someone suffers from certain mental afflictions or conditions, maybe long periods of meditation could be bad for them. All things come when the time is right. Is the time right now for you?

Do not measure your practice by the experience of others. My experience is mine; yours is yours. Indeed, I should not even try to replicate my own experience in zazen. What comes just comes— or it does not. The point is, whatever experience that comes is *it*. And whatever comes, goes. Even if it is the dark night of the soul, it comes and then it goes. Like Sengan, in brightness and in darkness, there I am still. There is really nothing to fear. The Buddha is not disturbed by anything at all. In zazen, we can be like this.

# A House of
# Many Rooms

*In Zen we do not emphasize graduated steps toward
awakening. It is not that we do not experience
each of the rooms of meditation as we sit; rather it
is that we do not label and name them. We pass
through the* jhanas *naturally, with nonthought.*

IF YOU ARE LUCKY, you live in a house with many rooms. But even
if you live in a cramped apartment, there is likely an infinity of
nooks and crannies in it. There is the place where you sleep, the
place where you eat, the place where you wash, and the place where
you sit. Above you is a ceiling. There are many distinct areas in
the place you live in. But imagine it was a large house with many
rooms: that there were four, five, or six stories, and above that an
area outside, where there is a roof garden. And even higher is a
staircase leading to a viewing platform, from which you can see
for miles around. And on this platform in the open air is another
ladder, leading to a snug crow's nest space, hidden high above the
house. As you might imagine, to be in each space feels different.
Each space has its own characteristics and energy. Meditation is
much like this. Your zazen is a house of many rooms. You might
even say it is a house with infinite rooms.

If you have started to practice, you will know that many feelings and sensations come along in zazen. You might experience

pleasant physical sensations, like warm feet and hands, or beautiful energy passing through the channels of your body. You might feel joy for no apparent reason whatsoever. This might transform into a deep contentment. You might feel profoundly at peace, where all the matters of the world and your life feel settled. These are pleasant experiences that make us want to continue with our practice. We may even take to the meditation cushion hoping to replicate some pleasant experience we had before in meditation. We may seek the "high" of these feelings, again and again.

The Buddhist tradition has studied these states of meditation with great care and attention over an incredibly long period of time. Each room in the house has been lived in by the ancestors that have been here before us. In the ancient teachings of the Buddha, these many rooms have been identified and described. In the tradition, nine *jhanas*, or levels of meditation, are identified. They include *jhanas* of form and *jhanas* without form, where one experiences vast spaciousness or an infinity of consciousness. Then there are the levels where one experiences the boundless and ever-changing stream of reality. And so on, beyond this, where the perceiver no longer blocks the perception of the direct truth of things.

In some traditions, these steps are meant to be practiced or experienced in order. Some say the Buddha entered deep states of consciousness following this order of the nine *jhanas*, and that as he came out of this deep state, he followed the *jhanas* again in reverse.

But in Zen we do not emphasize graduated steps toward awakening. It is not that we do not experience each of the rooms of meditation as we sit; rather it is that we do not label and name them. We pass through the *jhanas* naturally, with nonthought. The entirety of what we experience in zazen potentially includes all of the *jhanas*, and more. Realizing that the student might ardently seek out each *jhana* in turn and that this might become a blockage or obsession in practice, the Zen school does not categorize and systemize the levels of meditation. All rooms taken together make the house. This is the way we see it.

And yet the wisdom of the old Buddhist traditions, where the *jhanas* are taught, is precious. While we practice just sitting with whatever comes up, it can be helpful to have some language to talk about the experiences that emerge in Zazen. This is particularly true for those new to Zen, whose new experience in meditation may provoke many questions.

In my own practice, I remember having the disconcerting experience of heavy perspiration during zazen. Even in a cold room with no warm clothing, I would sometimes perspire heavily as I sat, as if I were in a hot sauna. I brought this up with Paul Haller Rōshi once, when I was sitting with his sangha in Belfast. At the time, I had been meditating only for a few years and I was preparing to take lay vows, or *jukai*, and formally enter the Zen path with Paul as my teacher. This was before I met Taïgu Rōshi, who was to become my ordaining teacher and eventually my transmitting teacher, passing on the permission to teach in our tradition. But having sat through an uncomfortable morning of pouring sweat, I asked Paul Haller what it signified and what I should do about it. He shrugged his shoulders. "Just ignore it," he advised. "Pay it no heed." It was good advice. I ignored it as if it were part of the scenery of my zazen, and shortly afterward it stopped. This is advice I have heard from time to time since, and advice I have given to my own students: do not cling to the bizarre and distracting experiences that emerge in zazen. Let them arise and disappear, as part of the totality of your experience.

And yet they will come, all sorts of things. One may have the sense that a short period of time is very long, or the sense that a forty-minute period of sitting passes in an instant. Time may expand and contract. Students have told me that they experience shaking or trembling during zazen; others may feel a vast spaciousness around them, as if they were very small—or the opposite, that they are very large, filling an incredible amount of space. Such experiences in zazen can be a little like Alice in *Alice's*

*Adventures in Wonderland*: at one moment tiny, at another huge. These experiences may arise but are rare enough. If they do, the advice to ignore them is very helpful. It's as though they have been thrown up as a distraction to divert you on the way. There is even a word for this phenomena in traditional Japanese Zen practice. They call it *makyō*, which are hallucinations and other visions and strange experiences that can arise during zazen. The mind and ego are able to produce any number of toys for you to play with in zazen to bring you away from letting go and becoming free. There is an infinity of rooms to explore in this vast and endless house; there are even halls of mirrors, where the reflections seem to go on forever, leading down an endless path of illusion. Best just to see them and let them be. Whatever room you find yourself in is right where you should practice. Wherever you are, that's the place to sit down and rest.

# An Ordinary
# Awakening

*If we can want what we already have, we can discover
a deep contentment. This is the art of appreciating
our own life. We do not have to be saints with
supernatural abilities. To be human is enough.*

W HEN ZEN CAME TO Ireland, and to the West in general, I think
there was a fetishization of the enlightenment experience.
Before Zen teachers arrived, books about Zen arrived. And those
books presented Zen as the search for enlightenment, which was
described as a heightened experience, something like an LSD trip,
but caused by spiritual intoxication rather than by drugs. There
was also a certain Orientalism to the reception of Zen in the West.
It was an exotic Eastern "philosophy," which the Western mind
could barely comprehend. It was something best practiced in distant Asia, in a monastery buried deep in the snowy mountains of
Japan, or in some hidden wilderness hermitage in China. Zen was
all about experiencing *satori* or *kenshō*—great experiences of awakening that shook the very foundations of your being and transformed you into a sage-saint, a blessed guru standing above and
beyond the ordinary person. Such a person could potentially perform all sorts of magical feats. They could read your mind. They
could control their heart rate and body temperature. Some people
even suggested that they could defy gravity and levitate. Certainly

these enlightened beings had to be special in some way. They had to be endowed with special powers. Otherwise, they were just like us. And that wouldn't do, now, would it?

This magical vision of Zen came to Ireland in the 1980s with these early books. It persisted throughout the 1990s, as there were really no Zen teachers in the country yet. News trickled back to Ireland of Maura O'Halloran, a young Irish American woman who had gone to Japan and ordained as a Zen nun. After three years, she intended to travel back to Ireland in 1982 and begin to teach Zen, but tragically this never happened, as she was killed in a traffic accident in Thailand before she could return to Ireland. She would have been the first Irish Zen ancestor. Indeed, in many ways that is exactly what she is. Our sangha honor her in this way, in any case. But in Ireland, she has been presented as a "Zen saint." She has even been depicted artistically with a halo, with all the iconography of a Catholic saint. This tendency toward hagiography seems irresistible. We expect our Buddhist masters of all traditions to be capable of superhuman feats. We want our saints to perform miracles. The miracle of water is not sufficient for us; we want our water turned into wine.

By the late 1990s, there were one or two actual Zen teachers offering the Dharma in Ireland. And later, as the unmediated teachings of the Zen masters became available in print, we learned that "ordinary mind is the Way." When the Zen student Jōshū asks his teacher Nansen, "What is the Way?" in case 19 of the *Mumonkan*, that is exactly the teaching he received: "ordinary mind is the Way." Not heightened awareness or supernatural powers or some kind of out-of-body experience. Nothing of the sort. Just ordinary mind.

Buddhism, like many religious traditions, is full of magic. There are stories that say an enlightened being has six mystical powers: they can know others' minds; they have supernatural seeing and hearing; they know their past lives; they can shapeshift or change form; and the sixth is the power to end excess. But for Master Dōgen, the mystical power of awakened beings is the consciousness we already have. This is the miracle of seeing and hearing, of touching and tasting. Imagine these powers did not exist and you had to invent them. They would be beyond comprehension and beyond our imagination. As the poet Ho-on[8] said, "Carrying water and lugging firewood" is a wondrous function. The true miracle is the ordinary, the very fact that we are conscious at all. Why is it that we want more? Isn't this dissatisfaction, this *dukkha*, really the heart of the problem, rather than our own human limitations?

Think back to a time when you were sick. I remember, for example, when I was told by an eye specialist that I would lose the sight in my right eye if I did not get a series of operations. Even with the operations, they were not sure that they could save my sight. The first thing I thought was: "What if I cannot see my children's faces as they grow up?" I was very upset that I would not know what they'd look like. The thing I had taken for granted might be taken away. Now I knew what a precious miracle my sight was, like a mystical power I never realized I had.

Gladly, after four operations, they were able to save my vision. I am so grateful for the gift of my sight now. But like any person, I often forget the blessings that I possess. I complain and I get short-tempered. I easily forget that I am alive and what being alive means.

But this forgetting is part of being alive, too. It is very human. What Zen does is bring us back to reality. Often, we find it quite hard to deal with reality. We prefer fantasy and escapism. The problem is, as we dream and fantasize, reality gets on with being reality, but we are not following it; instead, we are off somewhere else in intoxication. But we always have to return to reality at some stage. And if we have neglected reality too much, then there might be an awful mess to deal with when we return. If we cannot deal with it, we may seek solace in more escapism. And so the circle of neglect continues. It's like the cycle of addiction.

The practice of gratitude can help us here. If we can want what we already have, we can discover a deep contentment. This is the art of appreciating our own life. We do not have to be saints with supernatural abilities. To be human is enough. In fact, just to be human—an ordinary human being—is in truth to be wise and compassionate like a saint, with the most incredible powers one could imagine. The Dharma eye of Zen allows us to see this truth.

# Parental Mind

*It may be easier to blame others and not take
responsibility for yourself, but that is not the Zen
Way. In Zen, we take charge of our own behavior. We
take charge of our own life. As the Buddha advised us
on his deathbed, you must "be a light unto yourself."
This kind of inner light is very hard to extinguish.*

GOING ON RETREAT IS a bit like going to a spiritual boot camp.
You will find out for yourself if you ever go on a Zen retreat.
There is a full schedule of sitting every day, and each minute of the
day is accounted for—from the moment you rise in the morning to
the time the lights are turned off at night. Because we are spend-
ing the few days of retreat as a single, organic unit, everyone must
postpone their wants and desires, how they prefer to do things,
until the retreat is over. Many of us find this very difficult. But it
is precisely because it is difficult that it is such wonderful training. When at the end of the retreat we return to our normal lives,
we are so grateful for those lives. We return to ourselves renewed
and refreshed. Retreat is a wise and wonderful vehicle for this
transformation.

Because we are so used to doing what we want when we want,
many of us have become selfish and lazy. We can see the results of
this attitude all around us. Rather than put rubbish in trash bins,
we leave it on park benches or on the ground. Instead of cooking
a wholesome meal, we eat convenience food, which is bad for our

health and the planet. We do what requires the least effort and the least personal responsibility. We are like ill-mannered children that have not learned to clean up after themselves and respect the space they share with others around them.

Zen training counters these selfish attitudes. Even sitting zazen in solitude at home, we must commit to taking responsibility for doing this practice every day—but that commitment is heightened so much more on retreat, when we have to enter the group practice of the sangha. We are so used to putting ourselves first that having to put others first feels like an imposition and an inconvenience, and we may even resent it.

After getting up before dawn and sitting zazen for three hours, we are hungry and want to devour our breakfast. But on retreat we begin eating together. We do not start to eat while others are still working to ensure we have tea and milk on the table. We are considerate and wait. Even so, I have often had to ask people to wait, as they have started to eat while others are still getting things ready for the group. It is amazing how annoyed people can become when you ask them to wait. I understand this. With hunger and fatigue, I am often annoyed myself. But despite this annoyance, waiting with composure is a valuable lesson to learn. Zen retreats create the conditions for this training to happen. At mealtime, we learn about our own greed and our habit of putting ourselves before everyone else. For a few days in utter silence, we create a temporary society where we put others first—and the results are quite amazing and uplifting: the Zen retreat becomes a space of healing and mutual consideration.

Healing, however, is not an easy thing. It involves great patience. Like a hospital bed where we must lie and wait for the body to repair itself, in zazen we must sit on a cushion and wait— for nothing. We must give ourselves over to the moment and let things take care of themselves. Apart from sitting, we make no effort in any specific direction. We do not orient our zazen toward some aim. We sit expecting nothing. We get out of our own way and let things take care of themselves. This is the process of healing. But the difficulty is that we lose patience, even when we're sitting alone at home. We commit to sit every morning for twenty minutes, but then after ten minutes we are bored and give up. We are like a patient in a hospital that needs to rest for a week but checks out after two days and goes back to work. Soon we are sick again. When we vow to sit, we must stick to the vow. That is why the support of others is so helpful.

Sometimes on retreat, individuals try and ignore the request of group practice. I remember one woman that came on one of our summer retreats and after a day or two she decided to skip some of the schedule and go for long walks in the sunshine. Everyone else sitting in the silence of the zendo could hear her walking outside on the gravel. They probably could also sense that someone was missing from the room. Her walking outside brought the attention of others with her. No doubt she was totally unaware of this. She was just doing what she wanted to do. But it was not in the spirit of retreat.

This type of thing has happened quite a few times. People decide to sleep in and have a shower, instead of coming to the zendo in the morning. Others sitting in the meditation hall can hear them pottering around the retreat center and turning on the shower. The actions of one can break the silence of practice for all.

As a teacher, my role is often to challenge people when they behave in these ways, so that we can protect the practice space we have created together. Sometimes this leads to resentment. Because people do not like being told what to do, they can become aggressive and lash out verbally, because you are challenging their egocentric behavior. What is normal in everyday life is not normal in the special conditions of a Zen *sesshin*. In life, we often speak when we want. If we want to go for a walk in the sunshine, we just go. If we feel like heating up a pizza and eating it, we can do that whenever we like. But having agreed to enter the special conditions of *sesshin* willingly, a *sesshin* can fall apart if its participants decide to do their own thing. And when they are challenged, they often blame the teacher rather than themselves. They insist that centuries of Zen tradition around retreats should be reshaped to accommodate their desires, to reflect the way they see the world. To remain silent and just see what comes up is very difficult for so many people. That is because so many of us are really like children that want things all our own way.

In Zen, we become a parent to our child selves. On retreat, participants can become angry at the teacher, as a father or mother figure to blame and resent. But the teacher can never make you practice. Only you can do that. And to do that, you must cultivate a parental mind toward yourself and others. It is you that takes responsibility for yourself. It is you that looks after yourself and others. You correct and support yourself and others. You look out for your own welfare and the welfare of others. You cultivate a parental mind that is capable of love and care when needed and is also capable of offering correction and forthright advice. This is your responsibility. It may be easier to blame others and not take responsibility for yourself, but that is not the Zen Way. In Zen, we take charge of our own behavior. We take charge of our own life. As the Buddha advised us on his deathbed, you must "be a light unto yourself." This kind of inner light is very hard to extinguish.

# Macho Zen, Lazy Zen

*It's important to realize that this "Macho Zen"
I've mentioned also has a flip side: a lazy attitude
to practice that is indolent and sluggish. While
in Macho Zen the ego is strong in its controlling
self-discipline, in "Lazy Zen" the ego asserts
itself in an absence of discipline entirely.*

THE POINT OF ZAZEN is not to sit suffering and in pain—but neither is it to give up as soon as discomfort arises. The Buddha's Way is "the Middle Way," as set forth by him in the Dharmacakrapravartana Sutra. It is not a way of self-mortification; neither is it a way of self-indulgence in comfort and pleasure. It navigates a way between these two poles. Religion, however, often loves self-mortification. It loves bleeding stigmata and the suffering of crucifixion and martyrdom. With a dualistic understanding that hates the body and is intoxicated with the spirit or emptiness, it sees higher spiritual attainment being possible only at the expense of the corporeal. The Middle Way corrects this tendency.

In Christianity here in Ireland, we see this view of self-mortification being prevalent—now less so than it was, thankfully. When I was growing up, people like Matt Talbot were held up as an example of great holiness. He was a poor Dublin Catholic devotee who starved himself and tortured his body with chains. Members of the Catholic organization Opus Dei that engaged in self-flagellation were also held in high esteem, seen as saintly and pious. They wore chains with spikes under their clothes, and they beat themselves regularly with whips. It always struck me as a kind of religious masochism and as something deeply disturbing.

The Buddhist tradition is as guilty of self-mortification as any other religious tradition. Think of the story of Dazu Huike, who cuts off his own arm to display his sincerity when seeking teachings from Bodhidharma, the first Zen master in China. Or think of the tradition of self-immolation in East Asian Buddhism, where parts of the body are burned as an act of devotion, and in some cases even the entire body is set alight in ritual suicide. As spiritual practitioners, we are supposed to be awestruck and admire such acts, rather than be repelled and disturbed by them.

While these are quite extreme examples, we often see more modest manifestations of this misguided macho spirituality. Such a spirituality is often an egocentric display of sincerity and devotion. It is usually directed toward an audience, but that audience may also consist only of the insecure self, an audience of one. How it shows itself may be in extraordinarily long spells of spiritual practice, leading to physical pain. It may be in fasting to a point that is damaging to human health. For example, a friend once told me about a Tibetan nun who was on the point of near starvation she ate so little. But even in our own zazen, we must guard against such a macho attitude developing, in which we brag about the difficulty of the practice we engage in or attempt to martyr ourselves through extremes of practice.

If you are in pain, put up with that pain for a while. But if it persists and is intense, then your body is trying to tell you something. Find a more comfortable way to sit. Your body is not something bad and dirty, something to be rejected. This is a dualistic understanding. If you experience pain while sitting zazen, then your body is telling you that you are causing damage and that you need to change something. While some pain and discomfort are normal, especially when you are new to practice, you should not force your body into positions that it does not want to go.

You can make sitting easier by introducing some regular yoga into your routine. Then your body will become more flexible and pliant. Over time, you will find it is easier to sit zazen in one of the more traditional postures. If not, it is perfectly fine to sit zazen in a chair. But if you do sit in a cross-legged posture, or sit on your heels in the *seiza* posture, there will be some discomfort from time to time. This is true, even if you sit in a chair. Accepting this is, in fact, part of the practice. If you still find it hard to walk five minutes after rising, then maybe the posture is too extreme for you. But if you need a few minutes for your circulation to return after sitting, that is normal enough. It is not really a concern. If pain and stiffness continue long after sitting, then you need to review how you sit.

It's important to realize that this "Macho Zen" I've mentioned also has a flip side: a lazy attitude to practice that is indolent and sluggish. While in Macho Zen the ego is strong in its controlling self-discipline, in "Lazy Zen" the ego asserts itself in an absence of discipline entirely. On one hand, you have the person that insists on sitting all night in the meditation hall until the following morning's practice; on the other, you have the person who sleeps in and misses morning zazen, who skips blocks of practice to engage in some pleasure or other. One is as common as the other. For the first, *emptiness* is an intoxicating idea that they lose themselves in; for the second, Zen represents some attitude of laxity, relaxation, and effortless tranquility. But neither the austere spirit nor the lax spirit is the Zen Way. The path lies somewhere in between.

The Sixth Ancestor of the tradition, Huineng (638–713), well understood this. In the Platform Sutra, he teaches us to be free of these polar dualities.

> If you're confused about the outside, you're attached to forms. If you're confused about the inside, you're attached to emptiness. To be free of form amid forms and to be free of emptiness amid emptiness, this is when you aren't confused about the inside or the outside.[9]

Here *inside* refers to spiritual orientation at the expense of the physical world, while *outside* is the external orientation that is attached to sense pleasures. One can see this Zen master's clear and balanced teaching, pointing the way past both extremes. The perpetually strict and humorless need to lighten up, and the perpetual clown needs some sobriety.

Once, when I went to the Soto Zen Buddhist Association's biannual conference, I saw this lesson well demonstrated. I was there at the conference, in beautiful Maple Lake, Minnesota, to perform the Dharma Heritage Ceremony, in which new Zen teachers are recognized by their peers. It was early autumn, and the trees were beautiful surrounding the lakes of Minnesota. For many days, we sat zazen early in the morning and held workshops, discussions, and ceremonies throughout the day. It was a full and serious schedule, with many of the leading Zen priests of North America and Canada in attendance, as well as priests from Japan and further afield. As a Sōtō Zen event, it was full of formality and solemnity. But on the last night, a celebration was held. People played music, told stories, and laughed. A band played, and it was a wonderful sight to see some of the leading priests, whose teachings and published works I admire so much, waltzing and dancing around the dance floor like teenagers. All the seriousness and solemnity had vanished in celebratory abandon. It was beautiful to see the inside and the outside so much in balance.

# Knowing Contentment

*When we sit in meditation, we return to the eight
great states that the Buddha taught. We want for
little but to sit still, with the in-breath and out-breath.
We know satisfaction with the state of things the
way they are, and seek out peace and quiet.*

A GREAT CONTENTMENT IS TO be found walking the Middle
Way. With neither lack nor surplus, all things are in balance.
Craving is put to rest and there are sufficient things for life and
happiness to thrive. Our insatiable desires have been calmed, but
not suppressed; and we find peace, no matter what situation we
are in. Of the mind-states that flow from zazen practice, contentment is one of the most precious.

I have known many content people in my life. To be clear, they
were not people in dire poverty, whose wants of food, housing,
security, and other basic needs were not met. My mother used to
say, "poverty is evil." I think she was right. But these people were
not highly successful people either. They were not the people that
chased after high achievement and status. They were not usually
people in positions of power. They were ordinary people, living
ordinary and decent lives. They were people with little ego and
few cares in the world. They were free within the boundaries of
their own life. Often, they had a quiet faith in things, believing
that the flow of life would take care of itself and work out. In that
sense, they were in harmony with their surroundings, whatever

those surroundings were. They were people who gardened in the neighborhood where I grew up, finding silent pleasure in planting and tending vegetables or flowers. Or they were old fellows sitting quietly in country pubs, unconcerned with the busyness of the world, meditatively sitting near an open fire. What was common among them was their centered presence. Their full being was right there in the situation they were in. They were totally engrossed in the present task and the present moment.

Near the end of his life, the Buddha confirmed what the thoughts and reflections of a "great person" were. Among them is knowing satisfaction, being content. Many of the other thoughts are related, such as wanting little and enjoying peace and quiet. These sound like simple states—and they are. But what makes them so elusive for many of us is that we have constructed the world to run entirely counter to entering these states with any regularity. We live in societies geared toward endless economic growth. The whole commercial basis of how we have organized everything is based on the creation of wants through advertising. In this model, everything must be disposable and regularly replaced. Things we once craved quickly become obsolete and must be updated. Everything is assigned a value in a theater of prestige and fashion, rather than having a value in its own right. In this unhappy vision, anything can be turned into a commodity—even the ground we stand on.

I remember in the late 1980s when gold was discovered on Ireland's holy mountain, Croagh Patrick. The place had been a site of pilgrimage and contemplation for centuries, but now it was to be ripped open and mined for the seam of gold that ran along its western slope. Even one of Ireland's most sacred sites was under threat by those that wished to extract gold from the mountain's heart for short-term profit. The ordinary people of County Mayo, who knew something of contentment and the innate value of things, pushed back successfully and stopped the mining. But other battles were lost in the years that followed. Shell ran its infrastructure through scenic Rossport to bring in gas from off the west coast. In this instance, the local community were beaten off the roads by police. But there were other successes, including Carnsore Point in County Wexford, where nuclear power was resisted in the 1970s. And in recent years, there's been the protection of some of our peat bogs. Often, it was ordinary people of modest means that fought these battles and understood that things had a value all of their own, far beyond any commodity value. In contrast, the powers of state and commerce were under the delusion that all things could be bought and sold in an insatiable drive for more.

When we sit in meditation, we return to the eight great states that the Buddha taught. We want for little but to sit still, with the in-breath and out-breath. We know satisfaction with the state of things the way they are, and seek out peace and quiet. With effort, we bring our awareness to when and where we are, right now, cultivating wisdom and stillness. In this state we no longer objectify the world as something we can use for our own selfish ends. We intimately realize that we are deeply connected to the world around us. In truth, our true body reaches far beyond the boundaries of our skin. It is the air we breathe and the food that sustains us, grown in fields watered by rain that falls, brought here by clouds that have crossed the broad ocean. The ground that supports us as we sit in zazen is not merely an object or commodity; it is our body itself. It is the body of things that stretch out in every direction, filling the entire universe. And in a simple, quiet way, that total reality is just here where we quietly sit in zazen. To be present here is to be present with the true reality of all things.

Master Dōgen learned this when he returned to Japan from China in 1227. Having taken the dangerous journey there and back again, he knew that he did not need to abandon his own place and seek out "the dusty borders of foreign lands." He learned that "the truth is originally all around" and that "we do not stray from the right state."[10] Would he have learned this if he never made the journey to begin with? Maybe not. But this was a journey he made on behalf of us all. He returned to Kennin-ji temple in Kyoto with the teaching that everything we need is already with us. He taught this in his "Fuganzazengi," or "Universal Recommendation for Zazen," he addressed all people—not just monks and nuns. Zazen was for everyone and everyone everywhere, in all times and places. Wanting little and knowing contentment were to be found right where we are, not out in another faraway and unattainable place. This news of Dōgen's is very good news—and never have we needed this news more than we do now.

The eccentric Japanese poet Ryōkan (1758–1831) well understood this teaching of frugally wanting little. But even *frugality* is the wrong word in a Zen vision where even a particle of dust contains whole universes. For this hermit monk, even a few twigs were a treasure from which he could make a fire. Known as Taïgu, the "Great Fool,"[11] he spent his days sitting in zazen, playing with local children, drinking sake with farmers, and wandering around writing poems. He often wrote his poems and then just left them behind. He was offered prestigious positions as poet and priest, but he declined them all. He preferred instead to remain in his simple, isolated hermitage, living surrounded by nature, content with his simple life. Ryōkan has much to teach us. For him, even the sound of the rain was a precious gift.

Too lazy to be ambitious,
I let the world take care of itself.
Ten days' worth of rice in my bag;
a bundle of twigs by the fireplace.
Why chatter about delusion and enlightenment?
Listening to the night rain on my roof,
I sit comfortably, with both legs stretched out.[12]

# A Peaceful and Effortless Gate

*What heals us in zazen is giving up the quest to be
healed. It is allowing the healing to happen in the face
of It, all by itself. It is accepting the unconditional,
rather than always insisting upon the conditional.
This zazen is an act of unconditional love.*

THERE IS THE WEIGHT of the world and its counterweight, zazen.
Sitting in zazen, all the attention we usually direct outward
we turn in the other direction. Sitting with whatever arises, we
are aware that we are aware. We see the knower that knows. This
attention contains everything. It goes in all directions and is truly
boundless. It passes through walls to hear sounds outside the
meditation hall, where birds are singing in a nearby tree. It travels
through time, from the past to the future. It is uncontainable and
holds all the objects in existence within it, just like space. In zazen,
we enter this attention, this mind. It contains our birth and our
death. It is itself birthless and deathless. Starting with the self, we
end up forgetting the self. We see that everything is sentient, that
everything is the mind of Buddha. The distinctions between the
weight of form and the formless counterweight of zazen fall away.
The original balance is restored.

I think it is useful in beginning practice to think of zazen as
this radically free space, a kind of counterweight to all our worries

and concerns. Our entire lives involve effort and struggle as we make our way in the world. We must find work to do and a place to live. We have to try and get on with difficult people and look after our physical and mental health. Every day, we need to be fed and washed. We have illness and worry and seemingly endless responsibility. And everything in our life is working toward some end. We exercise to get fit. We study to get a good job. Everything has a utilitarian function. And as a tool, it is used and then it out-lives its use. When one goal is reached, another one looms. And so, we constantly struggle.

Zazen is different. In zazen, we give up the struggle—not in defeat, but because we have empowered ourselves to let go. Zazen is not another tool that we use to attain some goal and then dis-card. Zazen exists on its own terms, not on ours. As the great Zen teacher Kōdō Sawaki said, zazen is "wonderfully useless." It is not self-help. It is not something you master, and it is not a kind of knowledge that you attain. The "you" that sits zazen and gives up the struggle disappears in zazen. You do not control zazen. It is not about more control. It is letting things be as they are. So, you choose to give up the struggle and then you give up yourself too. Sitting zazen, the struggle of carrying your own weight is relin-quished. As you sit, the earth beneath supports you. As my teacher Taïgu Rōshi often says, "you do not sit zazen; zazen sits you." This experience contains you, but it is not just you. It is far vaster than that. It is the body of truth itself, far beyond the boundaries of your own birth and death. That this practice heals you is incidental, rather than essential. As your sicknesses and anxieties are yours, in leaving yourself aside, you also leave aside your sicknesses and anxieties. We are at our happiest when we are not self-obsessed, when we are no longer self-conscious and self-aware. This is when we are in our natural state. This is the state of zazen. It is also the state we find ourselves in when we are totally engrossed in something, when we are at one with our actions. Like this, in zazen we give ourselves over to this greater truth. And like a leaf in a stream, we are carried along. We are only a leaf, but having given ourselves over to the stream, the whole flowing power of the stream gives us strength.

The power of this stream is wisdom and compassion: its body is wisdom, and its powerful flowing movement is compassion. This is not just meditation to make us feel better. This is a force to transform the whole world. This is why this is soul-and-spirit practice. It is something closer to the sacred than the secular. It is poetry more than prose. And it is something far beyond "Buddhism." When Buddhism has been left behind, only this remains. It is elemental and natural, rather than artificial and provisional. It is the source from which everything flows. It has many names, but it is ultimately unnamable. When we name it, we limit it. And it has no limits. It is ineffable: too great to be described in words. It is what Christ wrote in the sand. It is the thing we appeal to when nothing has worked.

Unwilling to lead his monks astray, Master Dōgen refers to it only as *It*. The word is *inmo* in Chinese—something we do not need to explain. It is the meaning of things. It is the order we perceive all around us. We take its intelligence for granted and usually don't even see it. Because it is all around us, it is hard to see. Because it includes all being and also transcends being, we cannot pin it down. That is why the Zen tradition has developed so many ways to point toward it, while frustratingly (for many) refusing to name it. Because naming it is to limit it. It gives the wrong impression. Naming it suggests it can be known, rather than experienced directly. But it is too vast to know.

What heals us in zazen is giving up the quest to be healed. It is allowing the healing to happen in the face of *It*, all by itself. It is accepting the unconditional, rather than always insisting upon the conditional. This zazen is an act of unconditional love: for ourselves and for all things. It is returning to our original nature, which is not originally sinful, but is full of a wisdom and compassion that is far greater than us. This is the substance we are made of.

**The Heart-Circle of Zazen**[13]
Sitting with all at rest is love unconditional.
Sitting simply on the ground is to
Reenter the ordinary heart of love.

Touch the earth daily, morning and evening,
Let it ignite your whole body,
Your full being,
Into a bonfire of love.

Let the warmth of your zazen
Radiate in all directions.
For, in truth, this is a fire that has woken up,
Not one that was ever put out.

Fire without fuel,
Endless flame of being,
The coldness of the world is banished
By even one person sitting zazen.

From the still center of your sitting,
Allow a joyous river to well up within you.
Without trying,
Without directing its flow,
It will gush forth in all directions,
To relieve the parched throats
Of all who thirst.

Your zazen is just this particular portal
For a universal Dharma that flows through you.
Open the gates
And the water will flow by itself.

The world will be washed clean.
Even the grime of it will sparkle.

With the true Dharma eye,
Those that hate you,
Even the hurtful,
Will reveal their innocent hearts,
Though they are yet to be freed themselves.

Let your zazen be the stillness
Where all movement begins.
See that this movement is stillness,
That stillness itself is movement.

Do not point out others' actions,
But return the point of attention to your own heart,
As the source of wise words and action.

Allow your zazen to teach silently,
Because silence can reach the corners of the heart where
    words can never go.

Do not seek healing from your sitting.
When the body is ready,
The appetite returns.
After the night,
Wakefulness happens,
All by itself.

This sitting is a thing of nature,
A potato field with weeds,
A weir running
With leaping salmon.

But it is a Holy Well too,
Revered by the ancestors,
Where generations have been blessed.

It is a sacred peak to climb
By sitting on the earth.
A deep fishing ground to trawl,
Where the greatest prize is an empty net.

At the heart of this zazen
Is the heart itself.
It is unburdened and actualized
Only when it is shared,
In solitude with visiting birds,
Or in the clamor of cities,
Where play out the struggles of our kind.

Poised beyond peace and fury,
The heart anoints all.
Perfection beyond perfection.
Boundless love,
Beyond love's outer possibilities.
This is not something we can have
Or ever give away.
It is something others cannot give to us,
That we can only get from them.

Zazen's great matter is
The impossible matter of love.
All we can do is allow it open us up
As a feast to nourish the world.
And in nourishing the world,
We nourish ourselves.

This is the great circle of love.
The heart-circle of the Way.
The heart-mudra we make

With our entire body and all being.
The loving center of zazen
That is no more than our
Just sitting.
So we sit . . .

PART TWO

# Living

# For Self and Others

*In our zazen practice, it is important to realize that we do not do it for ourselves alone. We do this practice for all beings everywhere. It is the foundation of our actions in the wider world.*

THERE IS A GREAT meditation in the Buddhist tradition on developing loving-kindness. Called the *metta bhavana*, it begins with generating an attitude of loving-kindness toward oneself. Then it becomes progressively harder, as we move on to generate loving-kindness for loved ones, and then those we feel neutral about, before coming to the generation of loving-kindness for our enemies, those people we find most difficult to deal with in life. The *metta bhavana* ends with wishing well to all beings equally everywhere, no matter what our personal relationship is to them. It is a meditation that develops unconditional love—not love based on self-interest or what you can get from it personally. All utility is set aside. This is something much more akin to divine love. It is something that comes through us, not from us.

Growing up in Ireland in the 1970s and 1980s, there were awful tragedies on the news every other night. I remember clearly as a child watching on television the remains of a person being shoveled into a plastic bag after a bombing in Belfast. Every few weeks or months, a murder seemed to outdo all that preceded it in terms of violence and barbarity. Throughout all this warfare, there were still voices of loving-kindness that stood out. The Derry politician and civil rights advocate John Hume was one of them. He often repeated a quote often attributed to the pacifist Indian leader Gandhi: "An eye for an eye leaves the whole world blind." Despite being disenfranchised and brutalized by the British state, Hume always sought a peaceful way to resolve the conflict in Northern Ireland. He sought respect for both sides. Similarly, Gordon Wilson, a Protestant draper from Enniskillen, forgave the Irish Republican Army when they murdered his daughter in a bombing in 1987. "I bear no ill will. I bear no grudge," he said, even meeting those that killed his beloved daughter and calling for no reprisals for her death from the other side. Both these men were incredibly inspirational figures. They were people that managed to get beyond their own limited horizons and see the world with unconditional forgiveness and unconditional love. To them, their enemy was misguided rather than evil. And despite their own pain and suffering, they reached out to make a connection with that enemy, in search of mutual healing.

In the Buddhist tradition, we would call such people bodhisattvas, "awakened beings." While Buddhism is misunderstood as being only about personal meditation and spiritual development, in truth it is motivated by the bodhisattva vow to save all sentient beings and relieve their suffering. Mahayana Buddhism is clear on the importance of this vow. Pope Benedict XVI may have deliberately misunderstood Buddhism when he caricatured it as being nothing more than "autoerotic spirituality," essentially a kind of spiritual masturbation, where one gratifies the self and seeks no union with others. But the gross and willful ignorance he displayed with this comment betrays the limited understanding of Buddhism in the West. Maybe Benedict felt his Catholicism was under threat as Buddhism increasingly finds a presence in Western societies. In any case, the increasing popularity of meditation in the West has shored up this misconception, as the most popular forms of meditation tend to be secular, cut off from a Buddhist context. Such meditation lacks a solid philosophical and ethical base, and is concerned more with personal experience than societal obligations and the greater good. But even secular meditation has some benefit, for if individuals are more at ease and less anxious, then they will be in a better position to give to others. They will be better people all round. To some extent, the dichotomy of self-love and love of the other is a false dichotomy to start with. This is an important lesson the Buddhist wisdom tradition has to teach.

However, emphasizing meditation alone is not the eightfold path taught by the original Buddha. When we rise from meditation, we must take that practice with us out into the world. Three of the eight parts of the eightfold path are dedicated to *sila*, ethics. To engage in correct speech and action, and to not work in an unethical profession—these are among the very foundations of the Dharma, along with the development of wisdom and meditation. These ethical concepts later came to be codified in the Buddhist canon as the Vinaya, the code of conduct for the monastic order, as well as the precepts, which are taken by lay and ordained Buddhists alike on the bodhisattva path. The precepts are familiar guidelines that are shared by many faith traditions: respect life; be giving; live one's sexual life in a harmonious way; be truthful; protect the clarity of your mind; see what is beautiful in others; cultivate your own beauty without pride; give with generosity; pacify the angry heart; and embody awakening, wisdom, and compassion. Traditionally, these precepts are also articulated in their negative form: do not kill; do not steal; do not misuse sexuality; do not lie; do not abuse intoxicants; do not slander; do not praise self and criticize others; do not be greedy; do not harbor ill will; and do not disrespect the three treasures of the Dharma. The positive articulation of the precepts may resonate with some more than others, and so they are also stated like that. To live this way is considered a skillful way to live. The precepts are given to us to live and interpret skillfully and honestly, rather than as a set of authoritarian commandments we must follow to the letter. The spirit of these precepts is more important than the letter. We accept and live by them, knowing that the self and other are deeply interconnected, and are in truth one body. Based on the wisdom that knows the true nature of reality, for Buddhists there is no other way to live. From wisdom, compassion flows naturally. The self cannot be saved if all others are abandoned. What kind of salvation is that which sees all others abandoned to their fate? In the traditional Buddhist view, even the hell realms must be emptied before the bodhisattva's work is done. It is a radical vision that leaves none behind. Even the evil must be shown how badly they are misguided.

In our zazen practice, therefore, it is important to realize that we do it not for ourselves alone. We do this practice for all beings everywhere. It is the foundation of our actions in the wider world. By manifesting peace within ourselves, we can realize peace beyond the borders of the self. It takes great bravery to do this— the kind of bravery that John Hume and Gordon Wilson realized. It involves loving even our enemies, reaching out to those we disagree with—like that great statue in the divided city of Derry, *Hands across the Divide*, where two figures reach out to each other in friendship from each side of the conflict, setting aside their differences so that the circle of violence can be broken. The kind of dualistic spirituality that sets up the self versus the other cannot offer an inclusive vision that truly heals. A genuine practice knows that there is no such boundary as that between self and other. What is truly good for the self is good for the other. This is how things really are, once the delusion of duality is broken through. With such a view, the circle of delusion, the circle of suffering and violence, can be finally broken.

# Overcome by What Needs to Be Done

*Right where you are is where your power is. Right where you are is where you can heal the world or harm it. Look around you. This is the field for your activity. This is where your work is to be done.*

WITH OUR AWARENESS AWAKENED, it is easy to see just how much work needs to be done in the world. Every day of the week, if you watch the news you will feel paralyzed by how many problems need fixing. The "lungs of the world," the Amazon rainforests, are being cleared. Human beings are being abused and being trafficked as slaves. The icecaps are melting, and wars are raging in different parts of the globe. It is easy to be overcome by it all.

Social media makes these problems even worse. There are so many issues that come to your attention as you scroll down the page. With the collapse of distance on global social media platforms, all the problems of the world come to visit you at home on your small screen, concentrated and brought together into a toxically powerful form. Each individual problem is bad enough on its own. But brought into one place and time, filling your attention as you scroll, they become unbearable and unsolvable. Because these issues are happening simultaneously in parts of the world that are often far away, you feel disoriented and powerless in the face of what you have become aware of. Your attention is being pulled in twenty different directions at once. This makes you unable to act. Your mind follows one story, and then suddenly it is pulled in another direction, and ultimately you go nowhere, unable to respond in any satisfactory way to any of the things that have come to your attention.

Where we direct our attention is what becomes our life. Before global media was part of our lives, our attention was on the things that lay before us. For my grandparents, the circle of their awareness was very local. Living in rural East Galway, what mattered to them was the weather, along with local sports and news: who was getting married, who had died, how were the crops doing, and was the cow ready to give birth. The news was about people they knew and events in their lives that they could potentially have a bearing on. In contrast, what we do today in the face of events feels as though it has no effect whatsoever. We feel utterly powerless. We feel as though what we do really doesn't matter—only the powerful and rich can have an effect on the world. Because what are we but ordinary people? How can it matter what we do and say?

When I was in my late teens and early twenties, it felt as though there was an underlying shift in the way the whole world was structured. As a college student, I looked on as the crippling conservatism of Ireland was challenged. In China, ordinary people stood up for democracy. In Eastern Europe, citizens took peacefully to the streets and toppled long-standing repressive regimes. Then the free and open internet came along. The free exchange of ideas and information was possible among citizens. I was in my early twenties and the world looked like it was entering an era of enlightened equality and fairness. But soon the old powers exerted their influence again, and bit by bit they took back control in new and more subtle ways. What started out feeling like liberation flipped over to become something else. The thrilling prospect of freedom in distant places never materialized. The new global world we lived in had not delivered, but instead continued to trespass in our living rooms and homes, via 24/7 news channels and the World Wide Web. It's like a constant storm of news is raging now, and we are totally powerless in the face of its immensity.

In Zen practice, we find a refuge from this raging storm. We realize that to change one small thing is to change the world. As all things are without an independent, enduring self, all things are part of the same boundless reality. If you consider that this reality is one unified system or body, if one thing changes in it then the whole system has indeed been changed. In the ancient Avatamsaka Sutra, we see the interconnectedness of the universe illustrated by the image of Indra's Net, which has a jewel wherever the net's strands intersect. If one thing happens anywhere in this web, it is reflected in every other jewel throughout the web as a whole. No one jewel is cut off and independent from the entire system, but rather, the system is only made of all its constituent parts.

In light of this teaching, everything you do profoundly matters. When you make a cup of tea, it makes a difference if you put the teabag in the compost bin or in the garbage. It all matters: if you smile or scowl at the shop assistant; if you buy clothes made with child labor; if you support politicians that care little about environmental emergencies and growing inequalities; whether you speak with kindness or anger; even whether you make your bed in the morning or not. Every single thing matters. You are not powerless at all. Right where you are is where your power is. Right where you are is where you can heal the world or harm it. Look around you. This is the field for your activity. This is where your work is to be done. The people around you are the people you must work with and support. The things to take care of are right before you. Bring your attention there. Do not allow yourself to become distracted from the work at hand.

When Master Dōgen was in China, he met an old monk drying mushrooms in the sun. The day was scorching hot, and this old and experienced monk was charged with preparing mushrooms for the kitchen. As Dōgen looked on, he saw this man, who was his senior, taking meticulous care with each mushroom as he laid them out in the hot sun. The old man was tired and perspiring heavily due to the amount of work he had to do for the large monastery. Dōgen, much younger than him, approached and asked why he didn't leave this work to a younger monk and concentrate instead on his important spiritual duties. The old man impressed upon Dōgen how this was his work to do and his alone, and how it was as important as any other work he had to do as a monk. For the old monk, drying mushrooms in the sun was the most important thing in the whole world at that moment. This, he taught the young Dōgen, was true Zen practice.

What are the duties you must perform today? Do you have to prepare a meal? Do you have to write a document at work? Can you perform this task with your full attention, treating it as your own Zen practice, right here and now? What needs to be done should be done now—no need to become overwhelmed by what needs to be done later or elsewhere. What are your responsibilities? In the totality of the entire universe, nothing is as important as that individual mushroom that needs to be dried out in the sun.

# Holding Opinions Lightly

*While our opinions often come from lived reality, we have a habit of reversing this process and imposing our opinions back onto reality. Now we are not seeing reality for what it is. Rather, we are viewing the world through a thick and distorting filter.*

WE LIVE IN A time when opinion has more force than fact. Opinions are put forward strongly in a culture that is deeply polarized. In many countries, there are two main political and cultural camps. They shout at each other, neither listening to the other side. Each exists in a bubble of its own truth, where narratives that challenge their point of view are never aired. They are trapped in a dark echo chamber, where their own voice echoes back to them as confirmation of their own strongly held beliefs. Rather than being connected to the wider reality around them, they are disconnected. Everywhere they look, they see a mirror that reflects only their own face.

Never have we needed the teaching of Saint Thomas more. In the Gospel of John, Thomas will not believe that the risen Jesus has appeared to the other apostles until he can touch Christ's wounds himself as proof. He is the original Doubting Thomas, and this is where the phrase comes from. In the Gospel, Jesus appears to criticize Thomas for his skepticism: "because thou hast seen me, thou hast believed: blessed are they that have not seen, and yet have believed." Such faith may be necessary to follow a spiritual path, but it is just as important to have an equal amount of doubt. In the Zen tradition, it's said you need great faith, great doubt, and great resolve to awaken. Indeed, faith that is not balanced by doubt can be dangerous because to take things for granted is not to see things as they really are. To rest in one's biases and pre-formulated positions is to fossilize, while reality moves on in its dynamic flow of change.

One way doubt is engendered in the Zen Way is through the use of koans, or apparently paradoxical teaching stories from the tradition. For example, a Zen master asks her student, "Without words and without gestures, display your understanding." The student is flummoxed. She cannot find a way out. There is nowhere to go, and her habitual ways of thinking are useless. The usual thought patterns that have served her well for so long suddenly fall away, and she is faced with a great doubt. The Zen teacher is teaching something; but if the student is not ready, she will not hear it. She might dismiss the teacher's question as nonsense. She might decide this Zen thing is a waste of time and return to her usual way of living. Or maybe she is ready and there is a breakthrough.

We all have strong opinions, and we usually expect the world to conform to these opinions. We inherit these opinions untested from others, or we derive these opinions from lived experience. In the first case, we have not tested these beliefs ourselves, but merely inherited them. In the second instance, we formed an opinion in the past, but conditions have moved on since. While our opinions often come from lived reality, we have a habit of reversing this process and imposing our opinions back onto reality. Now we are not seeing reality for what it is. Rather, we are viewing the world through a thick and distorting filter. We do not see things as they are, but things as we imagine them to be.

Koans are a splash of cold water on the face. That is how they wake you up. We can resist the koan and get annoyed by it, or we can work with it and have a breakthrough. Zen practice is full of teachings that work like this.

For example, one time on retreat there was a controversy about the use of the *kyōsaku*—the slat-like stick used to strike meditators on request, in order to counter sleepiness and torpor. The *kyōsaku* has a long history in Zen as a means to help meditators stay awake—and there are stories from the past of it being used on monks with great force. However, usually it is used as I intended to use it—not with force. Despite involving a blow to the shoulders, it is nevertheless not an act of aggression. (If that were the case, certain types of massage and forms of medical treatment could also be construed as acts of aggression.)

But practitioners of Zen are mostly lay people these days, and so the monastic understanding and acceptance of the *kyōsaku* is absent. Many who are new to Zen may never have encountered the *kyōsaku* before, and, while it can appear to strike with great force, in fact it does not injure or inflict any substantial pain.

The *kyōsaku* is used only on request: the person asks for it because they feel it will help them, whether to stop them from drifting off or to give them renewed energy. It is administered with kindness, with the strike given on the shoulders with enough force to enliven, but not enough force to actually hurt. So, on this seven-day retreat, I was offering the traditional *kyōsaku* as an aid to meditation. I explained its use beforehand and gave a demonstration. I emphasized that it would only ever be given on request, not as some kind of punishment. However, despite all this, the strong convictions of a few people against the *kyōsaku* made it impossible for it to be used at all on this retreat. Why? Because they felt that striking another person with a stick was categorically a violent act, and that it disturbed everyone else in the meditation hall. They also argued that there could be those in the room with trauma from suffering violence in the past, and so the *kyōsaku*, they said, was simply inappropriate and unacceptable.

On that retreat, the discussion around the *kyōsaku*'s use became so heated that afterward, if I were to use the *kyōsaku*, then it would be against the strong convictions of a few members of the sangha present. Using the *kyōsaku* after such a heated argument would just be inappropriate, as it would mean imposing my own view on the group, in full knowledge that a few among us strongly disagreed with its use. Those that would benefit from it were therefore denied it, as a few held entrenched opinions against it.

It is a shame, as the *kyōsaku* can prove to be a great support to practice, as it has been for many centuries. It seemed to me that contemporary views of what constitute violence and acceptable behavior were being incorrectly applied, and in this context those cultural assumptions were being imposed on a situation where they resulted in a misreading of what was actually taking place.

Zen challenges us in ways that contemporary culture is particularly apt at resisting. It asks that we park our opinions and see what is there. But silent spaces where we contemplate before we speak are now few and far between. We are encouraged to have strong opinions: in our education; on social media; in debates and discussions. It is good that we can assess the facts and formulate an opinion that we can articulate. But when that opinion becomes a bubble from which all other opinions and contesting facts are excluded, then we are trapped in a prison of our own making. With this view, Zen training becomes impossible. The tradition and the teacher become not much more than an imposition upon one's individuality. Everything must measure up to notions of conventional logic and accepted practice. Koans become nonsense, and the *kyōsaku* becomes a weapon of power and abuse. Indeed, they may be like this, but wisdom lies in knowing when the situation is as you see it and when it is your seeing that has colored the situation.

# "Emptiness": What Goes Around Comes Around

*"Emptiness" is really about connection and co-reliance. But because of the word itself, it is often misunderstood as some kind of nihilism or an assertion that nothing really exists—that there is no meaning to existence. This is a total misunderstanding, and one of the pitfalls of the translation of the word* sunyata *as* emptiness.

I HAVE NEVER LIKED THE word *emptiness*. It has connotations of the void, zero, meaninglessness, and lack. In Buddhism, it refers to the reality that everything has no permanent, unchanging, independent existence. Take your own body, for example. It is impermanent. It relies on everything else in existence to exist itself. So, you need the ground you stand on and the air you breathe. You need the generations before you that led to you being born at all. You need the food you eat and the water you drink. Maybe you are alive now because someone once invented a medicine that you need to stay alive. The sun is still shining and warming the earth, which makes it warm enough for you to live. All of reality is supporting your existence in ways that you are not even aware of. This is what it means to arise interdependently with everything else. To say you are empty of essential or intrinsic existence is to say that you are part of a holistic totality. Others have preferred the word *boundlessness* to *emptiness* to describe this concept. The Vietnamese Zen teacher Thich Nhat Hanh uses the term *interbeing* to describe this truth.

But this philosophical observation is much less important than its practical consequences. At the moment here, we are in the middle of a global pandemic. Every day in Ireland, many people are dying because of it, and all over the world thousands are losing their lives daily and many are suffering terribly. Because of an initial transmission of the virus, when someone handled or consumed a sick animal in China, now the entire human population is in danger of getting sick, and over two million people have died globally already. International travel has ground to a halt, and millions have lost their jobs. The global upheaval has been staggering—and it all started with one incident in China. Now we are painfully aware of the truth of interconnection. We also understand that by looking after our own health, we look after the health of others. If we become sick, we pass that sickness on. The public mantra of the moment is "We are all in this together."

But this idea of togetherness has been much criticized also, because there have been glaring inequalities exposed by the pandemic. If you work in a low-paying, menial job, you are much more likely to get sick. If you can work from home and have the protections of a good salary and all that that means, you are in a better position. The rich countries of the world are hoarding the vaccines that have been developed against the virus for themselves, and poor countries can do little about it. Acknowledging these realities, there is little togetherness and social solidarity in evidence.

The great second-century Buddhist philosopher Nagarjuna saw that there were two truths about existence: there was the ultimate truth and the relative truth. From one point of view, all things are equally empty and interdependent. From the other point of view, relative phenomena have their own independent reality; they have an existence that we can identify as separate and apart. From one perspective, there is one seamless and boundless reality. From the other, there are big things and small things, rich people and poor people. It is important that we recognize that both perspectives are always there simultaneously. So, while we are all profoundly interconnected, there is also this independence and separateness, which allows us to deny the other reality of interconnection and act in selfish and egocentric ways.

But even though we act in a self-centered way, as if we were the only thing in existence that mattered, we cannot escape the ultimate truth that we are holistically bound to everyone and everything else. This plays out in our individual lives and in our society as a whole. The effects of actions on a collective level can also be observed. In the political sphere, we see the politics of "law and order," for example. Governments starve underprivileged parts of society of supports, and when that results in social unrest or a spike in crime, they react with policies based on law and order. What inspires these law-and-order or security-minded reactions is that the wealthy feel threatened by the spike in crime. But the wealthy are often those who were in favor of cutting back on social services and supports in the first place. Then, when the effects of these actions come home to roost, the response is based on a misunderstanding of the causes, as well as a delusion that they, as wealthy people, can somehow be protected and sealed off from the rest of social reality. Again and again we see this process played out: We encourage everyone to drive a car, and then we complain that there are traffic jams. We do not invest in education and hospitals, and then we take issue with a poorly educated workforce and an overwhelmed hospital system. We are so full of ourselves that we forget about emptiness—that is, we forget that we are all interconnected.

"Emptiness" is really about connection and co-reliance. But because of the word itself, it is often misunderstood as some kind of nihilism or an assertion that nothing really exists—that there is no meaning to existence. This is a total misunderstanding, and one of the pitfalls of the translation of the Sanskrit word *sunyata* as *emptiness*.

In the classic collection of Zen koans, the *Mumonkan*, or the *Gateless Gate*, there is a story that well illustrates this "empty" nature of things, this interconnected system of reality that all things are part of.[14] On a windy day, two monks observe the temple flag billow in a strong breeze. One monk asserts that the flag is moving; the other thinks, rather, that the wind is moving. Huineng, the Sixth Ancestor, hearing the conversation, suggests that both the monks are wrong. It is not the wind that is moving or the flag that is moving. It is their mind that moves. The monks are awestruck by this insight. But, in reality, each of them is both correct and incorrect at the same time. I think that is the point of the koan. In the "empty" nature of interpenetrating reality, the flag, the wind, and the mind all move with everything else in the universe. Each of the monks is partially right, but missing the bigger picture. Once we understand that we see reality from a single, self-centered perspective, we can act with wisdom in the face of the truth of emptiness. This is the beginning of enlightened activity.

# A Perfect Offering

*To give totally is to give with no residue left behind.
To give totally is to give and forget about the
giving, so that no indebtedness is left afterward.
Best of all is to give anonymously. This makes the
offering perfect. There can be no contamination of
the act itself. It is to give and not to seek reward. It
enters the world in purity, transforming the world
for the better, without seeking any self-gain.*

WHEN I WAS IN school, the Jesuit priests that ran the school used to get us involved in "social action" on the weekends. Usually, this meant doing jobs for the elderly or helping some poor families that lived in Galway City. I remember painting houses and delivering and stacking firewood. That kind of thing. I also remember serving Christmas dinner in the geriatric ward up in the city hospital. That experience opened my eyes to the realities of old age. Feeding some of the residents was quite an experience. I must have been no more than sixteen or seventeen at the time. And taking one of the old men to the bathroom was at the time a shocking lesson for me in the vulnerability of the human body and how it degenerates with time.

Once, I remember we went to paint an old man's house on a Saturday morning in the city center. He lived alone and in total squalor. Old plates and dirty dishes were piled up everywhere, left unwashed for days. The walls were filthy with dirt and food stains. I remember a pill stuck to the wall—some of his medication that maybe he had spat out. He himself wore dirty old clothes, and the tiny, cramped house he lived in smelled awful. We had to scrub down the walls before we could paint anything.

But when we were finished, the old man laid out tea and biscuits with such pride and gratitude that we had to take them. For him, a packet of biscuits was a real luxury, and he had spent the very little money he had on buying them. Now he was offering them to us. In offering us biscuits, he was giving more than a much wealthier person would be in buying you a nice dinner in a good restaurant. He was offering something really precious.

In Buddhism, *dana*, or generosity, is one of the six *paramitas*, or perfections. Real generosity is not a matter of what is given; rather, what's important is the spirit with which it is given. When a child gives you a flower, it is given totally and fully as an act of love. In giving the flower, the child allows a natural and spontaneous act of generosity and gratitude to flow forth. It arises before connivance and manipulative consciousness can exist. It is an expression of our natural and true state of being. This is who we really are. We are not originally sinful. Rather, we are originally giving, generous, and kind. This is obvious when you observe even a small baby. They constantly hold things out to give to their parents: toys, small objects, or scraps of food. It is their natural state to give—and to take. Because for a long time, a small baby does not see the difference. They do not see themselves as being separate from their mother. They consider that they are still part of the mother's body. We may think that their minds are simply underdeveloped and mistaken in this perception—but in another way they are totally right.

In the *ōryōki* ceremony of taking food on Zen retreats, we chant, "May we with all beings realize the emptiness of the three wheels, giver, receiver, and gift." From the point of view of ultimate truth, the person who receives the food and the person who gives the food are of one being. Because we are giving and receiving at every moment, in giving we receive and in receiving we give. Did you ever feel in receiving a present given in the wrong spirit that you were in fact having something taken from you? Maybe the present was given by the person so that you would be in their debt, a debt that would later be collected. Or maybe you were a prop in a public display of virtue. This is not truly giving. Rather this is giving to take. It is nothing like the child giving the flower. The child giving the flower is more like a stream that gives you water when you are thirsty, or the sun that gives you warmth when you are cold. It is the true giving that the universe is blessing us with at every moment. A flower or a smile can be a much more precious thing than money or an expensive gift. It all depends on the spirit in which something is given.

Once when I was visiting a friend studying in Canterbury, in England, we were walking through that beautiful town when we came across a homeless man sitting at the side of the road. My friend who lived there knew him, as he spoke to him regularly. And on this occasion, he sat down beside him to have a chat for a few minutes. I waited patiently as they talked, but noticed that the homeless man was totally unnoticed and invisible to most people that walked by. Even one woman that gave him money didn't really look at him as she passed. It struck me that the conversation my friend was having was precious. The pound coin that was dropped in his cup was no doubt very useful. In contrast, what my friend gave was nothing material, but something much more important. He gave him the gift of dignity. My friend was acknowledging him as an equal human being. He affirmed his humanity. Sometimes it is much harder to give these kinds of gifts.

Often, when it comes to the practice of giving, we are really looking for something in return. We tell others that we are giving so that we are appreciated or praised. But a perfect offering is hermetically sealed off from such exposure. The best kind of giving has no reason beyond the giving itself. It is truly giving, rather than giving for another motivation, such as improving our reputation or appearing like a good person to others. To give totally is to give with no residue left behind. To give totally is to give and forget about the giving, so that no indebtedness is left afterward. Best of all is to give anonymously. This makes the offering perfect. There can be no contamination of the act itself. It is to give and not to seek reward. It enters the world in purity, transforming the world for the better, without seeking any self-gain.

When our Zen community holds a *kitō* (chanting or prayer) service for those in our life or in the world that we know are suffering, one stipulation of the service is that we do not tell those for whom the service is dedicated. It is a service involving chanting and transferring merit to those that need it—like offering them a blessing in their time of need. Members of the community bring forward the names of those we will dedicate the ceremony to, but their names must remain a secret outside of the ceremonial setting itself. You cannot tell your sick friend that you had a Buddhist *kitō* service conducted for them. Often, people want to tell afterward, because it is a beautiful service, involving the offering of incense and the ritual reading[15] of the Prajnaparamita Sutra, with offerings of flowers and lights. But they are reminded that this should be a perfect offering and that they should not tell. It must be sealed off in secrecy to hold real power.

For me, I often think of the *kitō* service as being like checking on a loved one sleeping during the night. Although they are sleeping and are not conscious of it, you are looking out for their welfare and caring for them. When a child is asleep in their cot, they do not know that you have looked in on them. Especially as a new parent, you might check many times a night to make sure that they are still breathing. This is the kind of care that we take in the *kitō* ceremony. There is no practical intervention—like giving money—but still, something important has happened. Something has been offered and given, and that is pure and real. It is like this that we should give. And when we understand giving like this, we realize that we all possess immense wealth that we can share with others.

# Hope in the
# Present Moment

*To hope in the present moment is what makes
life possible. Not so much hope in the future—
let the future take care of itself. Take care of
the present and all will be fine as it is.*

RECENTLY, I WAS ASKED to participate in an interreligious service around the theme of hope. *Hope* is an emotive word with many positive associations. It reflects an optimistic frame of mind that is directed toward the future. We hope something will happen, and we hope for a good outcome. We hope people get better, and we hope all will be well. But in the Zen tradition, hope is not emphasized so much. This is because we emphasize the importance of the present moment, rather than the future. It is not that we do not hope for the future; it is just not where we place the emphasis. So, in the interreligious service I spoke in general terms about hope. Outside the context of Zen and the subtleties of its teachings, I felt the audience would misunderstand this Zen teaching as a dismissal of hope, which would not have been my intention at all.

Hope is always in the present moment. The future is insubstantial—unknown and unwritten. We can only imagine what the future holds. So when we hope, it helps us in the present rather than in the future. Like everything that exists, it can only exist in the present. "I hope you will have a long and healthy life." This is a frame of mind that changes things right now. And by changing things right now in the present, because of the law of causation, we see certain effects in the future. But unlike the present, these future effects are not guaranteed. You may live well and look after yourself, but that does not lead automatically to any outcome. It only makes an outcome more likely. It is always our actions in the present moment that count.

Hope becomes a problem when the present moment is neglected and all energy is projected into the future. This is very common: there is inaction in the present, with some vague hope that the future will be better. So, with this mindset, we do not practice Zen; we don't take the actions that will make us healthier, or the actions that will lead to a better job or life situation. We just hope for some abstract, better situation in the future. In fact, it is a certain religious disposition that we have inherited. In this view, the present world is just a shadow of no importance. The true world is in the life to come. We yearn toward heaven and put up with all sorts of suffering, inequity, and difficulty now. As my parents' generation often said, "your reward awaits you in heaven." This view encourages us to overlook any shortcomings of the present with stoic acceptance, because it is seen as being of no importance. And this view isn't limited to religion. In Plato's *Republic*, this world is just a pale reflection of a higher world, which is an ideal world of perfection. The theme that this present moment, this world here and now, is of secondary importance is a strong and recurrent strain in Western thought. It is so deeply rooted that even the contemporary cult of technology has adopted it. There is always a drive toward a better and more technological future. With cloud computing, even Plato's higher realm of forms has been reimagined as an immaterial, almost mystical, space. This technological future even promises something like heaven, where billionaires hope to upload their brains and cheat death. It is a fantasy based on the denial of material reality—which is ironic, considering it is from the secular world that such ideas come.

While Zen does not deny the immaterial, crucially it does not deny the material either. Both form and emptiness are affirmed equally. The work of Zen is work done in the present moment. Hope is a great support for many, but the real point is what we are doing right now. If we can make peace with the present, we have healed our life, which is here, not off in some posited future. Look around you now. This is the truth, even if the current situation is difficult. This is where the work must be done. Hope is useful only if it supports action in the here and now. In Zen, we do not yearn toward some heaven that is yet to come.

You might take it then that Zen is an atheistic religion. But it is neither theistic nor atheistic. It is a practice rather than a dogma. It is perfectly common to see atheists happily practicing Zen. It is also perfectly normal to see sincere theists on the Zen path. Zen is unconcerned with many of the usual preoccupations of religious faith. It has a totally different and refreshing take on things. It offers medicine we can take now, rather than placing us on a waiting list for a procedure we'll undergo sometime in the future. This is evident not just in the Zen tradition but right back in the original teachings of the Buddha. In the Majjhima Nikaya, for instance, we hear the "Parable of the Poisoned Arrow," where the Buddha refuses to answer speculative metaphysical questions, called the "Fourteen Unanswerable Questions." One who dwells on these questions is likened to a man shot with a poisoned arrow who refuses treatment until he knows who shot the arrow, what the arrow was made of, who made it, and so on. "All this would still not be known to that man, and meanwhile he would die," the Buddha says.[16] What the Enlightened One offers is a way to live right now in this situation that we find ourselves in. He has a method to remove the arrow—an immediate and urgent concern. It is what we face at this very moment. Life is too short to spend years in speculation about what may be. As time passes here, we may whittle away our life, dreaming of the future. The point is to wake up. Right now.

As I write this, the global coronavirus pandemic has been rag-ing for over a year. Millions have died and we have all been in lockdown, confined to our homes for weeks or months on end. It is a little like being under house arrest. I hope the freedoms of life have been reinstated by the time you read this, sometime in the future. But right now, it is the depths of winter, and the world has ground to a halt. It is snowing outside, and if I wander beyond a five-kilometer travel limit, I may be stopped by the police and turned back, or even fined. It's been like this for months on end. And while I have hopes for the future, it is this present reality that I have to deal with. Being fully in the present with acceptance is what makes every day possible. We have no idea when life will return to normal. It just seems to go on and on. To sit zazen in the morning and drink tea at noon—this is paradise, a kind of oasis in an endless desert. This is my life now. The point is to embrace it, not some idea I have of what it will be like in the future. To hope in the present moment is what makes life possible. Not so much hope in the future—let the future take care of itself. Take care of the present and all will be fine as it is.

# Right Livelihood

*For the Zen student, work is Zen practice. The same kind of focus and attention needs to be brought to work as is brought to zazen. We become one with our work. We engage in it totally. To truly work is to see our self fall away in work. We are at one with the task at hand, whatever that task is.*

ONCE, WHEN I WAS a journalist, I had dinner with a man that worked for arms dealers and big tobacco companies. As a public relations expert and lobbyist, his job was to advance these companies' interests. He presented their unacceptable business as acceptable, and he pushed politicians to make decisions that benefited his clients. For someone so morally reprehensible, he was pleasant company. He was an expert at conversation, able to make whoever was in his company feel at ease and steer the subject matter where both parties to the conversation would be comfortable and enjoy the chat. But every now and then his mask slipped. He spoke in racist terms about "all the Arabs" at the exclusive school where he had sent his children. He mentioned trade unions with naked and bitter hatred. His arrogance was presuming that, just because I was having dinner with him, I agreed with him and his various opinions. While initially appearing charming and good company, he could not hide the darkness inside him for long.

Because the work we do is so central to our identity in the world, we become what we do. By dealing in death, this man connected with the arms trade and the tobacco industry had aligned himself with evil. To the wider world he was wealthy and successful, even respectable. He wore impeccable suits and lived in a rich part of town. His children went to the best schools, and he supported public charity events. Yet he was still evil—in a banal and acceptable kind of way. He preferred to describe himself as "worldly." He was well connected and had friends high up in the Republican Party in the United States. He had contacts and clients throughout the oil- and gas-rich regimes of Central Asia. Wherever he did business had appalling human rights records. But, as he said, "life is not a bed of roses." And the kind of work he did ensured life was hell for many.

Right livelihood is an important part of the noble eightfold path. The Buddha taught that we should earn our living in a way that does not cause harm and that is ethical. The fact that one part of the path addresses what work we do shows what emphasis the Buddha placed on this matter. At the least, we are asked to do no harm. This is ethically neutral. But beyond that we are requested to do good and be ethically positive. So, there is a great request to us in how we engage with the world. Because of this, certain professions are traditionally not engaged in by Buddhists: anything that involves the slaughter and sale of meat; the selling and promotion of alcohol or other intoxicants; dealing in arms and weapons. If our way of earning a living causes us to break the ethical precepts, we should seek a new way to work. Our effect on the wider world is of the utmost importance. The kind of karma that we create will have a great bearing on the future. It is not a matter to be taken lightly.

But so many people only view the work that they do as a way of earning money. It is so much more. We may think that we can change the world through social action and activism—and these are important. But the main effect that we have on the world is through the work that we do. Work is our being in unified action with the rest of the world. We shape the world through work. Bridges and cities, the food we grow, and the structures we live in—all come about through effort and work. The efforts of many generations have given us what we see around us today. And our work today creates what we give to the future. Our work extends our presence far beyond the boundaries of our own lives.

In the Zen tradition, work has always been of central importance. Whereas the origins of Buddhism in India saw mendicant monks living solely on alms donated by the laity, Zen has always emphasized *samu*, or work. The Japanese word literally means "strenuous labor." The great eighth-century Zen teacher Baizhang Huaihai used to say "a day without work is a day without food," and he was known to participate in the group work of his monastery well into his ninetieth year. This work ethic allowed the Zen monasteries of China to survive and thrive. And work became of central importance in the community rules that Baizhang drew up; indeed, so it remains in Zen communities all these centuries later. For the Zen student, work is Zen practice. The same kind of focus and attention needs to be brought to work as is brought to zazen. We become one with our work. We engage in it totally. To truly work is to see our self fall away in work. We are at one with the task at hand, whatever that task is. And while *samu* often consists of manual work—such as cleaning and digging, sweeping or cutting vegetables—whatever work that you do can be transformed by the spirit of *samu*. Even if you work in an office, you can see your work as Zen practice—and those that work around you will see a great change in you and be inspired. Your zazen should find its way into your work like this. What is the reason to practice if we just confine it to our time on the cushion?

In our own meditation hall, it is so clear who has this spirit when they are carrying out a task. It is moving to watch most people as they engage in their work with such sincerity and heart. Whatever it is that they are doing—cleaning the altar, arranging flowers, or serving food at mealtimes—it is done as an act of loving-kindness. Their beautiful heart is there for all to see in their actions, although they do not see this themselves.

In truth, there are also those that act as though they were born to be served. They possess a quiet arrogance. They look on as others do things to help and support them, but rarely offer a hand themselves. Then, if they are given a task, they perform it badly and grudgingly. Often, someone else has to redo the task again after them because it has been so carelessly performed. So much about their character is betrayed by their actions in this way. And again, they are entirely unaware of what others can see in them. They serve the food, not with care and a loving attention to detail, but as if they were plopping food in front of a farm animal. They look at others as they bow to them, but do not return the bow. We must feel sorry for people such as this. They are so intoxicated by their own egos that they cannot forget themselves. Their zazen is misdirected and only strengthens their vanity and sense of self-importance. It is often impossible to teach such people, as even a thousand attempts to do so fall on deaf ears. They may never break out beyond the illusory importance of the self. Even their practice becomes another expression of their will.

So, right livelihood is concerned not only with what we do; it is also concerned with the spirit with which we do it. It is not an appendage to the eightfold path; it is integral to it.

Yet we should be careful about judging others as being hard-working or lazy. We all have different gifts and capacities. Some need more food; some less. Some need more sleep; some less. We practice and work as best we can. We are primarily responsible for ourselves. And when others need a helping hand, we should offer them our strength in a spirit of friendship and service. It is important to remember that it is better to inspire others than to scold them.

# The Miraculous
# Is Ordinary, the
# Ordinary Miraculous

*Zazen is like a holiday wherever you are, without going anywhere. In the midst of your life, you look again with open eyes, and everything becomes fresh and new.*

WHEN WE GET TIRED of the repetitive rhythms of our life, we like to go on holiday. We like to go someplace strange and sample another way of living. We go to other countries and eat strange food and listen to everyone speak a different language. Everything is new and fresh. We feel renewed by this experience, and after a week or two we go home. We reenter the familiar schedule of our usual lives. Then, after some time, we feel that we need a holiday again. And so off we go again.

Zazen is like a holiday wherever you are, without going anywhere. In the midst of your life, you look again with open eyes, and everything becomes fresh and new. In zazen, even a ball of fluff on the ground before you is an amazing vision. Your breath is a miracle. To have a body to sit cross-legged on the ground is itself a gift beyond words. Every day, this practice allows you to reenter reality as it truly is. This is the power and beauty of zazen practice. But isn't the point of a holiday that your everyday routine is broken? How can something you do every day always be fresh and new?

Often, my more dedicated students say that when they have been practicing for a long time, their zazen can begin to feel stale. Every day they find their way to the cushion at 7 a.m., and it begins to feel like nothing more than a routine. The practice that we do is called *shikantaza*, which means "nothing but sitting."[17] In the Chinese tradition, it was called silent illumination or serene reflection. It is the practice of letting go of everything and doing nothing at all. You literally sit there and do nothing else. It is exactly the opposite of all that you have habitually learned to do all your life—which is to do something, even when you are relaxing or on holidays. Just sitting, we meet again the rockface of being. There we are, and there is all existence too. We have gotten out of our own way and given up our calculations and manipulations. We have stopped the flow of the river, which has swept us away for years, and taken a radical step outside of that flow. It is so simple and at the same time elusive. It is allowed to emerge and cannot be grasped or achieved. Because we have stopped doing, our mind desperately searches for something to do in order to reassert our sense of self. Because distractions have been removed, the mind wants something to play with. It shouts out, "I'm bored!"

Boredom in sitting is normal. Boredom, like any other state in zazen, is just something we sit with. It is allowed to arise and fall away. Boredom is not a problem. Nothing in zazen is a problem. It just is as it is. When bored, it is you that is being bored. Eventually there will be no you to be bored anymore. When there is no you to be bored anymore, you have forgotten yourself and merged with the way of things. In the meantime, just be bored. It's not a problem. The question I have for you is: Do you get bored of breathing? Do you get bored of eating when hungry? Is sleeping something that is boring, because it is so regular and repetitive? What is key here is your mind. You must develop a mind that appreciates the present moment, whatever it holds. With our grasping and seeking mind we get bored of our jobs, our sex life, our selves. We become disenchanted with life. The whole advertising industry is built upon manipulating this fact. Zen training allows us to stop this seeking and grasping. It is the radical antidote to our addictive behavior, which is based on our bottomless wants and desires. Even becoming content to be bored is part of the training. But it is important to realize that it is a training with no end. Zazen is something we will do forever. There is no graduation ceremony where your achievement is crowned and publicly recognized. It is the very desire for such things that you are freeing yourself from. For the first time, you become content to be yourself *as yourself*. Making your Oscar acceptance speech is the fantasy. Sitting on your cushion with your breath—that is reality.

Still, I have suggested to students to change their zazen routine from time to time when the practice feels really stale to them. I've also suggested to take a few days off sitting, and then return to it renewed. I have never received this advice from a teacher myself, because there is such an emphasis on daily sitting in the Zen tradition. That's because it is vital that it becomes part of your life. But practice is dynamic and not static. It is alive and vibrant. If it stops being vibrant, why not take a break? You will quickly realize why you started to sit in the first place, and your practice will be reinvigorated. You might sit during the day rather than first thing every morning. Or you might change it for a while so that you sit before bed. You might even stop sitting totally for a few days or longer. As long as you return to it, you will reconnect with the practice and eventually you will move beyond stale and fresh with regard to your zazen. Your zazen will just be whatever it is. It will no longer need to be something special. It'll be miraculous and ordinary at the same time—because the miraculous is ordinary, and the ordinary miraculous.

This is maturity in practice. This maturity allows the practice to be like it was in the beginning. But before this maturity is rediscovered, we often want new distractions to entertain us. "Should I be doing something else?" students ask, after a time. Should I label my thoughts? Should I use a mantra? Should I repeat an affirmation over and over to myself while I sit? Should I sit in the presence of God? The student feels that there must be more. There must be second and third helpings. Is this plain meal I've been served all there is?

In Zen, we learn that the ordinary is extraordinary. Zen is simple and natural. It is more like a simple thatched cottage than an imposing cathedral. Its realm is the realm of our daily lives—where we spend most of our time. It is not so much like an exotic holiday—not that there's anything wrong with an exotic holiday. It's just that Zen reinvigorates us without our having to go anywhere at all. And it travels with us, no matter if we are in strange and foreign lands or sitting at home beside our own familiar hearth.

# A Coherent Practice

*"Do not set up standards of your own." When*
*we do, we often take the bits we like and reject the*
*bits we don't like. But it is more often than not*
*the bits we don't like that we learn from most.*
*All medicine cannot be sweet tasting. Some of the*
*medicine that is best for us is hard to swallow.*

To build a house, we pick a site and build there. If we scatter the building materials around a vast landscape, no house will result. When effort is unfocused and our energies diffuse, there can be no clarity or concentration. Zen practice is like this, too. If you are on the Zen path, then follow that path. It is best to concentrate on one way.

Recently, a man came to practice with us after many years of following another Buddhist path. For him, we offered the opportunity to sit with other people on a daily basis. From the outset, he made it clear that he was not following the Zen Way. Rather, he was following the Buddhist path that he had long followed, and was merely using us as an opportunity to have the feeling of practicing with a sangha.

We made him welcome and he practiced with us for many months, maybe even for a year. But he was always in the position of an observer. When we bowed, he stood aside and watched us bow. He kept himself outside the practice, and there was a certain aloofness to his presence. After Dharma talks or during group discussions, he questioned us all with great skepticism, always drawing comparisons with his own tradition, which he evidently felt to be superior. His presence was mildly disharmonious, but became increasingly an aberration, as he worked against the current of our sangha's practice. As the teacher, I let this go for a long time, feeling that his skepticism was a good thing, that it added an edge to sangha life. But gradually it grew into a disruption, and he would come to dominate the atmosphere during Dharma discussions, presenting the Dharma from the perspective of his own tradition, while suggesting in his demeanor that the Zen approach was not quite right.

Eventually I pointed out to him that he was not entering the spirit of sangha. I said that as Zen students we are all expected to participate in the life of the sangha in a certain way. That we were following a specific tradition, but that he was not, in fact, a Zen student. That it might be better if he practiced within his own tradition, rather than constantly comparing our tradition to his. He neither agreed nor disagreed with what I said, but after that he stopped coming to sit with us.

If practicing in a tradition, it is best to totally commit to that way, at least for many years. Of course, before committing it is a good idea to spend a long time exploring. And this is something I did myself. I sat with sanghas in the Tibetan tradition. I sat with the Friends of the Western Buddhist Order. I sat with various Zen groups. This went on for a number of years, but I kept returning again and again to Zen. Eventually I realized Zen was my Way, and I requested the *jukai* ceremony of formal commitment to the path. Later, I committed to practice with my teacher, Taïgu Rōshi, and was eventually ordained as a priest at his suggestion. In making this commitment, I gave up the other ways of practice to concentrate fully on the Zen Way. Like other Buddhist traditions, Zen has developed over millennia. It has many centuries of teachers, texts, and practices. Even ten lifetimes would not allow one to master the entirety of this rich inheritance. And it is the same with the various other, authentic Buddhist schools. It is not that one school is better than the other. It is simply that each school has developed in a certain way over a long period of time, and for complicated reasons. Each practice tradition has a coherence that has resulted from this history and development. If one is to take bits and pieces from one tradition or another and make them into an amalgam, then it should only be done after mastering the traditions you are borrowing from, and with great care indeed—if at all.

The problem with haphazard fusion is that it often does not work. To offer a banal analogy, I know this from an "Asian Fusion Restaurant" here in Dublin city. The food they do is not Thai. It is not Chinese and it is not Japanese. There is a mix of all of these, as well as some Vietnamese and Korean influences thrown in for good measure. The result is not very good. Things are carelessly thrown together, without enough expertise, subtlety, or thought. All of these great traditions are done a disservice in being used in this way. What results is a confused mess.

Like these cuisines, each of the various Buddhist traditions evolved in a specific geographical and cultural context. Through long trial and error, and for myriad reasons, they evolved as they did. It is not that there is some cultural purity that I am positing. The mixing of European, African, Asian, and Indigenous cultures in North and South America shows us how rich and coherent the results can be. Indeed, religious culture in each of the Asian countries I've mentioned is itself full of influences from other cultures. Buddhism in Japan, for example, is a hybrid of Japanese, Chinese, and Indian Buddhism. But it was many generations of people that contributed to this emergence, over a long period of time. It had an organic, natural development. Different religious customs married and settled together; they were not jarringly collided. There must have been pioneering individuals that brought in "foreign" influences to Japanese religious culture—for example, the first people to bring Buddhism to Japan. So, the dynamic tension between tradition and innovation should always be acknowledged. But this is something quite different from shopping in the global spiritual supermarket and putting whatever items take your fancy into your basket.

Maybe a better analogy is trying to learn three similar languages at once. If you study French, Italian, and Spanish at the same time, you will become confused. It is great to learn these languages one after another, but not all at the same time. Spanish and Italian will be all mixed up. There will be no coherency to it. It is best to master one thing at a time. That is the way to practice. To practice like this prevents confusion. It ensures that you are entering a coherent tradition, rather than making up a tradition of your own. As the eighth-century Zen teaching poem "Sandōkai" says, "Do not set up standards of your own." When we do, we often take the bits we like and reject the bits we don't like. But it is more often than not the bits we don't like that we learn from most. All medicine cannot be sweet tasting. Some of the medicine that is best for us is hard to swallow. An agitated mind finds sitting still painful; but that is what is needed. A sluggish mind needs a practice of focus and precision. The practice is meant to be challenging. We push ourselves and thereby we grow. It is for this reason that it is best to throw yourself into the practice completely, and not to opt out of the parts that don't suit your disposition or beliefs. If you do not like to bow, then bowing is your best medicine. If you like to bow too much, then you must stand up straight.

If you decide to practice Zen, then practice Zen wholeheartedly. Take all the medicine. Do not mix in some sugar and spice. It's not that other flavors are not as good. They often are. But it is necessary to make a committed decision. That is all.

# A Rational Religion

*The mind is now known to be so much more than the
conscious mind, the realm of our reasoning. The vast
majority of our mental activity is unconscious. So much
of what we do is not the end point of a process of reason.*

WHEN BUDDHISM WAS FIRST presented in the West, certain aspects of it were foregrounded, while others were
eschewed. A key moment of the westward transmission was the
1893 World Parliament of Religions, held in Chicago. This was
a time when reason and science were championed, just as they
masked the brutalities of colonialism and the subjugation of other
peoples by Americans and Europeans. In presenting Buddhism
as a rational, scientific "philosophy," an attempt was made to
appeal to the audience listening. A recalibration was at play:
"We are not backward and superstitious colonial subjects," these
early Buddhists appeared to be saying. "We have a rich philosophical tradition that is modern and reasonable." This "Buddhist
Modernism" gave Buddhism the reputation of being atheistic and
devoid of ritual and prayer. It was really a misrepresentation of
Buddhism, and it persists to this day.

First encounters with Buddhist traditions in Buddhist countries must have been confusing for westerners that had accepted
the modernist version of the tradition. The importance of devotion, chanting, and making offerings may not have been what they
expected. They want their Buddhism to be a "mind science," not

a religion. That's because they believe religion isn't rational, but instead primitive and naive, practiced by gullible and uneducated people that have received it unquestioningly with faith rather than reason. Certainly, many people that come to our zendo hold such views and are surprised or even put off by the service that follows meditation, in which we chant and bow and offer incense. "This isn't the Buddhism I signed up for," they seem to say. And probably we'll never see them again, before they have even discussed their reaction.

Once, I invited a local imam from a Muslim congregation in Dublin to join us in zazen and talk to us about Islam afterward. He sat well on the ground, but afterward in his talk he said that he was shocked that we seemed to be bowing to a statue in worship. In Islam, there is a strong prohibition against what they see as idolatry. It appeared to him that we were worshiping a piece of wood. So, I explained that it was just that—nothing more than a piece of wood. But for us it represents Buddha and his awakening. It reminds us of the teachings and the teacher. Our bowing, while oriented toward the statue, does not in fact involve an act of worship. We bow to the awakened nature of all things, including the Buddha nature within ourselves and others. We could just as well bow to a tree, a mountain, or a pile of old stones. The imam had applied his own frame of reference where it did not apply—just as the Buddhist modernist had done in dismissing our service. The imam was greatly interested in how he had read the situation through his own filter of experience. He felt reassured that he had not participated in an act of idolatry.

What's interesting is that early Buddhism did not make figurative representations of the Buddha in the way that Islam prohibits. Only after contact with Greek culture, which so loves the image or icon, did Buddhists start to depict the Buddha in art and sculptures. Before that, the Buddha was represented as two footprints—the empty traces he had left behind—rather than any depiction of his person.

When it comes to Buddhism being a rational religion, however, there is a solid basis to that view. There is a deft analytical character to much of the teachings. The Buddha unfolds the logic of his Dharma with great rigor and sense in the Pali canon. Then there is the Kesamutti Sutta (AN 3.65), in which the Buddha encourages us to thoroughly investigate truth before accepting it as true. He warns us not to rely on oral history, tradition, rumor—not even scripture and dogma—in determining truth. Anything based on greed, hate, and delusion should be rejected. He does, therefore, encourage rational enquiry, but without dismissing faith and the other religious elements of the Dharma. But Western commentators have grasped on to that part of the Kesamutti Sutta that encourages this kind of skeptical enquiry and made it into the be-all-and-end-all of the Dharma in its totality.

Meanwhile, the mind is now known to be so much more than the conscious mind, the realm of our reasoning. The vast majority of our mental activity is unconscious. So much of what we do is not the endpoint of a process of reason. We often act instinctually. We act on gut feeling. We can even react well to situations faster than we have time to come up with a rational and thought-out response. There is so much more going on than reason. We have premonitions. We gain insights in dreams. We fall in love for inexplicable reasons and make decisions based on feelings. We also are capable of acting in compassionate and altruistic ways that run counter to our "rational" self-interest. And we exist in a universe that contains much we cannot explain or fathom. There is so much that we simply do not know, and yet without this knowing we must act or choose how to act.

Brain science, cognitive psychology, and neurology have shown great interest in these areas in recent years. The idea that we are rational beings appears to be a somewhat one-dimensional explanation of our humanity. There is a lot going on in us other than reasoning. To start with, we are also feeling and dreaming, intuiting and perceiving, imagining and narrating. We use symbols and gestures in an aesthetic way to communicate poetic truths. We express gratitude, offload anxiety in cathartic activity, and engage in individual and group play through shared games and rituals, which serve deep psychological and social functions.

When we encounter the mythical, archetypal, or ritual practices of Buddhism, we acknowledge all of this. All the traditional practices of religion carry and address these truths. The rational mind is addressed in philosophy. But religion addresses it too, while also speaking to the body, the unconscious mind, and—for lack of a better word—the spirit. The bowing and chanting and incense offering in Buddhism are important parts of its holistic wisdom, and they cannot be dispensed with so easily. A reductive Buddhist Modernism might wish to cut away all of this, leaving behind only the rational and coherently philosophical. But to do this is to neglect the other aspects of our humanity that make up the whole of our being. The part of us that climbs a mountain and says "Wow!" when viewing the majesty of the view all around— this is the part of us that reason cannot reach. We may hold our arms aloft in jubilation. We may bow down in gratitude. We may take a rock with us when we leave as a memento, or make a pile of rocks as a marker that we have been there and passed on. Ritual is part of our DNA. It is the wisdom that flows through our whole being. The limited, Cartesian view of the self cannot accommodate this totality.

So, is Buddhism a "rational religion"? Yes—and much more besides. Clearly it addresses ways of knowing beyond the purely rational. It has a deep and massive body of philosophy, but it also has a deep inheritance of devotional and ritualistic practices that are religious in nature. It cannot, therefore, be reduced to a philosophy only. It is a religion with a philosophical underpinning, just like Christianity, Judaism, and Islam. It is rational, but not exclusively so. In other words, it is just like we human beings.

# Fighting Spirits

*From the perspective of emptiness, there is no
self and no other. In an ultimate sense, to be at
war with another is to be at war with oneself.*

IT GETS SO TIRESOME listening to the endless arguing on television news and talk radio. The discussion is always polarized and presented in contesting terms. No one really listens to anyone else. They just wait for an opportunity in the conversation to insert their own position. It's like a perpetual family argument or couple's row. Every position is fossilized and immovable. There is Position A and Position B, and little common ground in the middle. Everyone has a grievance and a well-nurtured wound. Each side is self-righteous and keenly aware of their rights, but less aware of their responsibilities. One side may indeed have a great grievance. The other side may indeed have committed terrible wrongs. Often this is the case. Arguments like this are often old quarrels, with little hope of resolution. To get past them, there must be growth, where new thinking comes along.

Growing up in Ireland, the argument in Northern Ireland was always in the background. The two principal sides dominated a polarized discourse about whether Northern Ireland should remain in the United Kingdom or join a United Ireland. The argument was divided along lines of ethnic origin, as well as religious affiliation and political conviction. It was a messy mix of identity issues that made identity the core of all existence, to the detriment of everything else. After a long period of peace and resolution, of late the argument has found new life, as a new wave of British nationalism has awakened many old sleeping ghosts. Again the familiar, intractable positions are being taken up. For each side, only its own grievances count; it is deaf to the other.

But this is the nature of fighting the world over. In the United States, a terrible polarization has emerged. The same is true in many other countries. What starts out as a war of words can easily tip over into actual violence. Those with long-held grievances have become eaten up with anger, so much so that they have become locked in a prison of rage. Those that dominate them have nursed the anger and hatred required to dominate for a very long time. You can only dominate those you despise and do not respect. Both the dominated and the domineering are not free in this interlocking wrestle. Someone has to release their grip. The choice is not only between winning and losing. There is another choice. There is the choice not to fight. In this case, the rigid rules of the game are rejected. More often than not, the rules of exchange have been maintained by the side that dominates. Refusing to play by these rules anymore is a much more radical choice than remaining trapped in the endless conflict that has been set up.

In Buddhist cosmology, there are traditionally six realms of existence. Although considered real and actual realms, they can also be seen as states of mind. One of these realms is the realm of the *asura*, fighting spirits that engage in perpetual warfare. They can also be seen in a positive light as protecting deities that guard the Dharma with their fierce presence. So, it's not all bad. Anger and aggression do sometimes, in fact, have a place. Anger can be the correct response in a situation. There are times when the right thing to do is to defend yourself and stand up to violence and intimidation. It is not just a simple case of passively rolling over and not ever fighting. Sometimes the correct response is indeed to fight. The wisdom is in knowing when.

Those that feel Buddhism is only about taking a passive approach do not know the history of Buddhism. Like any faith tradition, some of this is a history to be proud of, but there are also chapters of shame. During World War II, for example, the Japanese Buddhist schools largely supported a murderous imperial project of expansion and war crimes. Today in Myanmar, there are Buddhist monks that are driving on a campaign of genocide against the Rohingya Muslims in the western part of the country. There have also been more benign "warrior monks" in the tradition, the most famous of which are the monks of Shaolin in China. When one considers the complex history of Buddhism, there are many contradictions. How can a warrior monk reconcile the life of a soldier with the precept against killing? The same question must face any soldier today that practices Buddhism but remains a soldier. How can one be a U.S. Marine and a Buddhist at the same time? It is a difficult circle to square. When is an army an army of oppression and when is it an army of liberation? Is this just a point of view? After all, one person's freedom fighter is another person's terrorist.

To get involved in violent action is hugely problematic for a Buddhist. Acts of defensive action may be justified for protecting life, but these usually transform into acts of aggression with time, especially in prolonged conflicts. If we are to truly accept the empty nature of reality, we must recognize what that means for conflicts between self and others. From the perspective of emptiness, there is no self and no other. In an ultimate sense, to be at war with another is to be at war with oneself. In the relative sense, deluded individuals may attack and oppress others because they mistakenly think they have no connection or sympathy with the other. This delusion needs to be challenged and resisted, sometimes with defensive force. There is an apparent contradiction at play here that cannot be avoided. It is wrong to engage in acts of aggression, but sometimes acts that involve aggressive action are required. When it comes to the precept against killing, there is the letter of the law and the spirit of the law. An assailant should be challenged.

The problem is that life is rarely simple. Moral complexity means that right and wrong are not always so clear-cut. Part of the problem is the abstract nature of moral reasoning. Whether the concrete action right before you is right or wrong is the real question. The abstraction that allows bomber pilots to drop an atomic bomb on a civilian city to shorten a war has no moral weight. The action at hand involves mass murder and a war crime. Everything else is at a theoretical remove. The past and the future take care of themselves. Only the present moment has weight and reality. The question is, what you are about to do now—is that the moral and ethical thing to do? This is quite apart from the inherited wounds of the past and the potential outcomes of the future.

It has as much to do with our individual lives and relationships as it has to do with societal conflicts and conflicts between nations. There will always be the legacy of wrongdoing, the past that we have inherited. Engaging in ill will or aggression can always be justified "for the greater good," or for some imagined good outcome. But we only truly exist in the present moment. We can be *asuras* forever, as the bonfire of our anger has an endless fuel to fire it. Or we can extinguish that fire for good. Take the heat out of the situation right now. Leave the past to the past and the future to the future. The real question in this practice is always the same: What is happening right now?

# Desire of Love,
# Desire of Greed

*To say that there is no self at all is problematic.*
*There must be some sense in which there is a self.*
*Right now, some part of empty, boundless reality*
*is having these thoughts and writing this.*

JUST AS ANGER CAN be righteous or aggressive, desire can be motivated by love or by greed. *Desire* is a recurring word in the Buddhadharma. It is one of the roots of suffering. "Cut off the bonds of desires," the Buddha tells us in the Dhammapada.[18] It is right there in the Buddha's first teaching on the four noble truths. Desire is something to be rooted out and destroyed. It has no meritorious qualities. Particularly emphasized in the older Buddhist teachings is that desire of all kinds is inconsistent with the path. To become an arhat—the highest spiritual state in the Theravada Buddhist path—one has to fully eradicate all desire. It must be extinguished to enter nirvana and end all future births. In seeing that there is no self, the illusion of self is annihilated and transcended. This involves a complete denial of selfhood and its illusory desires.

Certainly, our state of mind is tranquil in the absence of desire. When we crave things, we are uneasy and irritable. The analysis that desire leads to suffering is a correct one. At its most basic, when we are hungry, we suffer. When we have satisfied that hunger, we ease the suffering. Then the hunger comes along again, of course. So, again the analysis is correct. Even temporary contentment turns inevitably into desire and suffering again. We are in a bind. Desire leads to suffering and contentment leads to suffering. Remove the desire and the contentment and the suffering is also removed. The way to do this is to remove the subject that is experiencing the desire and contentment. If we say that there is no one truly there to experience the desire and contentment, then we have solved the problem. Isn't that so? But who is asserting this teaching or analysis? There must be at the very least a temporary and illusory "I" to come to this conclusion and to seek the path of the arhat. This person must have had a fortunate birth to have been born a human being, so that they are able to follow the path. This is what the tradition says of a human birth. Indeed, they must have a mother and a father. In a very basic sense, even the arhat must have been born of desire.

To say that there is no self at all is problematic. There must be some sense in which there is a self. Right now, some part of empty, boundless reality is having these thoughts and writing this. I am not permanent, and I am not separate from the rest of reality. But in this relative realm of existence, I can be pointed out and identified as one thing of the myriad things that exist. I can be identified by myself and others as an individual. If you cut me in half, you may have made some profound philosophical point, but I would be dead. Even if one day I were to go on to become an advanced spiritual being like an arhat, it would be too late for me, having been cut in half. So, in a very real sense, there is a self. It may be a self lacking an inherent and permanent existence, but then nothing has an inherent and permanent existence. Things come and things go, but there are still things.

Nagarjuna brought the earlier teachings to a new level of understanding that can accommodate this complex reality. In the Perfection of Wisdom teachings, we see that there is emptiness, but there is also form. And where there is form there is desire. Where there is a human body, it must be cared for and nourished.

And there is only a human body because someone conceived that body in an act of desire. With no desire, there is no arhat. And with no desire, the human race comes to an end.

There were two classifications of desire in the Pali texts, and some commentators have argued that one is more benign—like the desire to practice, for example—while the other is wholly negative. *Chanda* is positive desire; *tanha* negative. Indeed, *chanda* is often translated as "zeal" and *tanha* as "thirst" or "craving". But it appears most commentators agree that all desire is basically viewed as negative by the earlier tradition. And that is my experience in my limited study, too. Indeed, the later Mahayana texts also view desire negatively. Meditation traditions have also grown up around this view, where the body and temporal forms are viewed with something akin to disgust. In denying the body, birth has also been viewed almost as a misfortune at times, and certainly being born into a body is seen to bring all the problems of desire with it. Along these lines, women have been viewed as the harborers of this misfortune by giving birth and bringing more people into the world. Male religious commentators, having felt sexual desire, have often taken that out against women. Even the original nun's order founded by the Buddha was stamped out in some cultures. The problem stems from patriarchy, but also from a failure to find an accommodation with desire. Desire is simply rejected as unwholesome and corrupting in most cases.

But this is a misguided approach so long as we are in a human body. The Buddha himself lived until eighty and required food and rest, like everyone else in this life. He had attained nirvana— perfect bliss and release—as well as full insight into reality. But it was only on his death that he attained *parinirvana*, or final nirvana, as his body dissolved and faded away. While alive, he still felt hunger and tiredness and heat and cold. Desire still had its role. But as such an advanced spiritual being, the early texts show us a man that had rooted out anger and malice and envy and the more negative desires we associate with harm and unethical action.

It seems to me that a rebalancing of our understanding of desire is needed in Buddhism. There is the desire of love and the desire of greed. The desire of greed leads to hatred and violence and acts of aggressive lust. It leads to war and exploitative pornography and the hoarding of wealth. But the desire of love leads to self-care and a thirst for justice; it leads to the beautiful and even sometimes the beautifully erotic. It leads to family life and the various generations of our community, and the gifts each one brings. It even leads to the birth of all those that enter the monastic life, as well as all those that choose other paths and that support the monastics on their way.

*Chanda*, even if it is not a clear-cut positive classification of desire, has an important need to be reclaimed and defined in a way that supports the flourishing of human life. If this world is indeed the Pure Land, as the Sixth Ancestor of Zen taught, then we must see it for the bountiful oasis that it is in an otherwise arid universe. This orange might be empty of inherent existence, but it can still feed me and support my journey. Its succulent juices might even be viewed as a good thing, and as something to be enjoyed.

# Knowing beyond
# Our Boundaries

*Knowing our boundaries and knowing there
is a vastness beyond them should engender
human humility. When we look at animals,
we can learn from their humility. Consider the
humility of a bird or a seal, a fox or a badger.*

A LL WE CAN KNOW about ourselves is that we do not know ourselves. We know things about ourselves, but the totality of it is far beyond us. Look in a mirror and you will see a one-dimensional picture of your body. But it is not your body truly. You might use your hands and run them along your shape to feel your form. But you will never see the back of your head. You might see a picture of it, but that is just a picture. You will never see it truly. And what are the unseen effects of our actions? How do they ripple out and change the world in ways that we will never see? What do people really think of us? How are we viewed by others? How many years will we live, and what will we be thinking in five minutes time? Even to ourselves, we are a total mystery. What then of the wider world? What of other people? How much do we really know?

"Those who greatly realize delusion are buddhas," Master Dōgen teaches us in the "Genjōkōan." Plato tells us that Socrates used to say "I know that I know nothing." This is not just a maxim.

It is the experience of realizing just how limited our boundaries of knowing are. This wisdom was also shared by the accomplished scientist Isaac Newton: "To myself I am only a child playing on the beach, while vast oceans of truth lie undiscovered before me." There is great honesty and humility in this realization. It is an encounter with the vast ocean of truth, and it fills us with awe. We can often encounter this in meditation, and it can fill us with bright invigoration or give us the feeling that we are drowning in insignificance. Beyond both is a deep peace beyond words or conventional understanding.

In our ordinary lives, it can be useful to remember how little we know. It checks our innate arrogance and helps us in our dealings with others. How often have you judged someone, only to find out later that they have some terrible suffering in their lives that has led them to act as they do? We constantly make judgments based on our own experience. But often our own experience is misleading and leads us to inaccurate decisions. We decide someone is rude only to find out they are shy. We think someone is miserly and then discover what dire poverty they live in. The person who ignores our question turns out to be hard of hearing, or the neighbor that does not return our waved greeting simply has poor eyesight and did not see.

Our limitations of perception are clear when it comes to scientific research. One look into a microscope shows us the deep universe beneath our very nose—a universe that is invisible to us with the naked eye. Everything that we see is far richer than we can imagine. The reality we think is real, exactly as we see it, is really just our limited point of view. It is a tiny and subjective slice of an infinitely large cake. Because we have human eyes and human ears, we see and understand things in a certain way. Cats and foxes and bees will perceive the things we see in totally different ways. Are the foxes and bees wrong while we are right? What is truly "out there" when it can be viewed in so many different ways? My two sons, for example, are colorblind. What is green to me is brown to them. They see the world in a totally different way than I do. In their universe, green is brown.

Dōgen investigates this truth in "Sansuikyō," the "Sutra of Mountains and Water." He says: "Water is neither strong nor weak, neither wet nor dry, neither moving nor still, neither cold nor warm." He goes on: "There are beings which see what we call water as a string of pearls." And: "There are beings which see water as wonderful flowers." "Demons see water as raging flames."[19] So, what is seen is different for each being that sees it. The question is, What is water truly? Dōgen says, "It seems that there is no original water." And yet there is something. When we look through our eyes and see water, we see something. When we look through a microscope at water, we see something else. But still something is seen. That our world is the seen world is important to know. And it is important to know that there is a vast and much bigger world beyond what we see.

Knowing our boundaries and knowing there is a vastness beyond them should engender human humility. When we look at animals, we can learn from their humility. Consider the humility of a bird or a seal, a fox or a badger. Perfectly in tune with their surroundings, they deport themselves with harmony and without arrogance. We humans, on the other hand, consider ourselves masters of all that we survey. We enter the world seeking to dominate it, to be "the pinnacle of the animals." We have forgotten how little we know. We are like a celibate priest, self-confidently lecturing couples on marriage. We do not know even what we are talking about. Dōgen advises, "We should not stick blindly in only the human sphere, we should move forward and learn water in the Buddha's state of truth."[20] From this enlightened perspective, we see that our view is subjective and partial only. We now know that there is a truth beyond it. In a sense, we now see that truth. And so everything is changed.

From this eye-opened place of seeing, we can meet people and situations as they are; not as we subjectively view them. This is the action of compassionate love. We do not dominate and make others in our own image. We cast aside self-obsession and false knowledge. The point is to love much more than it is to know. As Dōgen says, the "mountains belong to the people who love mountains." The mountains are beyond our human world. Dōgen reminds us that "we can never know the mountains with the human intellect."[21] We can, however, know them with the heart. Feeling can encompass the whole mountain. Cartography can only offer us a two-dimensional map. Maps are useful, but they offer only one view of something that is infinite. The same is true of each person that we meet. Our mental view of them is so limited, but they are truly infinite as well. This is the great mystery of being a human being. It is important to remember this when we come face to face with other people in the world—but also each time that we look in the mirror at ourselves.

# Becoming a Student

*A bit like acupuncture, Zen inserts needles in order
to relieve pain. It might seem at first that the needles
are just adding to the pain as they are inserted, but
stick with it and the needles will begin to work.*

WHEN YOU BECOME AN apprentice at anything, you are taken
on by your mentor and agree to follow his or her direction.
Often, you begin your life as an apprentice by sweeping the floor
or making tea. You may have strong opinions about how things
should be done, but you keep them to yourself and engage in the
apprenticeship with a spirit that is open to learning from others.
As an apprentice, you engage with your teacher through observation. Everything your teacher does, you look at closely and study
carefully. You have become this person's apprentice because you
know you have things to learn from them and you admire the
way that they work. You will be an apprentice for a long time; and
then you will no longer be an apprentice. You will be a teacher or a
master yourself someday. In pottery, in carpentry, in the fine arts,
and in crafts, this is how knowledge has been passed from one
generation to the next.

It is not always easy to be an apprentice. But that is the way
of learning and growing. When I was in Zen training, I was bad
at so many things. During ceremonies, I'd drop the incense stick
or trip over my own robes. I was always dropping candle wax on
carpets when tidying up the altar, or crossing the Buddha hall in

an incorrect way, so that it was showing disrespect to the Buddha. In the *ōryōki* ceremony of taking meals, I'd be chomping away for a minute before I'd realize that people were looking at me and I was not supposed to have begun eating yet. But despite my ineptitude, I do not think that I was a bad apprentice. That is because I was putting my full heart into it, and was just making mistakes. We all make mistakes. But what is really important is that we have the correct spirit. Having the correct spirit is trying sincerely and with all your effort. It's not doing things your own way because you think you know better, or just being lazy and taking shortcuts. This is the incorrect approach for an apprentice. But if you bring the right spirit to being a student, then who can fault you when you fail?

I have been a Zen teacher for ten years now and have met many students. Most people come to practice Zen with great enthusiasm. Then they find that the practice is difficult or hard to keep up, and so they stop. Good students come with an open and generous mind. But others come with their minds already made up of what Zen should be. Although they often know little of the tradition, practices, inheritance, or teachings of Zen, they have decided in advance that Zen supports a relaxed approach to doing things. Maybe they believe Zen is a way of spacing out. They think Zen is essentially the same as Hindu and yoga practices, that there is no distinction, or that it is atheistic or a type of self-help. Frequently, they think the Zen teacher should take a laissez-faire approach, allowing people to practice as they want, with great freedom and a permissive approach in the meditation hall. This might mean listening to meditation music with headphones while sitting, or getting up during meditation if you have had enough. It might mean arriving at meditation late, at a time that suits you, or opting out of group activities that you don't like. Then when you find out that Zen does not take an approach like this, you might become resentful. You might feel that the Zen teacher is overbearing, requesting that you do things the way he or she requires. You may think there are too many stupid rules in Zen and that it is too straitjacketed, not allowing you to do things as you want. You may resent that you have to curtail your individualistic way of doing things now that you are in a group practice setting, where you have to moderate your behavior in order for the wider group to function.

I have heard people say that it is now impossible to teach Zen in the West. This belief comes from the virulent individualism and narcissistic culture of the self now prevalent. People that assert this say that the deferential culture of the East is better suited to Zen, as it has the conditions of the mother culture that gave birth to Zen in the first place. In Japan, it is acceptable to behave in a less individualistic way, hierarchy is accepted, and teachers and older people are treated with reverence and respect. But I do not accept this. In any Western classroom, workplace, or university lecture hall, most people show up on time and do not do their own thing while the class or meeting is in progress. A teacher could not run a classroom where each student took their own approach. Medical students do not decide which parts of the curriculum they wish to respect and which parts they wish to ignore. We already have many contexts in which we can set aside our own desired way of doing things so that we can work under direction and in a group.

Zen is a bit like a treatment that gives us some of the disease in order to cure us of it. Life frustrates us because it doesn't turn out the way we want. So, what does Zen do? It creates a space where things are not the way we want, and this trains us to deal with that. It gives us constraints so that we can feel freedom when those constraints are lifted. In Zen, we learn to set our wants and ego aside, and this turns out to be a liberating experience, although it feels quite the opposite of that to begin with. A bit like acupuncture, Zen inserts needles to relieve pain. It might seem at first that the needles are just adding to the pain as they are inserted, but stick with it and the needles will begin to work. The initial discomfort will be the gateway to a greater and more profound comfort, if you can only stick with it.

The thing is, many of us do not want any discomfort at all in our lives. And having left childhood behind, we are too proud to follow the lead of others. As adults, many can find it hard to be taught at all. The teacher-student relationship in Zen can be a challenging one. It is not a master-and-disciple relationship in the traditional sense of following a guru, and it is not just a spiritual friendship. The teacher is there to support you and see things that you do not see about yourself. The teacher also points out things you would maybe prefer not to acknowledge. It can be quite a difficult relationship—so much so that the student might not want to continue after a time. Many of us do, after all, undertake challenging courses of change only to abandon them. We often underestimate the difficulty that the journey involves.

In traditional Zen, a new student is admitted to training only after proving their sincerity. This involves sitting zazen for many hours—maybe even days—in a special area outside the monastery proper before being admitted. Joining a monastery is deliberately made difficult, as only those with great motivation to practice will not be deterred and will persist in seeking the teachings. In many Buddhist schools, there is a tradition also of having to ask three times—and being refused twice—before a teacher will take you on as a student. While this has been somewhat ritualized in some contexts, it does show us the spirit that is required in approaching training as a student. Barriers are placed before you so that only those that are ready for the training will proceed. What is absent in Zen is some kind of proselytizing drive that seeks to catch as many adherents as possible. Quite the contrary. The Zen Way is not for most people. It is far too difficult in its discipline and practice. That is why the Zen monasteries of the world are not bursting at the seams with students. In most Zen centers today, these kinds of ritualized barriers are not there for lay students to begin the practice. However, there are other barriers: One must practice in a certain way in the zendo, according to instruction; one must respect the forms and customs of the practice hall; one must follow the direction of the practice leader, and so on. But even these are too much for some people new to Zen. Used to having things their own way, they expect Zen to be the same. Rather than being a student or an apprentice, they approach it as if they are a customer; they are buying a service, and "the customer is always right."

To become a Zen student, it is vital to bring both humility and a strong motivation. To be taught you must be open to learning. And you must be willing not to have all things your own way. Remember, every master starts out as an apprentice. Spuds must be peeled for a long time before you get to cook them.

# Honoring the Menial

*We do not waste our time wishing we had better*
*vegetables and fresher tofu; that we had the best*
*Japanese noodles or magnificent organic Irish*
*potatoes. What we do is deal with the reality*
*before us right now. This is the Zen Way.*

WITH THE AWAKENED MIND of Zen, our whole life is transformed. The things we neglected or paid no attention to
are seen in a new light. The people that serve us in shops become
bodhisattvas, and the chores of our life become treasured opportunities to practice. The point isn't that the world has been made
new. The point is that our mind has been made new. And so, the
world has indeed been reborn.

In Zen monasteries, even the most menial of tasks is a great
honor to perform. Washing the dishes or cleaning the toilets is
Zen practice of the highest order. To wear the *rakusu*, the robe of a
Buddhist practitioner, worn around the neck, is to wear the bodhisattva's apron of service. To serve others is a privilege. To receive
is also a privilege. It is not that one is better than the other. Rather
it is that the server, the served, and that which is served come
together in one action, one moment of perfection. In the ceremony
of taking food, from the very first chant we remember that giver,
receiver, and gift are all unified. From the perspective of an awakened mind, there is equality in the action of giving. Habitually, we
want to be the one to receive, the one to be served. But Zen practice

opens our eyes that this is the incorrect way of seeing things. That is why we are happy to volunteer for menial work when practicing Zen. With concentration and awareness, even weeding or cleaning up become Zazen.

In the Zen tradition, one of the most honored of servers is the *tenzo*, or cook. Indeed, after the abbot, the cook is one of the most important officers in a Zen monastery, and a whole tradition of temple cooking and cuisine has grown up out of Zen kitchens over the centuries. In 1237, Master Dōgen set out a set of instructions for the temple cook in his famous essay "Tenzokyōkun," or "Instructions for the Tenzo." It is a set of teachings and practical instructions for preparing meals for the monks. The instructions teach that chopping carrots and washing rice are the most sacred of occupations. These tasks should be approached with the same nondiscriminating mind that one brings to zazen.

> Therefore, although you may encounter inferior ingredients, do not be at all negligent. . . . Never alter your state of mind based on materials.[22]

It is of lesser consequence what is presented to you. What is more important is the mind you bring to it. Whatever ingredients we are given, we make the best meal that we can. We do not waste our time wishing we had better vegetables and fresher tofu; that we had the best Japanese noodles or magnificent organic Irish potatoes. What we do is deal with the reality before us right now. This is the Zen Way.

Dōgen tells us that we need three attitudes of mind in approaching our tasks: joyful mind, nurturing mind, and magnanimous mind. Dōgen asks us to cultivate a happy heart as we carry out our actions. This is the joyful mind. The nurturing mind, he says, is the mind of mothers and fathers. This is a mind of kindness, where we look after others as though they were our only child, who we dearly love. Finally, magnanimous mind is like the great mountains or the great ocean, Dōgen says. This mind is vast and is not biased or contentious. It is a big mind that contains everything, great and small, important and unimportant, prestigious and ordinary. The magnanimous mind makes no such distinctions.

For most of us, this is a great teaching. Most of us cannot escape the many tasks that come with being alive. We have to cook and clean the house; we have to scrub the shower and wash our clothes. Often, we see these things not as blessings because we are alive, but as drudgery, inconvenient jobs we have to do that get in the way of other, more important things. But Dōgen does not see it like this. In his masterwork, the *Shōbōgenzō*, not only cooking, but also going to the bathroom, washing the face, kitchen work, and cleaning are all treated as spiritual practice, not more or less important than sitting in meditation. He offers clear instructions on how to use the toilet and brush the teeth. This is a spiritual inheritance that he offers where the body is taken care of and cherished. It is not seen as something dirty and of a lower order. Even washing up after ourselves is the work of buddhas.

Have you ever noticed how some wealthy people, who never have to cook or clean up after themselves, can take things for granted? They might be obnoxious to servers and never fully appreciate what is served to them to eat. The food will never be satisfactory, and the wine will just be passable, unless it is incredibly expensive. Then it will be appreciated with a bored, detached air. We can only feel sorry for such people. How few of their meals they enjoy. How seldom are hotel bedrooms experienced as a treat and a source of joy. They are bored and lacking in appreciation. But when you bring Dōgen's three minds to a humble plate of pasta, then it becomes a treasure. Living in a tiny apartment, a clump of mint growing in a balcony pot can bring more joy than a stately garden; a glass of cold water can be finer than the best champagne. As the Buddha teaches at the beginning of the Dhammapada, "All experience is preceded by mind / Led by mind, / Made by mind."[23]

It is not that we should accept our lot and see our place in life as somehow ordained. There are the privileged that live in mansions and the poor that live in hovels, and this is unjust. Those that do menial tasks need not be subservient, bowing and scraping to their "betters." This is not it at all. But we can find honor and dignity in whatever situation we find ourselves in. The world is structurally unjust and needs to be changed. But the three minds of Dōgen will transform it in a much more radical way than the habitual mind that sees the server as inferior and the served as better. It is from this attitude that the problem stems. We must see the authentic truth of the way things really are, just as we navigate our way through samsara—our usual, mundane existence. Glaring inequality is the stuff of samsara; radical equality is the ground of nirvana. In this body and life, we can see that they are one and the same. But we must skillfully know at each instant when the rule of the material and the rule of the immaterial apply. We reject neither, seeing that they are two sides of one truth. With this whole vision, the custodian cleaning the office is underpaid and underappreciated. But we see also that she is a bodhisattva doing Buddha's work. It is not that one is true and the other false. With the eyes of wisdom, we see that they are both true at the same time.

# Just Enough

*Even if we do not come to like something, we*
*can come to a place where we can move beyond*
*discrimination and deal with whatever comes our way.*

ON THE RARE OCCASIONS that I eat takeout food, I enjoy it. However, sometimes afterward I feel bloated and full in a heavy way. I feel that I have filled my body without nourishing it. I certainly do not appreciate the food in the same way as when I have prepared it myself. And as the portions are too big—to satisfy customers that they have received enough food—I often eat more than I need when eating takeout. In buying it, I have become a consumer, someone to sell food to rather than someone to feed and to nourish.

The Zen ceremony of taking food has a lot to teach us. It is called ōryōki, which means "just enough." An ōryōki dining set contains three bowls that nest into each other, chopsticks, a napkin, a spoon, a cloth to dry up, and a cloth to wrap it all up in. Nothing could be more economical. In a small bundle is everything you need to eat and drink. And as hot tea is used to wash the bowls as part of the ceremony, there is no washing up once you're finished. It is so gracefully designed. The ceremony is circular, ending at the point where it began—the circle being a recurring motif in Zen. At the start, the bowls are wrapped and ready to use, as they are at the ceremony's end. And the bowls contain just enough food to leave you feeling fed—neither overfed nor hungry. Just right. It is a manifestation of the teaching of the Middle Way.

The practice of *ōryōki* has its origins in the begging bowls that Buddhist monks use to receive donations of food on their alms round. The bowl varies from one Buddhist culture to the next, but in *ōryōki* the largest of the three bowls is the size of the top of a human skull. It is in proportion to our body. And what it contains is in proportion to our needs. Now, some of us need more food than others, so there is a second serving in the ceremony that acknowledges this, where no food, some food, or a second full bowl can be accepted from those serving. We judge for ourselves how much food we need, without comment or judgment from others. Certainly, the ceremony does not overfeed you; nor does it underfeed, as the first serving consists of enough food to sustain health for most people. It is beautiful and aesthetic in its precise economy. And nothing goes to waste, as you must finish whatever you are served and accept.

Herein is another great teaching of *ōryōki*. As we must eat what we are given, we must set aside all our likes and dislikes and deal with what is served to us. Allergies and medical or dietary requirements aside, we cannot eat like children, refusing the foods offered. Even if we do not really like some of the food, we should eat it. And eat it all. It's amazing how we can grow to appreciate foods we once disliked. Even if we do not come to like something, we can come to a place where we can move beyond discrimination and deal with whatever comes our way. This valuable training helps us in our lives in so many unimaginable ways beyond the ceremony itself. That said, I remember one particularly disgusting soup I was served up early one morning on retreat. I had to do everything in my power not to gag. But I did get through it. And the soup stayed in my stomach. On so many Zen retreats in the years after, eating anything that wasn't that soup was so much easier.

Because we have been so well trained to be customers, we feel that we can always pick and choose things so that they suit our tastes. It is difficult at first to have this privilege suspended. When the *ōryōki* ceremony is unfolding on retreat, newcomers to Zen are always introduced to all these aspects of eating *ōryōki* at the start, and still so many find it hard to break with their programming. They discriminate which food they will take and which they will reject. They do not finish one or another bowl of food, despite having requested it when served. They start eating before everyone else, or get up to leave when they are finished but others are still eating. We are so unused to setting aside our own needs and thinking of others. We are so used to trying to have everything our own way.

To put it simply, in *ōryōki* we cannot eat the way we normally do, the way that we want. Because our wants are frustrated, we see them clearly. We are annoyed or angry that we have to eat in a certain way. We may even resent it. We see how we are always arranging things to suit us, and how irritated we get when things aren't set up the way we want. But by deliberately setting up things in a way that doesn't suit us individually, we see that we can learn to handle things when they aren't set up as we'd wish. We learn patience and restraint. We don't enjoy learning these things, but they are useful attributes to have. As many situations in life are not the way we want them to be, we can learn to bring this training to those situations. *Ōryōki* becomes a training for life. And like many things that are worthwhile, *ōryōki* takes application, persistence, and effort.

This ceremony also teaches us the preciousness of what we have. Every single grain of rice is eaten, with none thrown away. There is nothing wasted. Even the tea we drink is used to wash our bowls before we drink it. And as part of the ceremony, we chant; acknowledging with gratitude the many generations of people, past and present, that have brought us this food and the recipes that make it. As I like to say, the meals our great grandmother prepared are still sustaining us. We also ritually remember and offer a little bit of food to those that are hungry and not satisfied, the hungry ghosts. When we do this, I often picture the emaciated bodies of my own ancestors from the Great Famine, those that walked the countryside in starvation, even resorting to cannibalism to survive. Only one hundred and fifty years ago, the lanes and country roads where we hold our retreats were full of the starving and desperate. It often strikes me how fortunate we are to have enough food to sustain and nourish us. In only a few generations, we have learned to take all this for granted.

When I started practicing Zen, I really disliked the *ōryōki* ceremony. But I have grown to deeply appreciate it. In eating, we cannot deny our interconnection with all things. In eating, the world of crops swaying in the fields and the world of fruits sun-ripened on the trees become part of our bodies, in a real way. Emptiness, interconnection—we actually experience these if we pay attention. In *ōryōki*, when we look down into our bowl of swirling tea, if we look closely enough, we can see that the entire universe is right there. The tiny particles of rice and a few seeds left over: they are stars and galaxies spiraling in the night sky of our black bowl. Always exactly where we find ourselves, all time and space are present. This is not some mystical statement. It is just something ordinary, right under our noses at all times. None of these teachings are hidden. They are plain to see. All you have to do is make a cup of tea and look deeply into it. You might find something unexpected. Look closely. You might see what has always been there all along.

# PART THREE

# Celebrating

# A Buddhist Year

*Ritual is where time and eternity are reconciled.*
*In holding our palms together, the relative and*
*the absolute come together in perfect expression*
*and balance. This time and all time collide.*

ACH YEAR WE CELEBRATE our birthday. It is a celebration that
helps us locate ourselves in time and navigate our way
through life. Marking the fact that we are one year older, we take
stock of where we have come from and of what we are turning
toward. Our birthday reaffirms who we are and is a chance to joy-
fully recommit to our life again. It gives our life a sense of overall
direction.

Our first birthday is a great occasion to be marked by all
around us. Later, when we are ten, we turn from one digit to two.
It's a big deal. If we are to add a third digit to our years, we must
reach one hundred. There is the significant birthday of thirteen,
when we become a teenager and finally leave childhood behind.
Then there are the culturally significant birthdays of twenty-one
and forty. The first marks our entry into adulthood and the second
our halfway point through life. These dates are in some way arbi-
trary and in some way not. They vary from culture to culture but
are determined by the actual trajectory of a human life. This architecture of life is captured in many ways through folk sayings and
native wisdom. Like the saying that gives its title to the memoir by

Muiris Ó Súilleabháin, about growing up on the Great Blasket, an isolated island off the west coast of Kerry in the North Atlantic.[24]

> Fiche bliain ag fás;
> Fiche bliain faoi bhláth agus
> Fiche bliain ag meath.

> Twenty years a'growing,
> Twenty years in bloom
> and twenty years of decline.

Such wisdom helps us make sense of life and the time we have. It allows us to pace decisions and actions. It makes us aware that we do indeed have limits, that our individual life is not unlimited and is bound by the restraints of years and seasons. This awareness is a great cure for our tendency toward arrogance and excessive pride. Estranged from the natural world, we often forget that we must operate within its boundaries. The degradation of the ground that supports our very life has resulted from our forgetting this.

Growing up in Ireland, the seasons are well defined, and the feast days and festivals that come with each separate season helped to make sense of the turning of the year. Apart from birthdays and anniversaries, a mix of Christian and older Celtic or Druidic festivals mark out each of the twelve months. The winter solstice and Christmas; Saint Brigid's Day and Bealtaine in springtime; the summer solstice, followed by Lughnasa, the harvest festival. And in the autumn, a favorite of all children is Samhain (pronounced "SAH-win"), now popularized as Halloween, when the door between this world and the next is open. And so, one year becomes the next. Time passes but the traditions remain.

These traditions came out of the land. They were of their place. Over many thousands of years, the Celtic festivals developed here, and specific sacred places were associated with the old religion. When Christianity came, it overlaid Christian meaning on this Celtic bedrock. The two thousand years of Christian heritage are deep and profound in Ireland, as they are in the West generally; but they disguise a much older sacred sensibility below. The Christian heritage is the tip of the iceberg, while hidden under the water is the massive solidity that holds it all up: the depth of an ancient reality below.

In Buddhism, a similar process occurred. The Dharma overlaid the older practices and faiths in the countries it came to. In Japan, for example, the local *kami*, or spirits, became part of Buddhist practice, with local deities absorbed and recognized by the new Buddhist religion—just as the pagan origins of Saint Brigid were in the Irish context. This was a natural and slow process. It took time. But it must have been marked by specific individuals making specific decisions at specific points in time. Tradition emerges naturally from innovation. New influences are brought in. And what is new becomes an ancient tradition with time, always reacting to specific needs and contexts.

We still need rituals. But what happens when we feel estranged from them? When we no longer identify with or support the authority that defines a tradition, what do we do? The bind is that new and improvised rituals can lack the sense of tradition and authority that comes with rituals over many generations of practice. Because ritual needs to be a container much greater and bigger than one human life, it should be passed down through the ages. So, to draw on an older authenticity, Christianity makes Samhain into All Saint's Day and the winter solstice into the birth of Christ. It summons to its side the ancient authority of the seasons themselves, as they die and are reborn. It taps into something much more basic and profound than culture: the natural world, which underpins everything.

Having left Christianity behind, having taken the Buddhist path, we still need rituals. Unable, in all conscience, to baptize and die in the Catholic Church, we remain in need of the vessels of ritual that carry us across this life. Thankfully, the Buddhist tradition is even more ancient than the Christian one. It comes to us from the ancients fully formed and with the authority of centuries. It taps into that deeper reality of life and death, of the turning of the year that underlies all the great religious rituals of the world. And just as it adapted to become a Chinese Buddhism, a Vietnamese Buddhism, a Japanese Buddhism as it traveled, so will it become an Irish Buddhism, a European Buddhism, an American Buddhism as it journeys on. These expressions of the Dharma will inevitably draw on the same deep and ancient roots that Christianity and Islam have drawn on as they traveled. These expressions of Buddhism will be the ancient spirit animated in the present moment, in this time and place. And that is something that all ritual is, as it is made new and revived from the ancient past in each specific instant of expression. That is because ritual is where time and eternity are reconciled. In holding our palms together, the relative and the absolute come together in perfect expression and balance. This time and all time collide in a recognition of our limited life and the wider limitless reality from which we have never been separated from the very start. This is the power of liturgy. It is dance and theater and literature and all the arts in their purest form as sacred expression. It is the choreography of the earth and the moon and the sun. We do not ask what it means that we welcome the sun on our faces in springtime and gather yellow leaves in autumn. Its meaning is its own reality, above and beyond interpretation and utility. It is the breath of life rather than breathing in a conscious way. It is innate and instinctual and healing, in a deep and natural way.

So, how do we mark the year as it passes? What is this great choreography we perform in community, along with the seasons and the turning of the earth?

# Bodhi Day

*What Buddha sees is for all beings, not just for himself. It is even for the great earth and the entire universe. It is like the whole universe has woken up and realized the truth. This is what we remember.*

I N IRELAND, I'M OFTEN asked if Buddhists celebrate Christmas. It is such a big festival in the year that the whole culture is taken up with it. I know for many Christians it has become an over-commercialized festival of indulgence in which people eat, drink, and spend too much. Indeed, I know of an Irish writer who, every December, goes to a Muslim country where there is no Christmas, just so that he can escape the orgy of overindulgence—especially the booze-sodden parties that are so common around this time of year.

But my family does celebrate Christmas. In truth, living in a largely Christian country, it's almost impossible to escape. Having kids in school also means that they are surrounded by it every winter. They make Christmas cards, and we put up a Christmas tree. We exchange presents and have a special Christmas dinner. We visit family, just like everyone else. But our Christmas is a little different. Sitting under the Christmas tree is a statue of Buddha on a small altar. That's because for Zen Buddhists, December brings the anniversary of the Buddha's great awakening, over two-and-a-half thousand years ago. December 8 marks what our sangha calls Bodhi Day, or Jodo-e, as it's known in the Sōtō Zen school.

*Bodhi* means "awakening," and it's on this day that Siddhartha became the Buddha and was enlightened as he sat under a sacred fig tree known as the Bodhi Tree. In our house, the Christmas tree has become a Bodhi Tree, as we remember that event when all of Buddhism began.

An ancestor of that original tree is still at the location of Buddha's enlightenment in Bodh Gaya in India. I have never been, but I hope to visit one day. Saplings of the tree have also been planted in Sri Lanka, Japan, and other places in India, as well as in Hawaii and California. I spoke to someone from the botanical gardens here in Dublin once about the possibility of planting a sapling of the sacred tree here in Ireland. He led me toward the Bodhi Tree that they already have, growing indoors in warm conditions. Although it is not actually a sapling from the original tree at Bodh Gaya, it is nevertheless the same species of tree. He said the plant could only survive indoors due to the Irish climate, and since they already had one *Ficus religiosa*, they would not take another one—even a cutting from the religiously significant tree in India. And so my plan of planting a sapling of the Bodhi Tree in Ireland ended there—for now, at any rate.

In the Japanese Zen tradition, Bodhi Day is also known as Rōhatsu, which literally means the eighth day of the twelfth month, when tradition says the Buddha experienced his awakening. Zen Master Keizan in *The Record of Transmitting the Light* tells us that according to tradition, Buddha achieved his great awakening on seeing the appearance of the morning star after a long period sitting in meditation. Keizan tells us the Buddha's reputed words at this moment: "I and the great earth and beings simultaneously achieve the Way."[25] At that moment, everything changed for everyone and for all time. What he sees is for all beings, not just for himself. It is even for the great earth and the entire universe. It is like the whole universe has woken up and realized the truth. This is what we remember at Rōhatsu.

Our sangha in Ireland usually has an intensive retreat in the days leading up to Rōhatsu. We rise at 3:30 in the morning and sit fifteen blocks of fifty minutes in meditation a day, with ten minutes walking meditation every hour. We break for breakfast, lunch, and an evening meal, and hold no ceremonies until the final morning, concentrating only on zazen. The schedule is based on the schedule at Antaiji Temple, near the western coast of Japan, and the whole retreat is in the style of Kōdō Sawaki, one of the most famous Sōtō Zen teachers of the twentieth century, and a predecessor in my own Zen lineage. It is a beautiful style of retreat: simple and sparse, with so much seated meditation that you can go very deep in your practice. Entering such profound silence can happen only through such single-minded practice. There are no distractions, only total silence for the few days of retreat. After a while sitting like this, even a dust ball on the floor becomes a universe of treasures.

On the last day of the retreat, we hold a ceremony at dawn to mark Rōhatsu. I remember one year the retreat center was buried deep in snow for the final day of the retreat. Before the sun came up, we went out to a large stupa on the grounds of the retreat center and offered candles in the snow. The stupa looked so magical with the candles burning all around it in the fading darkness. It really felt that a great light was appearing in the world. We circumambulated the stupa numerous times, and I remember clearly seeing the morning star in the heavens, before returning to the hall for our Rōhatsu ceremony. After not speaking for days, it was like attaining the mystical power of speech to be able to chant the sutras in the ceremony that morning. Sometimes speaking after a long silence can seem like speaking for the very first time.

In many ways, this festival of light is an archetypal winter festival. While we hold a ceremony for the winter solstice also, it is Rōhatsu that stands out in Zen as our winter observance. In ancient Celtic times, the winter solstice was certainly an important time of year, with the passage tomb at Newgrange in County Meath, still annually seeing its dark interior lit up by the sun on the morning of the winter solstice. It's incredible that a structure older than the pyramids and Stonehenge can still faithfully light up like this each year in alignment with the rising sun. Since 3200 BCE, it has given hope to people at the darkest time of year, as it still does today in our much-changed world. And just as Christmas marks the light entering the world, so too, for Buddhists, does Rōhatsu. The Buddha's enlightenment may be celebrated at varying times depending on the specific Buddhist tradition, but I think the winter observance of it fits well with Western and Irish culture, considering how we need to turn to the light for comfort when it seems that all light has gone from the world. In the depths of winter, to mark the coming of the light of Dharma is profoundly moving and reassuring. The hope that the Buddha brought at that moment is still alive and urgently with us each Rōhatsu. As Master Keizan reminds us, from this original spark, the fire of the Dharma has spread throughout the world.

Later, Buddha transmitted the Treasury of the True Dharma Eye to Mahakashyapa, and it has passed down from Mahakashyapa through generation after generation since, to the present day. Truly, it has been transmitted through India, China, and Japan, where the practice of the true Dharma endures. And so, after more than ninety-six generations, it has arrived here. It is young compared to the hallowed ages that Newgrange has seen. But it carries an ancient truth, much older than the original Buddha himself. It is at home here and is in no way foreign. It is universal, for all times and places. And yet in each instant it finds a unique expression: in the stones of Newgrange; in the chapel walls of St. Ciarán's in Clonmacnoise, on the banks of the River Shannon; each time we light a candle at Rōhatsu; and when we greet the morning star.

# Welcoming the
# New Year

*Like art that changes your life, the magic of
ceremony can operate only if you go with it, suspend
temporarily the critical mind that questions all
the time, and enter the truth of things on a level
that is deeper than the literal and conventional.*

A s one year passes and another one rises, we reflect on what
has gone and look forward with hope to what is to come. In
Zen it is no different, as we ring a temple bell one hundred and
eight times to welcome in the year as it arrives. In Japan, the temple bells are magnificent. Called *bonshō,* the large bronze bells are
housed in a small, roofed structure, and are struck using a large
swinging beam suspended on ropes. They are beautifully reso-
nant and atmospheric. It's truly dramatic to see them rung with
force and gusto. In our community here in Ireland, we do not have
such a magnificent bell. Still, we respect this Zen tradition, and
we ring our more modest *densho* bell in the same way. It marks the
beginning of our New Year's ceremony.

In the ceremony itself, we ritually read the Perfection of
Wisdom Sutra.[26] This is really something to behold when it is done
in its totality. The full ritual, called Daihannya Tendoku, takes
many monks to perform and involves all six hundred volumes of
the Great Sutra on the Perfection of Wisdom being ritually read

in a theatrical choreography of great beauty. It is the longest sutra in the canon, and in the past the whole thing was actually read in its entirety. However, an abbreviation of the full ritual evolved, whereby the books bound in accordion-like concertina form are cascaded dramatically through the air, in a "rolling reading" from hand to hand. During this performance, lines from the sutra and their various titles are shouted out. Incense smoke fills the room, bells ring, and the overall effect is really something impressive. It creates a "wind of wisdom" that has quite an impact on those witnessing the ceremony, which is dedicated to everyone's health and well-being, as well as to the peace of the world and the country. In Ireland, we ritually read a shorter Perfection of Wisdom text, as we do not have the full six hundred volumes, nor the resources to perform the full ceremony. But that does not matter. The intention and meaning are the same for all those that participate. The ceremony becomes a focus for our intentions for the year ahead, and we make an inner commitment to start afresh and recommit ourselves to practice in the coming year.

As part of our ritual, everyone is given a flower and blessed with "water of blessing," which is simply water that has been blessed by the officiating priest. Every single person is told by the priest leading the ritual, "You are precious, and you are loved." Or the whispered words might say, "May you be well and happy and free from suffering." Most people receive this blessing well and feel healed and uplifted by it. Some others may even be a little upset by it, shedding tears, as the idea that they are precious and loved is something they find hard to accept. Maybe they have low self-worth and low self-esteem. I think these people particularly need to hear these words. Certainly, when you see people participating in the ceremony with meaning and commitment, the whole experience is transformed from an empty ritual of gestures into what ceremony should always really be about: a gateway to transformation, a shared vessel that carries us all on a healing journey. Blessed with the sutra book and anointed with the blessed water, sprinkled from a freshly picked pine branch, each person has focused their intention to begin again with the New Year. They receive a flower to take away with them—maybe the only flower that they have been given for a long time. They are asked for nothing in return. It must be unconditional to have any truth to it.

The mix of warm joy and deep sadness that can come from our New Year's ceremony is nothing more than the emotions that we carry in our hearts. It is not that the ceremony creates these emotions; they are already there. Rather, it is that the ceremony becomes a conduit for their expression and release. The joy of starting the year afresh, or the regrets we may have and our fears for the future—these are all being carried about inside us. By expressing them we feel liberated and free. We feel lighter. In many ways, the effect of ceremony is similar to the cathartic effect of theater. Upsetting emotions can be woken up and purged in the release of catharsis. The energy and intensity of participation in a ceremony can be like expressing deep and profound emotions in a play. On one level, it is just acting. But on a real and deep level, there are genuine emotions and psychic energies being felt and realized. It is like the ceremony becomes a safe container for all these volatile thoughts and feelings that we suppress, concealed even from ourselves. Through the medium of ceremony, we feel able to deal with this truth in a more manageable way. For it to work, we must suspend disbelief, which is required for any drama of transformation to take place. If one does not dive in and participate, merely viewing the ceremony as a skeptical observer, then the effect of the ceremony will never be realized. For a drama to unfold, we must forget that it is not real—or, more accurately, we must allow it to become real. Like art that changes your life, the magic of ceremony can operate only if you go with it, suspend temporarily the critical mind that questions all the time, and enter the truth of things on a level that is deeper than the literal and conventional.

What I am suggesting here holds true for popular and secular ceremonies also: the New Year's Eve fireworks in the city center, the countdown to midnight and the popping open of champagne, singing "Auld Lang Syne" arm in arm: all these experiences are really no more than conventions. However, when invested with energy and emotion, they become something greater and very real. They may even be remembered as high points in our life, a pivotal moment when things changed for us. Each year, our New Year's ceremony has the potential to be this.

But in truth, every single moment has this quality. The ceremony of transformation is right here and now. Where you are at this very moment is at the center of a silent ceremony. Listen. Look carefully. You will see it.

# The Buddha's Passing

*It is easy to see nirvana as a kind of annihilation or
nonexistence, which could easily seem no different
than just atheistic extinction. But nirvana transcends
notions of existence and nonexistence. It is the final
state of liberation that we cannot map or comprehend.*

As winter recedes and spring freshness arrives, we remember the passing of the Buddha. His time of death is a time of rebirth in the world. The snowdrops have appeared and early shoots of daffodils are showing themselves. There is an icy newness in the air, and Irish people's thoughts turn to Lent, to Easter, and to Saint Patrick's Day in the weeks ahead. The spring equinox is not far away, and the long nights are ending.

According to the accounts we have, the Buddha died at the age of eighty at Kushinagar in India, not too far from the Nepalese border. After taking his last meal, given to him by a local blacksmith named Cunda, he fell ill, possibly with dysentery, and died shortly thereafter. His close attendant Ananda made a resting place for the Buddha in a grove of sala trees, and there, lying on his right side, he gave his final teaching and passed away. Passing through the four degrees of meditation, he then passed through the four immaterial levels, finally entering *parinirvana*, the final nirvana when the human body is transcended. In the days that followed, his body was cremated, and relics taken and placed in various stupas. Mounds were raised over these holy places, some of which can still be seen today. And so, the First Buddhist Council was convened, where the Buddha's teachings were all recited and Mahakashyapa became the first in the Buddha's long line of successors.

So it is that each year on February 15 we remember these events on Nehan-e, the day that remembers the Buddha's *parinirvana*. We also remember those that we have lost during the year at this time, and place photos of them and mementos on the altar as part of our ceremony. For this ceremony, the usual statue of the seated Buddha on the altar is replaced by a depiction of his death scene, in which he is lying on his side. The traditional offerings of light, incense, flowers, food, and drink are made, and the verse in homage to the Buddha's relics is chanted. At one point in our ceremony, everyone goes to the altar, bringing up a picture of someone they have lost. They offer incense and a silent prayer or intention, and then they place the picture below the Buddha and in his care.

Often, the whole question of death is discussed around this ceremony. It is one of the fundamental questions that people come to spiritual practice with. As I've learned, many people that come to Zen have experienced grief or loss of some kind. In our sangha, there are people that have lost sons and daughters suddenly and tragically; people whose parents have died young; people who've lost close siblings when they were themselves young and delicate. The founder of our school, Master Dōgen, also lost both parents very young. When he was seven, his mother passed away, and he is said to have had a deep realization of the transiency of life at his mother's funeral, as the incense smoke rose up around her and the monks chanted her funeral rite. This understanding of transience is deep in Buddhism. It is one of the marks of existence, taught by the Buddha early on. So, what happens after death? Where do we come from and where do we go? How do we tackle these fundamental questions?

There is mention of heaven—or more accurately, heavens— in Buddhism. Indeed, there are numerous heavens mentioned in various sutras, like the Tusita Heaven, where future Buddhas reside. This is where the tradition says the historical Buddha resided for many thousands of years before he appeared on earth. It is also where the future Buddha Maitreya now resides, awaiting his birth here. So the Buddhist worldview includes heavens, but these also are only temporary parts of the cycle of death and rebirth. But nirvana transcends notions of existence and nonexistence. It is the final state of liberation that we cannot map or comprehend. The Buddha is considered to have entered nirvana while still alive. But it is only at the death of his physical body that he entered *parinirvana*, or final nirvana. That is what we remember each February 15.

In the Mahayana Lotus Sutra, we are given the good news that Buddhahood and nirvana is what awaits us all, without exception. Indeed, in the deeper Mahayana view, there is, ultimately, no birth and no death at all. We appear as individual lives because of causes and conditions: We were conceived by our parents. They had ancestors before them. We were nurtured as infants. The planet remained habitable to sustain us. Our body remained healthy, and nuclear war did not wipe out our society. The list of causes and conditions that make our lives possible ultimately links to everything else in existence and, equally, everything that did not come to pass. So, it is not that we were born from nothing. Rather, the causes and conditions arose within the body of reality that brought us into existence. Those causes and conditions will eventually fall away again and cease to exist. Like a wave on a great ocean, we rise and fall. We do, indeed, disappear—but not in the way of nihilistic extinction. Because, in truth, we also do not entirely disappear either, just as, although we may be identifiable as individuals, ultimately we never were individuals cut off from the rest of reality to start with. So, we are beyond easy distinctions, beyond conventional notions of birth and death.

And yet the Buddhist teachings understand that there is something that moves from life to life, from rebirth to rebirth. But what is it that is being reborn? Is it the stream of energy and karmic consequences that we create? Is it the deepest part of our consciousness, which in Buddhism is called our "storehouse consciousness"? Is this a linear process that continues throughout samsara, and that ends in nirvana? Does some mind continuity exist, until it enters the final truth of things at nirvana?

These questions have been debated and written about for many centuries by Buddhist thinkers. As Buddhists, we may have many readings and understandings in relation to these questions—but the truth is that we do not know. What we do know, however, is that we come from causes and conditions, and when those causes and conditions have passed, we, too, have passed.

To ask to where have we passed is to apply the logic of time and space where it simply does not apply. We have not gone to a place. Place no longer has any meaning. We do not persist in another time. Time itself has been left behind. We are here (wherever here is) and then we are not here. How do we respond to this?

In the Nehan-e ceremony, we respond by acknowledging and honoring this mystery. We remember the last words of the Buddha, as told to us in the Mahaparinirvana Sutra: "Behold now, I exhort you: All compounded things are subject to vanish. Strive with earnestness." Such ordinary words, really. But they also go no further than what we know to be true: this life is brief and precious. We can sleepwalk through it until we find ourselves near the end. Or we can wake up now and see the truth and beauty all around us. If even a greatly awakened teacher like the Buddha passes from this life, what will stop us from passing? The wooden *han* that is struck to call us to meditation bears an inscription to remind us of this miraculous truth:

Great is the matter of birth and death,
Life flows quickly by,
Time waits for no one.
Wake up! Wake up!
Don't waste a moment!

# Buddha's Birth

*We celebrate coming out of the long winter, and our*
*hearts are glad to see the flowers again. Quite simply,*
*it is a time to express the joy of just being alive.*

BY APRIL, THE FORESTS around where we hold our retreats in rural County Cavan are carpeted in bluebells. But more often than not we are in the city, not on retreat—but flowers still bloom there. The spring equinox has come and gone, and we have observed it with a short ritual. Now we pick wildflowers (or flowers from our urban gardens) and adorn a special altar for Buddha's Birthday Assembly on April 8.

According to tradition, Buddha was born on the eighth day of the fourth lunar month. But since the Meiji Restoration, Japan has adopted the Western calendar, so April 8 is deemed to be the date of Buddha's birth. However, the date varies across the Buddhist world, depending on regional variations. In southern Asia, the festival is known as Vesak, and usually held sometime in May. Once I was an Irish delegate at the United Nations International Day of Vesak in Vietnam, and saw that many of the traditions common to Japanese Buddhism are widely practiced throughout the Buddhist world. It was an amazing experience to be with thousands of other Buddhists from every corner of the Buddhist world that spring in Vietnam.

On the altar for Buddha's Birthday, we place a small statue of Shakyamuni Buddha as an infant. Born in Lumbini, in present-day

Nepal, around 500 BCE, there are many stories that surround his birth. He is said to have walked from birth, taking seven steps in each of the cardinal directions before pointing at the earth and the sky, predicting the path that lay before him and proclaiming: "Heaven, earth, and I are all one person." And this is how he is traditionally depicted on the altar for the celebration of his birth, as he points to the earth below and the heavens above. The statue is placed in a kind of small pavilion, which is covered in fresh spring flowers. People take turns bathing the statue in sweet tea with a ladle as they make a prayer or intention. The sweet tea evokes the story that fragrant rain fell at his birth, and in Japan it is a popular festival with children, who take part in a parade before ritually bathing the Buddha statue. Central to the children's parade is a white elephant figure, which symbolizes the premonition or dream the Buddha's mother had before his birth, which told her of her son to come. The whole festival is the centerpiece of the Hana-matsuri Flower Festival, an important time in Japan when Japanese people appreciate the spectacle of cherry blossoms every spring.

I have witnessed Hana-matsuri only once, and it made a great impression on me. At a temple in Tokyo, I was surrounded by flowering trees, with the flower pavilion housing the infant Buddha statue set up outside the main temple building. The parade of children brought a flower each to offer to the Buddha. It was so beautiful in the fresh spring air, with all the cherry blossom trees shedding their pink petals onto the breeze. My wife and I had no children at the time and were on honeymoon. But offering sweet tea at the flower pavilion, we both thought the time was right to start a family. It was a magical time in Japan. In Ueno Park in Tokyo, the blossoming trees lined the pathways, and local groups of friends and their families ate and drank in a great celebratory mood under the flowering branches. So, I have a great affinity with Hana-matsuri. It's a great ceremony that is very close to my heart.

This need to welcome the spring is found throughout human culture. In Ireland, it was the feast of Bealtaine, held between the spring equinox and midsummer. Bonfires were lit and the cattle were driven through the smoke between the fires to purify and bless them. And in the past, everyone doused their winter fires, relighting them from the flames of this communal bonfire. Flowers figured greatly, too, with doorways to homes decorated and venerated with spring flowers and flowering bushes and trees. Ancient sacred wells were visited at this time of year and, when Christianity arrived, devotion to Mary was centered around May in particular, with the celebration of flowers and new growth greatly associated with this Marian devotion. It is no coincidence that birth and motherhood are given such emphasis at this time of year, be it Christ's mother Mary or Buddha's mother Maya. As the earth itself is full and fertile in the spring, we naturally find ritual forms to express these deep sensibilities and deep realities in our devotional and religious cultures. We celebrate coming out of the long winter, and our hearts are glad to see the flowers again. Quite simply, it is a time to express the joy of just being alive.

When our two boys came along, we also held a naming ceremony for them at this time of year. It was a lovely May day in the garden of our house, and Ingen, a priest from Suzuki Rōshi's lineage, came to perform the ceremony. There were offerings of incense, light, and flowers, and the boys' names were announced to friends and family. Ingen gave a beautiful talk about the act of naming, but unfortunately he could barely be heard, his voice drowned out by the wailing and talking of our youngest. It was a great lesson in the realities of having children. Still, it was beautiful, and Ingen did a great job. After the ceremony, we had food in the garden. And although it was only May, it was already warm, with people taking off their jackets and women wearing summer dresses. The boys loved making a racket with the Buddhist ceremonial bells, banging out their music until the bells had to be hidden from them. It was real life. Perfect as it is. That is all.

# Spring Does Not Become Summer

*The passage of time confounds us. It seems like
a dream is flowing by. Only where we are right
now has any solidity. The past has evaporated,
disappeared into thin air. The future is like a
mirage without form. We all have this sense
because it is the reality of our experience.*

IT SEEMS LIKE ONE moment the bluebells are out and the next
thing the crops are tall and yellow under the summer heat. We
see our breath bloom in the frigid air, and a moment later the road
before us shimmers with the heat of summer. We say that winter
has become spring, which in turn has become summer. But Master
Dōgen tells us this is not exactly so.

> Firewood becomes ash. Ash cannot become firewood again.
> However, we should not view ash as after and firewood
> as before. We should know that firewood dwells in the
> dharma position of firewood and has its own before and
> after. Although before and after exist, past and future are cut
> off. . . . This is like winter and spring. We don't think that
> winter becomes spring, and we don't say that spring becomes
> summer.[27]

Dōgen is telling us that spring is the bluebells and the frogspawn, and that summer is the yellow crops and the frogs. The bluebells of spring do not become the crops of summer. All the causes and conditions that make up spring are what spring is. These causes disappear and new ones arise. So, first there is spring; then summer follows. But it is not that spring becomes summer. We think that, but we've got it slightly wrong. Everything exists at its own moment and in its own position. Where have the bluebells gone in winter? In a sense they are still there; they are just latent, and they will emerge when the causes and conditions of bluebells come about. Dōgen is drawing our attention to the ultimate reality of the present moment. Yes, there is a before and an after within this moment—but at this moment, this is what is real. In winter, spring is like a dream. In summer, winter is like a fantasy.

Did you ever find yourself saying on a warm summer's day, "It seems like Christmas was only recently"? Or in the heart of winter: "I can't believe we were sitting out there taking the sun only a few weeks ago." The passage of time confounds us. It seems like a dream is flowing by. Only where we are right now has any solidity. The past has evaporated, disappeared into thin air. The future is like a mirage without form. We all have this sense because it is the reality of our experience. So, intellectually we think spring becomes summer; but our experience is otherwise. Our actual experience is only the experience of the present moment; everything else is a kind of dream. There is a before and an after at any given moment, but only this moment has any weight. Everything else is weightless.

To think of it another way: Where has the child gone that you were? You as a child, playing by the ocean many years ago. Has the child been somehow annihilated? Has entering the past killed off that child? No, it has not. The child can never be separated from that moment of being a child. It belongs at that time, just as you right now belong in the context of now. How could it be otherwise? We are time, as Dōgen tells us in "Uji" ("Being Time"). Not that we are *in* time—we are time itself. Time and being are the same substance perceived in two different ways. That is why time travel is only a fantasy. An object is inseparable from the time it is in. It cannot be ripped from that time and placed in another time. For each of us, there is only this time now. There is a past and a future, but they are only real in this now, in their presence right now in this instant. Spring does not become summer. There is spring, and then there is summer. That is what Dōgen is saying. It is important not to miss your life, which is happening right now.

This view of time has many implications. It allows us to find freedom from the weight of the past. It enables us to live with presence of mind and in reality, rather than in some fantasy of the future. It also allows us to come to terms with the idea of our own death. It is not that the child by the ocean is dead; rather it is that they remain at that moment of time from which they cannot be separated. Each moment of our lives is like this. We are bound to it, and it cannot be taken away. Right now is right now. Another moment has its own causes and conditions, and whatever flows from that. This is not a denial of the future. Rather it is an affirmation of the present, where all things are. Dōgen compares this ever-presence of all time to climbing a mountain peak and seeing many other places at once: "yesterday and today is just about moments in which we go directly into the mountains and look out across a thousand or ten thousand peaks."[28] This instant is the peak you stand on, and all time stretches out as other realities—other peaks that you can see if you turn around and look behind you. It's a beautiful image of time as a three-dimensional object, where different things have different locations in the landscape. It is not that when you are at one location on the map that other parts of the map do not exist. They do. But they are just not your current reality.

There is a kind of contradiction here. Dōgen emphasizes the present moment and suggests that there is an unreality to other times. Yet he is also affirming the ever-presence of all time in this moment. At different times, Dōgen brings together the relative reality at hand and the ultimate reality of eternity. He is happy asserting what can seem like a contradiction. But he is only being faithful to the way reality is. The only reality is the one before us, but this reality has a past and a future. Dōgen honors the truth of things, while waking us up to our life in the here and now. He makes us aware of the "suchness" of reality, *tathata* as it is known in Sanskrit. A fifth-century Chinese text describes it:

> In its very origin suchness is of itself endowed with sublime attributes. It manifests the highest wisdom which shines throughout the world, it has true knowledge and a mind resting simply in its own being. It is eternal, blissful, its own self-being and the purest simplicity; it is invigorating, immutable, free. . . . Because it possesses all these attributes and is deprived of nothing, it is designated both as the Womb of Tathagata [Buddha] and the Dharma Body of Tathagata.[29]

When we recognize things in the moment as truthfully just as they are, we say to ourselves: "Wow! That's it." We wake up to reality. It cannot be put into words. It is the truth of things. We see the bluebells or the yellowing crops. We hear the river flow, or our name being called by a loved one. Life is being lived. We feel, "this is it now." We are at that moment in touch with the way things are, and we feel and know it beyond any ability to express it in words. We feel alive. We are shot through with exaltation. This is what Dōgen means by "spring does not become summer."

# Midway along the Journey of Our Life

*The dualistic and Cartesian mind sees the earth and
seasons as something external to our being. This is
greatly mistaken. We are spring breathing the spring
air. We are summer with the sun on our face. How
could we be separated from this time and place?*

B Y LATE JUNE IN Ireland, the nights are much shorter than the
days. Close to the summer solstice, there is a great, ungrasp-
able magic in the air. Daylight still hangs in the sky close to midnight, and it never truly gets fully dark. There is that exalted
feeling of being at the height of things. It feels like the world is
immortal each midsummer, in the way that youth feels indestruc-
tible when in the midst of it. A frantic wakefulness stirred by the
light keeps people up at night, and living on earth is like living on
a planet blessed with a great and luminous treasure.

On any journey, the midpoint has a special significance. It is
the ridge from which both the track traveled and the path to come
can simultaneously be seen. It is a place of reflection. Like Dante,
when taking stock at the midpoint you might feel a course correction needs to be made: "I had wandered off from the straight
path." And often new energy is required for the journey to come.

By the midpoint in life, you have a keen awareness of time.
You understand what twenty years are. You have seen *"Fiche bliain*

*ag meath"* (twenty years of decline) firsthand, as your parents and grandparents have aged or gone. You possess the wisdom of years but still enough of the energy of youth. These together can make you restless. You ask yourself: Should I change my life? Have I made the right choices? Should I radically alter course? At this point, it is easy to wobble. You fully appreciate the great gift that is your life and that is now beginning to fade. You feel that you have a magic power that you haven't fully used. The boundaries of existence appear before you.

In youth, we feel that there are no boundaries. Later, we see that there are boundaries to our life. If we rebel against this fact, we can create much more suffering for ourselves. To rebel may be an appropriate enough response, but it will not change the outcome. It may even hasten it. To go wild at middle age might be fantastic fun, but it has a higher price and greater consequences. But the restlessness of midsummer is real and intoxicating. Your days are about to get shorter, and it feels that right now is the time to stay up all night and celebrate.

In many cultures, midsummer is an important time of year. Across Europe, Ireland included, fires are lit in late June for Saint John's Eve. I remember as a child in East Galway seeing the fires at summertime. People would light them in their gardens and at their gateways. Carnivals and festivals were held at this time of year. And I've seen the same in France, too: massive bonfires in town squares, with carnivals and festivals happening in so many rural French villages. In Scandinavia, midsummer is an especially big celebration. As night has temporarily been banished, it's as if light has finally overcome darkness. Once I was in Roskilde, in Denmark, for Midsummer Eve, and the youth of the city were out in full force for a night of revelry and fun, all centered around a big bonfire, just like elsewhere in Europe.

There is an innate human need to respond to the seasons in this way. That's because the seasons are not external to us. The seasons are in our flesh and bones. At midsummer, we are midsummer. We express that through festival and fire. The dualistic and

Cartesian mind sees the earth and seasons as something external to our being. This is greatly mistaken. We are spring breathing the spring air. We are summer with the sun on our face. How could we be separated from this time and place? Our very context is us.

In "Zenki" ("Undivided Activity"), Master Dōgen uses the image of a journey on a boat to express this truth. The complete, seamless reality of all things, taken together, is what is unfolding at any moment. We are in no way alienated from creation. Life is living me, as much as I live it.

> Life is like a person in a boat. Aboard the boat, one uses a sail, holds a tiller, poles the boat along. Yet the boat carries you and without the boat you are not there. Riding the boat is what makes it a boat. You must study and penetrate this very moment. In this moment, the whole world is this boat. Thus "life" is what I live and "I" is life living me. Getting aboard the boat, this bodymind and all that is around are all the complete activity of the boat. Both the whole world and the vast sky are the boat's complete activity. This I that lives and the life that is I is just like this.[30]

So, it's that midsummer makes me and I make midsummer. In reality, they are inseparable in this moment of midsummer. All things taken together make up midsummer at this place and time. Meanwhile, in the southern hemisphere, it is midwinter. So it turns out that summer and winter are the same thing, just at two different poles of their development. When it is at the apex one way, we call it midsummer. When it is at the nadir the other way, we call it midwinter. But when we are here, we are not there. We live at this relative point of existence: so, it is summer for us. From an absolute point of view, it is summer here and winter elsewhere. Taken from this big view, it is neither summer nor winter. It is both and neither at the same time. It is beyond summer and beyond winter. Still, it is summer here and winter in the south. So, both are true at the same time. For me, it is summer in my experience. But it is also winter. The relative and the absolute exist simultaneously and are really the same thing, just like summer and winter. They are just the same thing experienced in varying ways. This is the contradictory nature of reality. And because of these contradictions, Western philosophy has struggled with reality for centuries. Zen, however, makes its homeless home right at the heart of this contradictory reality. As reality confounds conventional logic, so does Zen. That is why I feel that Zen sees the way things really are. But as a Zen priest, I would say that, wouldn't I?

Midsummer is marked by our sangha, just as the equinoxes and midwinter are. There's no philosophical reason to hold a service to mark midsummer—it just feels correct to do so. In chanting and making a dedication of merit at midsummer, we are in step with the rhythm of things. To ask us why we do this is like asking why people hold carnivals and festivals and light bonfires on the longest day of the year. It is just moving to the music of this earth, which is our home. And when there is music playing, why do we tap our feet? That's just what we do.

# Summer Sesshin

*We have listened to the teachings from this place
of deep silence and been greatly moved. We have
seen our wounds and found the strength to heal.
We have touched deeply our innermost heart and
mind and remembered again who we really are.*

SINCE THE TIME OF the Buddha there has been a tradition of intensive meditation practice each summer and winter. The tradition
comes from the rainy season where the Buddha lived, which lasted
for about ninety days and made it difficult to travel, especially
before there were roads as we know them today. Outside of the
rainy seasons, monks usually wandered around teaching, as they
had no permanent monastic buildings or dwellings. It must have
been something like the hedge schools of eighteenth- and nine-
teenth-century Ireland, where Catholics and Presbyterians were
illegally educated due the discriminatory laws of the time that permitted only Anglican schools. I imagine the monks' teaching must
have been conducted in a similar ad hoc fashion, perhaps at the
sides of roads and pathways, in fields and beneath trees, as well as
often in other informal settings, such as houses or barns. But come
the rainy season, they came together and settled down temporarily
as a monastic order. And as the tradition grew, this turned into the
*varsika*, or rainy-season retreat. Soon it was included in the monastic code, the Vinaya, and all travel was forbidden for monks for the
retreat period. In the Zen schools, this tradition was maintained

as the *ge-ango*, the summer retreat, and the *fuyu-ango*, the winter retreat. And the summer retreat tradition is something that our Irish sangha respects in our practice each July.

Our retreat is not a full *ango*, as it does not last ninety days. However, in all other ways, in terms of our practice, it is an *ango*. We follow the schedule and the *shingi*, or monastic code of practice, for seven days. We rise early to sit zazen and eat our meals in the traditional *ōryōki* way. The whole day is focused on zazen, with some work practice as well. There is a tight schedule for the week, with little free time. Speaking is largely prohibited, and everyone is expected to follow the routine without exception. There are opportunities for *dokusan*, which is a private practice interview with the teacher, and each morning there is a morning service, with an evening service before bed.

While our winter retreat is all about intensive zazen with little else, on our summer retreat we get to practice some of Zen's most important ceremonies. We hold *kitō* services for the living, where we bring our intentions forward to relieve their suffering. We hold memorial services for the dead. We conduct services that involve circumambulation, as is common to many religious traditions. We circumambulate the altar and meditation hall as we chant, just as Catholics circle holy shrines, Muslims turn around the Kaaba, the moon circumambulates the earth, and the earth circumambulates the sun. We have a service for children, and each day we chant all the names in our full lineage, starting with the seven buddhas before the historical Buddha, through the historical Buddha and his successors, and all the way through the ninety-six generations of ancestors, right up to Nishijima Rōshi, my teacher's teacher's teacher, who died in January 2014. We chant the names of female ancestors, too, on every alternate day—from Prajna Paramita to Maha Maya, the Buddha's mother; through Yasodhara, the Buddha's wife; and Mahapajapati, the founder of the nun's order; and all the way up to recently alive female teachers in the Sōtō line. It is amazing to chant the full lineage, realizing that each person represents a face-to-face transmission of the teachings, from living person to living person, right back to the historical Buddha over two-and-a-half thousand years ago. Even if modern scholars think there is a fictional element to some parts of the lineage, it does not detract from the human chain that it represents across time and space. It is humbling to be part of that necklace of human-to-human transmission in a tradition that has endured for so long a time.

What has allowed the tradition to endure is its "family style." There is the idea that we belong to a "bloodline" stretching back to the Buddha, and at ordination one receives a chart detailing the entire lineage. Each name appears in black, and a red line goes through each name in the lineage, starting at the Buddha's name and ending in the ordainee's name, before the line returns again to the Buddha's name, the source of it all. This inheritance has been handed down the generations through the ordination of new monks and nuns. It has proven an effective way of preserving the teachings and the tradition, as it has endured until now. It is a tradition, therefore, that contains the wisdom of many generations. Yet it must be made new in each generation. What has been tested with time can continue. But what is flawed and no longer serves can be set aside. This will inevitably happen. The fundamental practice of zazen itself is what is most important. And this experience of the unconditioned is beyond such matters as cultural relevance and contemporary mores. It is unfortunate, however, that the primacy of zazen is often mistaken as a recommendation to reject the other elements of the tradition that contain much healing wisdom. Rejecting the liturgical forms, the rituals and rites of the Zen tradition, as mere superstition and religious codswallop is shortsighted and ignorant. It impoverishes the richness of what we have inherited and reduces Buddhism to secular science. It removes human experience, the rhythms of life, and the culture from Zen, turning it into an arid and technical utilitarian practice. Rejecting the Zen tradition reduces visions and dreams to mere hallucinations, and unconditional love and joy to nothing more than chemicals or hormones. To face the mystery of existence, we must accept that what we are facing is indeed a mystery, and rest in a space of not knowing.

The summer retreat is when we ordain new priests and lay students in our sangha. It is a moving ceremony every time. Each person has spent many months or years preparing. They have sewn their Buddhist robes and studied the ethical precepts of Buddhism. It has the atmosphere of a baptism or a wedding. We usually hold these ceremonies on the afternoon of the last day of the retreat, so that friends and families can join the solemn occasion and the celebration afterward. By the time the last day of the retreat comes, we have spent a week in deep silence. You can almost hear leaves falling from the trees outside the meditation hall, your ear is so aware. That is how it feels. It has been a week of sitting and walking meditation outside, through the forests and overgrown paths of the retreat center. In the distance, the summer crops are ripening in the fields, and you feel a great kinship with them, as well as with the dog that follows us as we walk through the forest in silence. You feel kinship with the ground and the trees and the birds that fly up before us as we approach. During the week, rain and sunshine have come and gone, and we have sat through it all. The life of the world has unfolded before us, and we have seen it in all its beauty and transience. We have learned something of our physical and emotional limitations, and we have become stronger for it. Having passed through the fire of *sesshin*, we are made new, just by giving it the time and space to happen. There is nothing mystical about it, other than the reality that everything inspires this sense of mystery and awe if we look closely enough. We have listened to the teachings from this place of deep silence and been greatly moved. We have seen our wounds and found the strength to heal. We have touched deeply our innermost heart and mind and remembered again who we really are. Now we are ready to return to our lives. We do not stay in this place of supported balance. We must return again to the busy street of life, but this time with composure and an ability to be at peace, no matter what is happening all around us.

Then the last day of *sesshin* comes, and our family and friends arrive for the ordinations. We see them freshly again and appreciate them like never before. We take our vows and receive the robe of Buddha and the lineage papers from all the ancestors that have gone before us. We bow in the direction of our hometown and of our parents, alive or dead, and thank them for this life and everything that they have given to us. We enter the Buddha Way, and it is the start of a new life. It is a rite of passage full of joy and celebration.

It was very moving to see one of our priests, Kōzan, bow to his aging father during his ordination. Without knowing at the time, it was the last time he was ever to see his father, as within the week his father was dead. It was so important that he had had this opportunity to thank his father for everything before his father died. I can still see the moment: Kōzan bowing to his father. It teaches us to thank our parents while they are still with us. To make peace with things now. Not to wait.

On *sesshin*, we are alone and not alone at the same time. No one is in your zazen apart from yourself. It is the original luminosity of the self that sits at the center of your zazen. This is the flame. The fire of *sesshin* is all the flames together, and the flame of all things shining. Ultimately, the reason it is impossible to do zazen on your own is because you are never separated from the warmth of life. It is our delusion that we are totally alone. But in reality, we are always with the light of all things, called *kōmyō* in the Zen tradition, which can be translated as "radiant light." It is what all things possess, without exception. Call it what you will, but it is ultimately unnamable. A Buddhist might call it Buddha nature. You might say it is suchness or thusness. It cannot be pinned down and its boundary cannot be found. We are not only in it, but we are also of it. So, while we do our practice, we see that we are one manifestation of it. That is why Dōgen says that when one person sits zazen, the whole of reality sits zazen. Indeed, zazen was being sat all along, you could say. We have just recognized it by sitting down and arriving at that awareness.

# Clouds and Water

*Our winter retreat honors the spirit of winter and involves only long hours of silent zazen, with almost nothing else. Come summer, our practice is full of color and sunlight, with beautiful rituals to heal and transform us, to allow us to grow again in the light.*

AFTER OUR OWN SUMMER retreat in Ireland, I often go traveling. I try and go to a Zen monastery in Europe or off to North America to practice. In 2024, I was honored to practice at the two head monasteries of the Japanese Sōtō Zen school—Eiheiji and Sōjiji—for the very first time, taking part in ceremonies to commemorate the great Sōtō Zen co-founder, Keizan Zenji. It is important to find inspiration and fresh perspectives in Zen practice centers elsewhere. There is always something to learn about this tradition.

This habit of going to monasteries elsewhere comes from my years of training as a Zen priest. My teacher encouraged me to go and learn elsewhere, from other masters. It's a part of the tradition, as novice monks are called *unsui*, which literally means moving clouds and flowing water. Monks wander from monastery to monastery, master to master, to learn the Way. They encounter various teaching styles and varying expressions of the Dharma, much like apprentices learning a craft. All this lends itself to a deepening in understanding and the emergence, over time, of their own style as a teacher of the Way. They travel light and with few possessions.

This lightness of movement is like clouds and water, and the term *unsui* refers to Zen postulants generally, who undergo a number of years of training before they are permitted to offer teachings and conduct religious services.

My own training consisted mainly of participation in residential retreats in Europe and America. Often, these were during the summer holidays with my teacher, Taïgu Rōshi. We held retreats in Belgium and France and Virginia. Sometimes these were winter retreats, but more often than not they were during the summer. I have wonderful memories of these times: sitting zazen in the pre-dawn heat in a garden in Marseilles; serving as head monk (*shuso*) in the summer heat of Virginia, where a chorus of frogs at a nearby lake chanted along with our evening service; the cold austerity of a winter monastery in Belgium, where I was originally ordained in 2011; the rural Zen monastery at Lanau, in the center of France, buried in deep snow, where we nearly froze to death in our beds, and we could see our breath in the freezing meditation hall during the long hours of zazen.

Before my Dharma transmission—empowerment as a Zen teacher—Taïgu also sent me to Kanshōji, the Zen monastery in the lineage of Deshimaru, in rural France. It was a magnificent experience, where I met some wonderful people. The abbot there is Taiun Jean-Pierre Faure, and in that lineage the style is to offer *kusen*, which are spoken teachings during zazen. I think it is a style that comes from Deshimaru himself, and I found it quite unusual that *teisho* (long Dharma talks) were never offered while I was there. The whole emphasis was on zazen with *kusen*, with the usual ceremonies and a big emphasis on physical work. In my case, this work involved digging a drain for water pipes with a pickaxe. It was summer in France, and I'd sweat in the dirt with my pickaxe for a few hours. Then the bell would sound, and I'd have five minutes to run to my room at one end of the monastery, shower, and change into my robes, before running to the other end of the monastery where the meditation hall was, where I had to be seated before the teacher came in to offer incense before the door was closed. It was good training. Very hard. Maybe that's why it was good. Still, I was glad when my job was changed to proofreading the English-language versions of the transcripts of Taiun Jean-Pierre's teachings that were printed in book form and sold in the monastery bookshop. I felt less comfortable with the pickaxe than with the pen.

Some of these retreats in France were so different to the Zen retreats I had first done with Paul Haller, of San Francisco Zen Center. A Belfast native, he was the guiding teacher of the Belfast-based Black Mountain Zen Centre, a lay sangha that held its retreats in a Christian monastery in Benburb, in County Tyrone. In his style, formal ceremonies were kept to a minimum, while the whole emphasis was on zazen and *dokusan*, or private interviews with the teacher. There were no spoken teachings during zazen, but Dharma talks were given every day. There was no *ōryōki*, or ritual eating, and the whole atmosphere was one of quiet austerity, even in the robes that Paul wore: simple and plain browns, with no silk or brocade materials, as are often seen in ceremonies. But again, there were very few ceremonies.

Practicing with my Dharma brother Dainin in France, who received Dharma transmission at the same time as me, the style could not have been more different. A former Benedictine monk, Dainin taught me many of the more esoteric forms and rituals of the Zen tradition, which he had in turn received from other teachers. A master of liturgy, his style was closer to the spirit of Keizan, who popularized Zen in Japan, than it was to Dōgen, who practiced with his few monks in the wilds of western Japan. These two are the founders of the Sōtō Zen school in Japan, and each has a contrasting spirit, which is evident in the inheritance of Paul Haller and Dainin. Whereas Paul shied away from the theatrical transformation of ritual, Dainin was all about ritual. Dainin's Zen was full of color and silk brocade. It was theatrical and moved the heart. I even remember being on retreat with his sangha in France and sipping rosé in the French sunshine in robes after zazen, as that most French institution, the aperitif, was served after zazen and before lunch. I can't imagine that happening on the Northern Irish retreats led by Paul Haller. Northern austerity was more the spirit there.

Looking back, I feel both these approaches have something valuable to teach. For those intoxicated with the aesthetics of form, one should emphasize the discipline of just zazen. For those in whom only doing zazen has seeded an isolated and austere coldness, the group intensity of ritual can thaw it. Acknowledging both styles, our winter retreat honors the spirit of winter and involves only long hours of silent zazen, with almost nothing else. Come summer, our practice is full of color and sunlight, with beautiful rituals to heal and transform us, to allow us to grow again in the light. They are like the sun face and the moon face of practice. Both have their place, as Dōgen reminds us:

> Know that the sun face and moon face have not switched over since ancient times. The sun face emerges with the sun face, and the moon face emerges with the moon face . . . the entire body is illumination.[31]

Everything has its place in this great vision of Dōgen's. There are the moment of youth and the moment of old age. There are the day and the night. There are even life and death. Yet whether it is the sun face or the moon face, there is still great radiant light. Because we cannot see the light traveling through the air does not mean that it isn't there. When it falls on objects, then this illumination is evident. In instances it shows itself. Sunlight or moonlight, the darkness is dispersed by both.

# Honoring Lugh

*With culture and religion so intertwined, how can
we tell the deeper meanings behind these beliefs and
customs? The original source of religion lies deeper
than a Christian cassock or a Buddhist robe.*

ALREADY IN AUGUST, THERE are dry, fallen leaves on the ground.
The verdant days of summer take on a maturity that leans
toward autumn. Crops have yellowed in the fields, and berries
have begun to show in the hedgerows. Summer retreats are over,
and our formal practice schedule is wound down to a bare minimum, as people rest before the onset of September.

In Ireland, this is the time of Lughnasa, the festival of harvest
in honor of the god Lugh. While only remnants of the old festival
remain, it is still a time for climbing mountains and high places,
for sporting contests and harvest festivals. The Gaelic games of
hurling and football reach their final highpoints around this
time of year, as is fitting with ancient tradition. And in late July,
"Reek Sunday" sees people climb Croagh Patrick (Mount Patrick),
in a Christianization of the Lughnasa rite of a pilgrimage to the
heights. This need to climb a mountain is common to many religious traditions. To climb a mountain is to raise oneself up above
the ordinary concerns and to enter the open and empty realm
of the sky. On mountaintops is where the solid world begins to
fall away, and the immaterial world takes over. Solid rock seems
to vaporize into mist and illusion, where whole vistas that were

invisible can suddenly show themselves for just an instant as the clouds momentarily clear. Mountaintops are magnificent places to sit zazen in solitude. I have sat zazen on some of the mountains here in Ireland, using a rock or pile of earth for a cushion, chanting the Heart Sutra on the top of the Reek. I love the custom of making spontaneous stupas on the tops of mountains. Climbers pile a few stones together and leave a marker to show that they have passed.

Pile of stones stupa.
Lone mountain memorial.
No name remembered.

We do not know who has come and gone, but we see the mark of their presence nonetheless. The mystery of coming and going is evident in those tiny stupas near the peaks of mountains. They are balanced perfectly someplace between absence and presence. They perfectly encapsulate the wonder of our own existence between birth and death. They are much truer than an ostentatious and declamatory headstone. They are testament to the raw, elemental nature of our lives. They represent our true legacy, which comes from the natural world and returns there again, leaving no permanent record, although we desperately try to leave an eternal mark. Sitting zazen in high mountain places, we can easily see these truths. That is why I love the practice of climbing mountains at Lughnasa and arranging a seat to sit.

Sadly, there is little left of the holiday of Lughnasa itself. Like so much of our culture, it has been wiped away by colonialism and Christianity. What remains is a feeling. It is an ancient sensibility that feels the weather and the landscape of this particular place. Its spirit is subconsciously honored by these mountain climbs and harvest festivals, but its true identification is barely felt, rather than really known. The god Lugh must have been like a real being to people of the past. He held his fiery spear and unleashed his slingshot; he presided over the time of harvest and was warriorlike and athletic, credited with inventing ball games and horse racing. Now we have become disenchanted, and Lugh has no real meaning for people. This once-revered god now only haunts corners of our life with a residual presence, in place names like Louth and the Gaulish city of Lyon. Just as we have been cut off from the harvest, so we have been cut off from Lugh.

In Japan, the arrival of Buddhism did not supplant the older religion. Rather, it found an accommodation with it. Before the Dharma, the trees and streams and mountains were dwelling places for the *kami*, the spirits and divinities of Shintoism. Similarly, in Ireland, the *aos sí* were thought to be members of the magical Tuatha Dé Danann race, forced underground and living beside us in a parallel world. While the *aos sí* (or fairies) were suppressed by Irish Christianity, the *kami* were honored by the new religion as local deities. It seems that monotheism felt that it had to put down the many expressions of the one, while the multivarious Dharma could live with plurality. The local *kami* were therefore enshrined in altars and paid tribute in regular rituals. And these older rites and beliefs are still evident in Japanese Buddhism. In contrast, what remnants of the older faith remain in Ireland are tolerated with embarrassment by the Christian Church, if not met with outright hostility.

This in-between place, between the old religion and the new, is a place of ambivalence rather than certainty; it should be a place of accommodation rather than of exclusion. In Japan, even today the religious exclusivity prevalent in the West is absent. Many Japanese are happy to have a Christian wedding, but later a Buddhist funeral. They will go to one religion's temple as happily as they would to another's. This attitude is not something we find in North America or Europe. Such fluidity is frowned upon, viewed as an irreverent lack of commitment to one faith or the other. Yet when I enter a mosque, I feel the urge to bow toward Mecca; and when I enter a church, I see nothing wrong with taking some holy water.

So, I am happy to pay tribute to Lugh. With culture and religion so intertwined, how can we tell the deeper meanings behind these beliefs and customs? They are all historical and provisional; they belong to a time and place—especially Buddhism. Time and place can change, as history shows us, but the Dharma is a doorway into the unutterable truth. The original source of religion lies deeper than a Christian cassock or a Buddhist robe. It is the same source where Lugh dwells. At harvest time, it is the harvest. On the mountaintop, it is the peak. In the fields below, it is the flatlands. It is only ever right where you are and at this very moment. So, at the time of Lughnasa, it is Lugh himself. It is in the ripe, offered barley and the sporting efforts of August. It's even found in the shape of a goat, crowned each August as "King Puck" at the Puck Fair in Kerry. This goat is no more or less holy than Saint Peter's Basilica. And Saint Peter's Basilica is no more holy than Lugh.

# Feeding the
# Hungry Ghosts

*The assembly taking part in the ceremony are asked
to acknowledge their own dark drives, their selfish,
greedy, or desiring side. Having acknowledged
rather than suppressed these aspects of ourselves,
we allow them to be released and sent away.*

O F ALL THE ANCIENT Irish festivals, it is Samhain that is most
alive today. As the harvest season comes to an end, we mark
the beginning of winter with this magical festival. Known as
Halloween in popular culture, that word does no justice to the
resonance of the word *Samhain* (pronounced "SAH-win"). Indeed,
Halloween is a more recent invention, the result of merging
the older Samhain with the Christian All Soul's Day, which the
Church moved to November 1 in order to Christianize the popular
Samhain holiday. While I was growing up in Ireland, this festival
did not have the crass commercialism that it had elsewhere. It was
a genuine people's festival, with popular, old, living traditions that
are still practiced today by many people. We played traditional
games, and we carved turnips—and later pumpkins—in which
were placed candles to guide the spirits of the dead. And as children, we went mumming in homemade costumes from house to
house, singing a song or playing a tune on a tin whistle, receiving
payment in the form of apples, sweets, or money for our efforts.

As a child, Samhain was full of mystery and the thrill of freedom. We were out at night in the darkness, walking the streets. It was like the children had taken over. Crowds of us were out in droves, our true identities hidden by masks. We believed that the door to the other world was open on this night, and we walked in a world that was fused with the spiritual. Spirits could visit us and we, in turn, could enter their realm. I remember Samhain as always being foggy, although many years it was not. And from this otherworldly mist, people emerged that looked like ghosts themselves, until you recognized their voices as your neighbors'. Samhain was a time for harvest fruits and nuts. Local teenagers would comb the fields at sunup to find "magic mushrooms" to make their experience of the walking dead even more intense and psychedelic. But mostly, it was a time of wild bonfires. When I was growing up, these bonfires were unregulated festivals of anarchy. They were family friendly and fun early in the night but became wilder and more insane as Samhain wore on, with people leaping over the flames on a dare, or throwing explosive materials in the fires so that everyone had to run for cover. Certainly, at Samhain, the normal rules and regulations of life were suspended, and the winter was welcomed with wild defiance.

At a deeper or religious level, this was the festival of the dead. With the door between the worlds open, our ancestors remembered their dead on this night, and even believed that on the night of Samhain the dead could return to visit. Taking this belief, the Christian festival of All Soul's Day encouraged visiting the graves of relatives on the first day of November. And so people visited their departed parents or family, cleaned their graves and left fresh flowers. In Japan, the festival of Obon bears a remarkable similarity to these beliefs and traditions. Indeed, Obon (literally "ghost festival") corresponds well to Samhain or Halloween for Buddhist practitioners in the West. Some version of this ghost festival is practiced all over the Buddhist countries of East Asia.

In the festival, the "feeding of the hungry ghosts"—dead beings suffering from unsatisfied desires—and the care of departed loved ones has been conflated into one observance. Based on the Buddha's teachings in the Ullambana Sutra, a ceremony called *segaki* (literally "feeding the hungry ghosts") developed in Japanese Zen Buddhism and is practiced by our sangha today. While the rite is observed in August in Japan, it makes more sense in our culture to observe it at the time of Samhain, similar to how many North American Zen communities celebrate it at Halloween. It has an actual resonance for Irish people at this time of year—so much so that our sangha was invited by the national broadcaster, RTÉ, to perform the *segaki* ceremony on national television during the COVID pandemic. We dedicated the ceremony to the many thousands that had died due to the pandemic, and we made an offering in their name.

In the actual ceremony, the departed ancestors, going back to ancient times, dwelling in mountains, rivers, and earth, as well as rough demonic spirits from the wilderness are summoned and offerings made to placate them. This ancient practice of offering food and drink can be seen in East Asian rites that pay tribute to the ancestors, as well as in the offerings of bread and wine in the Christian Mass. In Zen practice, the assembly taking part in the ceremony are also asked to acknowledge their own dark drives, their selfish, greedy, or desiring side. Having acknowledged rather than suppressed these aspects of ourselves, we free ourselves from them by allowing them to be released and sent away.

For this ceremony, the traditional statue of Buddha is covered up, as it would scare away these wandering and unsatisfied spirits. A notice is hung on the altar with words written to welcome them, and the offerings are placed on a special *segaki* altar adorned in a seasonal way with apples, nuts, autumn leaves, and carved pumpkins. Percussion figures greatly in summoning and then sending back the now-satisfied spirits to where they came: sangha members crash bells and drums and cymbals, which is really great fun for all involved. People are also encouraged to take part in the ceremony in costume, which makes it all very festive, especially for the children that take part. Then, at the end of the ceremony, the atmosphere becomes more reverent as we remember our dead. People are invited to place photos and mementos of the dead on the altar, offering incense as they do so. And we ask that the departed finally depart the round of samsara and be born in pure lands, as the ceremony comes to an end.

# The Meaning
# of Bowing

*We bow to ourselves as well as to all others. It is not
a gesture where there is a subject here bowing to
an object there. In bowing, we actualize the reality
that there is ultimately no subject and object.*

MOST BUDDHIST CEREMONIES INCLUDE various physical gestures that are common to all of them, particularly *gasshō*
and *sanpai*.

Often, the hands are held in *gasshō*, for instance, with the palms
together and held to the front, fingers pointing upward. This is
a gesture well known to most familiar with yoga, or Asian cultures generally, where it is understood to be a gesture of respect
or reverence. It is a gesture of greeting that has even become common enough in the West, especially during the COVID pandemic,
when shaking hands was discouraged as it led to transmission of
the virus. And so the *gasshō* gesture was used more frequently,
even by presidents and prime ministers who would never have
been seen using it before—unless they were visiting a Buddhist
country.

In the Zen tradition, this gesture is understood to be a mudra,
or ceremonial hand gesture with a symbolic meaning. As the two
sides of the body come together at the palms, it expresses nondual-
ity, the oneness of all things. Apart from being a simple greeting,

it can accompany a bow from the waist, which may be directed at another person or an enshrined image of a buddha or bodhisattva. While those new to Zen may find the gesture strange at first, its growing familiarity and resemblance to the gesture of prayer means that the *gasshō* gesture is often accepted quickly enough. But when it comes to full-floor prostrations, there can be a much greater level of resistance.

In many Zen contexts, one might perform three full bows, all the way to the floor. Known as *sanpai* when a *pai,* or bow, is performed three times, as prostrations most often are, the gesture involves bowing, kneeling, placing one's forehead to the floor, and then raising the palms upward beside the ears. The overall movement of the body is simple enough—kneeling and touching your head to the floor—but the details of how this is done are quite specific in the Zen tradition.

Many people might misunderstand this gesture as an act of worship or subservience. Or it might feel alien to them, or perhaps they see it as an affront to their dignity or self-worth. Others may feel it has no place in a modern, democratic culture. Some may even react quite strongly: "I will not bow down to anyone!" For these reasons, those new to Zen practice are not required to do it in our sangha. When it comes to performing *sanpai* in a Zen ceremony, there is an awkward moment when some of the people present do not participate in the bows. I say "awkward" not because the priests leading the ceremony feel that people must bow, but rather it's awkward for the person that feels they should be bowing and cannot bring themselves to. Perhaps they think, "Why would I worship a statue of the Buddha?"—mistakenly reading the situation as a room full of people worshiping a graven image. It is for this reason that I usually tell those new to Zen practice that they do not need to bow, before they feel the awkwardness of not participating in the bow. All that is required is a respectful *gasshō*. And usually, people are happy enough with that.

But sometimes people become curious, and they ask, "Why is it that you bow at all?" How best to respond to this question? They are hoping for a rational explanation that can be understood with the intellect—but this is utterly useless in this context. It is easier to say why we do *not* bow.

We do not bow in an act of worship. The statue is just a carved piece of stone or wood. It is neither more nor less holy than a block of concrete. We do not bow to the teacher because they are better than us and we are their inferior. We do not bow in submission, and we do not bow to grovel and garner favor from our "betters." So why do we bow?

Well, we just bow. Try it now. Tell me: What is the meaning of bowing? What did the experience of the gesture convey? What feeling did it evoke? What was the physical experience? Why is it that people in different times and different cultures have bowed and continue to bow? What does it mean for the human body to touch the ground in this way, to come to one's knees and touch the ground with the forehead?

A bow can be reverent or full of gratitude. It can be resigned or joyful. It is an acknowledgment of all that is greater than us, all the chance and fate and fortune of all that we cannot control. It acknowledges our birth and death, and it affirms the very patch of earth on which we stand. It recognizes that there are many things that we cannot master and, despite this, gathers our body in a gesture of dignity and respect for all in the natural world and all in existence. We pay tribute to the earth from which we have come and the sky that is our natural home. We bow to ourselves as well as to all others. It is not a gesture where there is a subject here bowing to an object there. In bowing, we actualize the reality that there is ultimately no subject and object. Both have fallen away in the realm of boundlessness, which is the true nature of things. If there is a shred of subservience in the bow, the result will be unbalanced and off kilter. If it is received by a teacher as an act of worship, then you need to find a new teacher, because the one you have is sick with ego and is not manifesting the great Way of the buddhas at all. If after penetrating the Way, you yourself are incapable of bowing to this reality of all things before you, then it is you that may be sick with ego; it may be your clinging to the importance of your self that is blocking you from the great teaching found in bowing.

There is a great story my teacher told me once about Rempō Niwa Zenji, the seventy-seventh abbot of Eiheiji monastery in Japan. He was my great-great-grandfather in the Dharma, and Nishijima Rōshi's teacher. Once, when he was officiating at an important ceremony, Niwa was waiting outside the Buddha hall where the ceremony was to take place. He was standing with the *jisha*, his attendant for the ceremony. It was a hot day, and Niwa was in the shade of a tree to take cover from the sun. To those passing in the glaring heat, he was invisible in the darkness of the shade. However, for each person that passed, Niwa reverently made a standing bow to everybody as they filed by into the Buddha hall for the ceremony, even though they could not see him bow. After a time, a dog trotted by and the *jisha* standing behind Niwa could not believe his eyes when Niwa bowed to the passing dog with equal reverence. Even a passing mutt was worthy of the respect of the seventy-seventh abbot of Eiheiji! And in that bow there was no Niwa, no abbot, no dog, and not even the bow itself. This is the true meaning of bowing.

# To Give of Oneself

*In offering, we move beyond our personal needs
and boundaries and are united in community
and sangha. Even if offerings have no practical
utility, they have a value in their own right.*

IN BUDDHISM, THE TRADITIONAL offerings are incense, flowers,
and light, as well as food and sweet tea. In Japan, I've seen sake
offered. And in an Irish Buddhist center, I've even seen Irish whis-
key offered once.

By *offering* I mean something offered at the altar, usually
placed ceremonially at the feet of the Buddha. Why is this done,
and what does it mean? Most people that ask this question have
grown up in a Christian context in the West, so they understand
the whole idea of offering bread and wine at the Mass—or even
the grisly slaughter of animals in certain traditions—as offerings
to God. The idea is that the favor of God is won by acknowledging
him and making offerings to him. Usually, people that come to
Zen or Buddhism in the West want to reject such practices, seeing them as a superstitious approach to spirituality. Buddhism has
been presented in the West for the past century or so as a "rational
religion" that does not engage in things like animal sacrifice or
seeking to placate some god. Many find this "rationality" attractive, and because of that, many meditation centers have removed
all of the form and ritual from their presentation of Buddhism.
But doing so is a break with the teaching of the tradition entirely,

which includes making offerings among other things. Indeed, the practice of making offerings sits deep in the human psyche. The idea of making offerings in a religious setting is common to many cultures: we see it in the ancient Greek and Celtic religions, and many indigenous spiritualities have some version of the practice.

Offerings generally come in two forms, practical and symbolic. Practical offerings include money and other practical supports that we see at churches, temples, and even secular meditation centers. These supports are given to keep the religious or spiritual center going. By practicing *dana* (generosity), the electricity is paid and the lights are kept on in the meditation hall. In "Kuyō Shobutsu" ("Making Offerings to Buddhas"), Dōgen talks of the four offerings appropriate to Buddha and to Buddhist monks and nuns. These are nourishment, clothing, bedding, and medicine. Traditionally, the lay sangha supported the monastic order with these practical supports, and in return they received merit. The practice and concept of merit is of vital importance in Buddhist practice and is tied closely with the teaching of karma. Essentially, merit is produced through good actions, which results in good karma for the practitioner. This merit can also be offered to another or for a cause, in a transfer of merit, which is a central process in many Buddhist rituals. Practical offerings generally come from the motivation to contribute to the greater good. Such offerings have myriad expressions, from feeding the hungry and supporting the homeless, to fixing the temple roof and cleaning the altar, to helping financially support the religious community. These practical offerings are easy to understand and make perfect sense. But what of symbolic offerings before a statue or in a ceremonial context? What purpose do these have?

To put it plainly: they have no purpose. In the accountancy of action that has become our default reason for acting in the marketplace, everything must have a purpose. Everything must have a utilitarian function and must be capable of being put to some useful end. Therefore, when a forest is not being used, it can be felled for firewood. When a lake just sits there, doing nothing in the deep wilderness, then how can it matter that it is polluted in the process of putting it to some profitable end? In contrast, symbolic offerings have no end, no purpose, and no utility. They are more like beautiful clouds that we admire. They drift away, with nothing gained and nothing achieved. If they have any function, it is to act as a counterweight to the world of gain and loss, where everything is calculated and functional. They are not even "symbolic" as I have termed them: they stand in for nothing else. They simply are given, with nothing more to it. They have worth in their own right. They are offered, pure and simple.

But why are fruits placed at the feet of a Buddha statue? Why is incense placed before the statue? Why a candle lit? Could it be that certain values are finding a material expression? Could it be that gratitude is being realized and expressed? Gratitude is a healthy mental state: gratitude for our life, our friends and family, the food that keeps us alive, the flowers that gladden our hearts, the water that makes life itself possible.

To make an offering is to move beyond the selfish self and to give of oneself. To give is to reenter the circle whereby we are always receiving and always giving; where the boundary between what is given and those that give and receive finally dissolves away. This is where the original unity of all things is reasserted and realized again. A symbolic act of giving is experienced as real, just as we might scream at a horror movie or recoil from a cliff edge in virtual reality. The simulation has a reality all of its own, and it spills over into conventional reality. Just as we practice for real life in simulated environments, so it is that ritual giving is not sealed off and separate from the secular or conventional world. But there I am again, falling into the trap of looking for utility.

When it is a mother's birthday, a four-year-old child, without money or ability to make anything, gives his mother a leaf as a birthday present. When a family returns from holidays and are reunited with their pet cat, the cat captures a small bird and places it before the family as an offering. In offering, we move beyond our personal needs and boundaries and are united in community and sangha. Even if offerings have no practical utility, they have a value in their own right. And even after closer consideration, such "useless" offerings are not sealed off simulations from the rest of reality, but rather they feed back into the unified system of life. And so it is that we light incense and place flowers on the altar. We leave seeds out for the birds in winter and offer a rock on the summit of the mountain we've just scaled. It just feels right. And for those that make offerings, it has a deep wisdom all of its own.

# Wearing Robes

*It is not just a matter of clothing. Indeed, it strikes
me that the choice of wearing the robes or not isn't
mine to make. This is something far bigger than my
preferences and inclinations. That is the point.*

WHEN I FIRST ORDAINED, I felt strange wearing robes. It felt
like dressing up in medieval clothes and playing a part. I
was acting as a priest, rather than being a priest. Because they felt
unnatural to me, I didn't wear them often. Then, as I began to take
on public roles as a Zen priest—officiating at weddings and funerals, representing Buddhism at interfaith events, offering readings
at public events—I slowly stopped feeling like an imposter and
began to realize that I was, indeed, a Zen priest. Now I realize
that this is how we all feel in many situations as we take on new
roles. When we begin a new job, we feel for a while that someone is going to find out that we're a fake. We become something
by acting as that thing. We play the role of college lecturer when
teaching a room full of students. We play the role of parent when
speaking firmly to an errant child. At family occasions, we all fall
into our constructed roles accordingly. We construct selves according to the need. There is nothing essential about it. We are playing
roles, and that becomes a reality all of its own.

So, after playing the role of priest for a long time, I became a
priest. In this journey, the Buddhist robes were vital. Gradually the
robes stopped feeling like dressing up and I became comfortable

in them. I filled the robes, if you will. I also began to understand just how useful they are. By wearing the robes, you stand out. You are no longer representing yourself. Rather, you are representing a tradition, of which you are part. Because you are not representing yourself, there is no self-consciousness about wearing robes. It has nothing to do with personal identity—that's for when you're lounging around on the weekend. In wearing the Buddhist robes, you represent a lineage of teachers stretching back over time. You represent the Buddha and his teaching and values. If someone treats you with respect or derision when wearing the robes, it has nothing to do with you. It is not you that is being respected or derided. In many ways, you have given up your personal identity, and you even go by the name that you were given at your ordination, your Buddhist or Dharma name, given to you by your teacher.

Robes are useful in the way that uniforms are useful. They add a certain formality to interactions that facilitates a seriousness of study and effort. I only wear robes in Dharma practice contexts or when I am representing my sangha. But on these occasions, they make me immediately recognizable as a Zen priest, which is useful, as the robes do a lot of silent explaining in these situations. Without opening my mouth, wearing the robes shows that I am a Buddhist priest, representing that tradition and coming from that worldview. It eases the way for me to fill my role and function, just as it does for a doctor wearing a white coat, or a police officer wearing a uniform. When people are looking for the doctor, they know she's the woman in the white coat. When looking for a police officer, they know he's the guy in the uniform. A whole lot of questions and explanations are dispensed with. It makes things easier.

I recognize that many people don't see it like this at all. For them, robes suggest dusty old tradition, formality, and even worse, hierarchy and power. And it is true, to some extent. They do represent tradition and formality; they do represent hierarchy, to an extent; but they represent service, rather than power. There are good things about these things, too, as well as downsides.

Tradition is something bigger than the horizons of our individual lives. Tradition may be the wisdom of the ancestors, the wisdom of the ages. Informality is lovely, but there are also moments to be solemn and serious: moments of birth and death, of transformation, or those times that we look the meaning of our existence square in the face. Even hierarchy has its role. Students need to know that they are seeking guidance from someone that has spent time learning and considering what they are teaching, someone that is living the meaning of the Way, rather than an inexperienced person not fully versed in what they are teaching. Hierarchy should be nothing more than the experience of years of practice. It should mean something, rather than be nothing more than position, prestige, and power. Prestige and power are as worthless as inexperience and permissiveness in teaching the Dharma, where every opinion is as valid as the next, and the Dharma is whatever you think it is yourself in the twenty-first century, rather than a wisdom tradition spanning thousands of years.

The Buddhist robes embody a teaching tradition and a body of practice and knowledge. But these are just the main Buddhist robes that I am talking about. I am not talking about the *okesa*, the outer robe common to all the Buddhist schools since the time of the Buddha himself. The main robes I am talking about are the kimono and *koromo* that are worn under the *okesa*. Taken all together, these three layers represent the history of the transmission of the Dharma to Japan. The *okesa* is Indian, the *koromo* Chinese, and the kimono Japanese. The Dharma traveled from one country to the other, and this is reflected in the formal robes of a priest in the Japanese traditions of Buddhism. But while the *koromo* and kimono are manifestations of Chinese and Japanese culture, the *okesa* is understood to be an essential and sacred robe, worthy of veneration in the tradition, as it comes directly from Buddha himself. To us, it is handed down from the historical Buddha, and represents not only the teachings but also the Buddha's body. Because of this, the *okesa* is worthy of respect. It is not just another robe.

I remember once meeting Panchen Ötrul Rinpoche, a teacher in the Gelugpa tradition of Tibetan Buddhism. Both of us were wearing very different robes. His was reddish maroon in color, while mine was black. However, both of us wore an *okesa* as an outer robe, and both were yellowish in color and of the same basic pattern. It was moving to both of us, as we examined each other's outer robe. Although all the other robes we wore were different due to history and culture, the basic robe of the Buddha was the same. Despite my being Irish and his being Tibetan, despite the many centuries and thousands of miles that separated our two Buddhist traditions, still the basic robe handed down to us from the Buddha was wrapped around our bodies. The robe had traveled through all that time and space and was there in that meeting. Had either of us given up wearing the robes, this collapsing of time and space would not have happened. It is not just a matter of clothing. Indeed, it strikes me that the choice of wearing the robes or not isn't mine to make. This is something far bigger than my preferences and inclinations. That is the point.

# Birth, Marriage, and Death

*These are times of heightened emotion; and somehow religious ritual provides a vessel to carry and contain that emotion with dignity and appropriateness. It provides a meaningful outer expression of a collective inner intention.*

ONE OF MY FREQUENT jobs as a Zen priest is to provide the ritual context for life transitions. Because many other schools of Buddhism in Ireland have their guiding teachers based abroad, and because the majority of people running meditation centers and Zen practice places either do not practice rituals or have not been trained in ritual forms, I often find I have to perform funerals in particular, not only for followers of Zen, but also those of other Buddhist schools based in Ireland, in order to provide a ritual context.

There is a long tradition of Buddhist priests providing funeral services. Also, it is not uncommon to offer blessings to newborn children at the Buddhist temple. But in many Buddhist cultures, marriage has long been seen as a matter for the civic authorities, and so marriage ceremonies are a recent innovation in Buddhism, especially in Western societies. Many of the naming ceremonies for children are also newly devised, sometimes created specially for each particular occasion, as are wedding ceremonies. I have officiated over both naming ceremonies and weddings, and in each case, I started from the basic template of how a Zen ceremony is structured, and simply worked with the participants involved to finalize a form that they were happy with. The structure of a Zen ceremony—entrance, incense offering, bows, chanting, dedication, and eventual ceremonial exit—usually provides the basic shape of the ceremony. And within this structure other elements are added, according to the needs of the specific occasion at hand. As per Buddhist tradition, the baby or couple may be blessed with water. In a wedding, rings are usually exchanged, while in a naming ceremony, words of welcome are often offered by those attending. Music may be included, and readings given, such as poetry—sometimes religious, other times secular. Usually, I will say a few words as the officiating priest. Once, with a Vietnamese family participating in one of the weddings I did, we included the traditional tea ceremony, where the couple offered tea to their parents. The basic ceremony structure offers an architecture that can accommodate these innovations and improvisations. It makes the ceremony meaningful and personal for those involved, while giving the occasion the sense of import and reverence that a religious ceremony brings.

Funerals, however, have a much clearer form in the tradition. Indeed, for many Buddhists in Asia, funerals are the main contact that they have with their local Buddhist temple. In Japan, for example, people usually get married in a Shinto context, as that religion has strong ties to the state and its history. But it is the local Buddhist priest that does their funeral. It may be that they have almost never set foot in a Buddhist temple their whole life. And yet it is traditional that it must be a Buddhist funeral. This tradition has a long history, and clear forms have emerged for conducting funerals in the Buddhist and Zen traditions.

For a layperson, the funeral consists essentially of an ordination for the deceased. The form varies a bit for the funerals of monks. The precepts and vows are taken on behalf of the deceased, who also receives a new Dharma name and a set of lineage papers, tracing their Dharma line back to the original Buddha. Their hair is cut—often just a symbolic snip—and sutras are chanted, before they are taken for cremation. Words may be spoken by loved ones, and, after more than a month, a memorial service is held, while the family are given a special prayer to say each day for forty-nine days after the death, when the deceased may be passing through the bardo, or the intermediate state between death and rebirth. After that, there is a whole series of annual memorial services, based around the *ihai*, or spirit tablet, on which the Dharma name of the dead person is written, and which represents the deceased during these services. The *ihai* is kept on the home altar, with another one kept in the local temple. After thirty-three years, the tablet is ritually burned by the local temple, as the dead person's final destination has been reached.

Most of the funerals I have done have been for ethnic Chinese or Chinese Malaysians here in Ireland. But I've also conducted funerals for Irish and African Buddhists here. In one case, I had to offer last rites in the Mater Hospital, as one young man was dying of lung cancer, surrounded by his wife and young children. In that case, they were Malaysian and told the Mater Hospital that they needed a Buddhist priest. I was the only priest that the hospital could find, even though we were not from the same school of Buddhism. But I have learned that lay practitioners are often not that concerned about the Buddhist school you are from; they just want Buddhist prayers and a Buddhist ceremony around the death. Then around the core ceremony they bring their own national or regional elements: using a particular kind of incense or placing a tray at the threshold that must be stepped over after the funeral. They may also play Buddhist chants in their own language over their smartphones, as they did in the Mater Hospital, while that young Malaysian man, Calvin, slipped away.

There are various challenges in offering Buddhist funerals in Western countries, as the whole system is set up to provide for Christian rites rather than the rites of Buddhists and other religious traditions. But that is changing slowly, just as the rites that

Irish people want in the twenty-first century have changed drasti-cally. But remarkably, even when it is an Irish Buddhist funeral, it is still very much a traditional Irish funeral: an old-fashioned wake, essentially, just with an outward Buddhist appearance. The Irish funerals I've done have been traditional in many ways: with a big gathering in the house, involving food, drink, and stories; and a home wake, followed by a removal for the religious rite. The only big difference is that most prefer cremation over burial—but that is also the case for many Irish Christians nowadays. And increas-ingly, fewer people in Ireland are choosing a Christian burial. Nevertheless, public structures around funerals haven't evolved to accommodate these cultural and religious shifts.

These issues are less important with weddings and nam-ing ceremonies, which are often conducted in private homes or in rented private spaces, such as hotels and community halls or gardens. But again, like funerals, these life celebrations tend to be traditional and Irish in their form, just with the religious rite itself being Buddhist. Everyone dresses up for weddings and naming ceremonies. It's a big party, with family and friends gathered. The baby is blessed with water. Vows are exchanged. What is strik-ing is just how universal so many of these ceremonies are, and likewise the elements contained within them. These are times of heightened emotion, and somehow religious ritual provides a ves-sel to carry and contain that emotion with dignity and propriety. These rituals provide a meaningful outer expression of a collec-tive inner intention for the person passing, for the joyous arrival of a newborn child, or for a new couple setting out on their life together. It is a great honor to be with people intimately at these times of joy, difficulty, and change. It is one of the most important roles that a priest can have in our society—in many ways, it is our primary means of service.

# Meaning in Movement

*It is in the face of all that is unknown and
that we cannot control that we practice the
predictable rhythms of ritual. They center us and
acknowledge our humanity. They carry teachings
from one generation to the next, in potent and
concentrated, extra-linguistic forms. They root
us right where we are, in time and place.*

A T 6:30 IN THE morning, my alarm goes off and I get up. I go
to the altar and offer incense and bow. Then at 7, I sit zazen,
followed by a recitation of the Heart Sutra during morning service. In winter, it is totally dark outside and nothing in the world
is stirring. In summer, it is already dawn and the birds are singing in the garden, from where a morning fragrance of flowers
comes into the house. I let the cat out and I have breakfast. Then
the day unfolds. Not every day is like this, but many are. After
breakfast, I brush my teeth, shower, and get dressed. The working day begins.

The way we move through our days is the ritual of our lives.
In this choreography, we ascribe meaning to things. Meditating in
the morning puts our practice at the very start of the day, giving it
a central location of importance. How we move through our days
and weeks and years is how we make meaning in our lives. It is
the central function of ritual in action.

Here, I have touched on just some of the rituals central to the Sōtō Zen tradition. There are many others. When we install a new statue or buddha image in our homes or practice centers, we have an "eye opening" ceremony. We similarly close the eyes of the statue when taking it out of service. We have the "mountain seat" ceremony to install a new Zen teacher or abbot, and they have a "stepping-down" ceremony when they end their period of service. There are ceremonies around food preparation and eating, and verses we chant in monastic or retreat settings when engaged in various ordinary tasks like washing the face, going to the toilet, or taking a bath. The Sōtō Way is designed to make all of life an act of devotional awareness. Ordinary life is, after all, the place of practice. So, the rituals not only carry teachings into the cycle of the year but also into the hours of the day, as we eat our meals and go to bed at night, as we wash and cook, and even as we take care of our bodily functions and personal needs.

To be honest, many of these rituals I do not practice outside of a residential or monastic setting, or on retreat. Like any religious practice, they can become a kind of obsessive sickness; just another burden to carry around, rather than the door into awakening that they are meant to be. It is important to be skillful and wise in incorporating such rituals into your life and practice. Like a familiar word said over and over again, these rituals can become meaningless through mindless repetition. They must be used carefully and with respect if they are to maintain their meaning and power. Therefore, there are certain rituals that I practice every day and others that I observe only during *ango*, or periods of retreat or special practice. Just as there is a time to put on the robes and a time to set the robes aside, so it is with our rich tradition of rituals. A spell used too often loses its power.

But when it comes to rituals generally, even contemporary atheists are beginning to recognize their importance. Some might say a version of grace before meals, for example, because they recognize the psychological benefits of gratitude. This psychological aspect is also evident in rituals of marriage and death. Funerals help in the grieving process, as does the *mizuko kuyō* ("water baby") ceremony in Buddhism, which helps parents that have lost or aborted children to grieve and to process their emotions. Even in public life, this need for ritual is evident. We see calls for a national service of remembrance at the end of the COVID-19 pandemic, to remember all those lives that have been lost. We see rituals held at the sites of historic abuse, such as in the church-run detention centers for unmarried mothers, the mother-and-baby homes that were dotted all over this country. We even see ritual at play in the secular sphere, where national holidays are marked, or the war dead remembered. As the earth moves around the sun every day and every year, we find ways to mark and map this great movement, and to give it depth, significance, and meaning in our lives.

But what kind of meaning is it? This kind of meaning does not require articulation and justification. In ritual, reason is only the tuft of hair on the head, and beneath that is a whole body of meaning. It is the organization of time into days and seasons. It is the meaning evident in the truths of life and death. It has as much to do with the body of reality and the heart of our emotions as it has to do with reason and the intellect. When a cat rises, he stretches. When a squirrel feels winter approaching, she stores acorns. We do not need to say "good morning" to each other, yet we do. We could just incinerate the dead without ceremony and be done with it. We could have a new child and get on with things, having no celebration of welcome at all. But to act like this would be to suppress the truth and the meaning of the mystery of our existence. It is in the face of all that is unknown and that we cannot control that we practice the predictable rhythms of ritual. They center us and acknowledge our humanity. They carry teachings from one generation to the next, in potent and concentrated, extra-linguistic forms. They root us right where we are, in time and place, and so dispel the disorientation and confusion that comes with every day being the same, and with all life transitions being treated like nothing out of the ordinary.

In northern Europe, the winter nights are long, and we welcome the return of the sun. When the spring flowers appear, we exhale with relief that we have survived the cold. In October, the evening sky is smeared orange, and we know the dead are near. The long June days intoxicate us into thinking we will never know death. And right in that moment, nothing is closer to the truth.

# PART FOUR

# Zen Here and Now

# How I Came to the Dharma

*What appealed to me about Zen was that it was about an experience rather than about a dogma. I could sit on my own and meet an unmediated reality, without any institution or priest getting in between.*

GROWING UP IN THE 1970s and 1980s in Galway, on the western coast of Ireland, was to grow up Christian. Even Protestants were exotic and not to be entirely trusted in this uniform and ethnically homogenous population. There was one black man in Galway at that time, and everyone knew him to see. There was also one black woman from Kenya, a mother of one of my childhood friends. Almost everyone else was Catholic, white, nationalist, and played Gaelic games. The wealth of doctors and barristers gave us the only real demarcation of class. Everyone else was pretty much the same, except for the very poor, who were objects of contempt, although we pretended that they weren't. The poor were despised in what was an aspirational middle-class reality, as we had all been poor only a few decades before.

I was baptized a Catholic and did my Holy Communion. At the age of nine, I enthusiastically greeted the Pope with my family when he visited Galway in 1979. Ireland at that time still felt like a theocracy. People had undue respect for priests and bishops. Sometimes the local priest called for tea to check up on us, and we would take out the best china for the occasion. He was met with great deference and was served in the "good room" at the front of the house. As Irish people, even when we still had no state, we had the church. It was a marker of identity to be Catholic. It was a mark of resistance to British oppression. It was an ethnic and political identifier. On our walls were portraits of the Pope and the Sacred Heart of Jesus. These pictures are still hung with pride on the walls of my parents' house. To turn my back on the church was not only to ensure that I was going to hell, but it was also a betrayal of the tribe and the nation. Apostasy was no small matter.

So, despite my nagging doubts, when it came to my confirmation I still complied. I was confirmed in Christ the King Church in Salthill, Galway, by Bishop Eamonn Casey, a jovial, well-liked, and stocky Kerryman. He was later accused of being a sexual predator and serial pedophile, and he fraudulently misused Church funds to deal with the fallout from his abuses. But in the early 1980s, all of that was still unknown. Indeed, everything that we would later learn was wrong with the Church was known to us only as a kind of undercurrent, subterranean knowledge. As boys, we knew which priests to avoid, as they were "touchy feely." We didn't have the language available to us to understand that these men were predators and pedophiles. It was more of an atmosphere of private knowing, rather than an overt and solid knowledge of what was going on. In any case, those that had directly encountered the truth had covered it up. And in those days, you'd be more likely to be arrested for making accusations against a priest than you would for actual clerical child abuse.

It was only when I was in my twenties that all the Church scandals began to unravel, thanks to the work of certain individuals that came forward and to the journalists that uncovered the truth. And while this led me to ultimately and formally "defect" from the Catholic Church, my interest in Buddhism and the Dharma had started much earlier. I did not know anyone that was Buddhist, but translations of Buddhist texts had begun to filter through to bookshops in Ireland by the 1980s. As a young teenager, I read the Diamond Sutra in O'Gorman's Bookshop on Shop Street, as I didn't have the money to buy it. Then at sixteen I bought Suzuki Rōshi's *Zen Mind, Beginner's Mind*, which had a big influence on my life. Published in the decade before I read it, it was my first introduction to Zen, and I began to try to meditate in my room on my own, aiming only for an experience of stillness. Then, I did not really understand how to sit Zen, as I had no teacher. But again, there were no teachers of Zen at the time in the country. They were only to come in the 1990s.

What appealed to me about Zen first and foremost was that it was about an experience rather than about a dogma. I could sit on my own and meet an unmediated reality, without any institution or priest getting in between. It was simple and quiet, and had nothing to do with the pomp, power, and repression that the Catholic Church represented. I must have been looking for something, as I had become intensely interested in Judaism before I came to look into Zen. I'd even secretly made myself a tallit, or Jewish prayer shawl, as a young teenager, which I kept hidden in my room. I'd looked into Hinduism, too. But it was Buddhism that really spoke to me when I first encountered it. Just the image of the Buddha sitting in meditation communicated something deep and beyond words. When I was about ten or eleven, I remember being struck by the picture of the Great Buddha at Kamakura in an encyclopedia set that my parents had bought. It made a huge impression on me. The grace, poise, and serenity of that being was something to aspire to. No words needed to be said. It was all there in the cross-legged posture. It was simple and serene.

I recall now that I used to draw images of buddhas a lot as I grew up. I'd sketch them on bits of paper. In art class at school, I'd draw Zen monks sitting in meditation. I didn't see this in any way as religious activity, as I increasingly had no time for religion. For me, it was something beyond religion. It was not a public declaration of faith but dwelled in a secret space of interiority. It was like being a dissident with a hidden conviction, despite the prevailing politics and culture all around. With no public show of faith, I continued to sit meditation in my bedroom, spontaneously sitting a kind of objectless meditation. Then later I found some books on Taoism in the alternative health food shop in Galway, and in these were basic descriptions of how to do meditation. So, that brought it all on a bit. But there really were no Buddhist groups or teachers that I knew of. Buddhist groups did exist in Ireland since the 1970s, but these groups had no visible presence in society, and their teachers were mostly based overseas, making only sporadic visits. Laurence Cox has done pioneering research into all of this in his book *Buddhism and Ireland*, which I highly recommend. But from my own experience, Buddhism was still an activity "in the closet," especially in the conservative and Catholic atmosphere of the west of Ireland in the 1980s. The small, isolated Buddhist groups that did exist from the 1970s on were discreet and hidden, with very few members. They certainly never were visible or accessible to an interested teenager in Galway in the mid-1980s. It wasn't until the 1990s that things began to change.

From the mid-1990s on, Buddhism had more of a presence in Irish society, I recall. There was a Zen teacher from France, Alain Liebmann, leading a Zen group in Galway, and he also held retreats. And in Belfast, native Belfast son Paul Haller from San Francisco Zen Center had founded Black Mountain Zen Centre. There were also various Tibetan Buddhist groups at this stage. But still there was the issue that Buddhist teachers tended to visit from overseas, rather than base themselves in Ireland. Paul Haller did have Dharma transmission[32] but was in the country only twice a year. So, the sanghas that existed were mostly lay sanghas, with no guidance from a fully empowered teacher based in Ireland. The Tibetan Buddhist groups, also, were mostly lay in nature, relying on teachers to come from abroad. So, the center of authority was located elsewhere for Irish Buddhism, making it a kind of outpost or satellite of a Buddhism whose power center was in another country. This meant Irish Buddhist priests were not fully empowered at the time, which would have ensured that Buddhism really put down roots here. And that remained the case for many years.

I did practice in both the Zen centers in Galway and Belfast over the years. When I moved to Dublin in the late 1990s to go to college, I also explored the Friends of the Western Buddhist Order, a new Buddhist movement that started in the 1960s, and I did one of their introduction to meditation courses in Dublin. Then, on my various travels—Paris, Boston, Cork—I continued to sit meditation and tried other Zen groups, as well as various Tibetan groups. But I kept coming back to Zen again and again, as it was the practice that seemed to fit best. So, eventually I began to go on retreats with Paul Haller in Northern Ireland, and took *jukai*, or lay ordination, with him in April 2010. It had been a long journey to this point, and this represented a clear commitment to the Zen Way. But in the months after taking *jukai*, I began to feel that my practice was frustrated by being able to talk with Paul Haller only on the two occasions he visited Ireland a year. It was still a problem that Buddhist teachers were mostly based abroad. But by now the World Wide Web was closing the gap, and some Zen communities had embraced it. And so it was that I met my Zen teacher, Taïgu, based in Osaka. And for the next five years we met almost weekly for an hour or so together online, he in Japan and me in Dublin. What had been impossible before had become possible. Through the online Treeleaf Sangha, set up by Jundo Cohen, I now had a real and deep relationship with a guiding teacher. Taïgu and I held *dokusan* (a formal student-teacher meeting) every week and began to hold retreats together: first online and later in person, in Europe or North America, during the extended winter or summer holidays. Within a few months, Taïgu suggested that I should ordain, and so I sewed my robes and ordained at the end of a retreat in the winter of 2011, held in a Catholic monastery in Kortenberg, Belgium, on the outskirts of Brussels. My training continued online and at in-person retreats, and Taïgu sent me on residential retreats in established Zen monasteries in France, like in Kanshōji, in the Dordogne. I did not know it, but he was preparing me for Dharma transmission, which he gave me in Paris, in December 2014.

From about 2014 on, there were priests with Dharma transmission based in Ireland for the first time. Alain Liebmann, the French monk based in Galway, had now received the authority to ordain as a transmitted priest, but he decided to leave Ireland at around this time. Ingen Breen, a Dublin native who had trained at San Francisco Zen Center, returned to Ireland after many years abroad, also at this time. He set up a community first in Dublin before moving to the west of Ireland to begin something there. Other longstanding Zen groups continue, in Galway and Dublin, led by dedicated and authentic Zen practitioners, priests that Alain Liebmann had ordained over the years: people like Mary Lehane in Dublin and Tom Cleary in Galway. There are probably other groups I don't know about, with visiting teachers supporting them. And in recent years, Mary Lehane in Dublin and Djinn Gallagher in Belfast have received Dharma transmission, meaning potentially a great growth for Irish Zen lies ahead. And then there is me.

Having newly received transmission in 2014, I decided to set up a sangha here in Dublin. The idea was that priests would be ordained over time, and that the sangha wouldn't focus only on lay practice. Maybe that way an Irish expression of the Zen tradition would eventually emerge and endure. That's how Zen Buddhism Ireland came about.

# Zen Buddhism Ireland

*We were a uniquely Irish expression of the Zen school: we were practicing this ancient path right here and now, in this place and time, with all its specific character and flavor.*

A T FIRST, MY INTENTION was to act as a supporting priest to Ingen Breen, who was based in Dublin in 2014. However, for various reasons that did not work out—especially because he decided to leave Dublin. I then set about trying to set up social media platforms for all the fragmented Zen communities around Ireland to communicate. These online platforms I collectively named Zen Buddhism Ireland, and I sent out invitations to everyone connected with Zen here to participate. But as no one responded or appeared interested, gradually the fledgling Zen group I had started began to use these platforms instead. I had called the new group Three Rock Zen, and we met in the Lantern Centre on Dublin's Synge Street every week. As people began to discover the group on social media, they called the group Zen Buddhism Ireland. So, after a while, that became the group's name.

The first time this group ever met, however, was for a Midsummer's Day retreat in 2014 at the Oscailt Centre in Ballsbridge in Dublin. But from 2015 on, we met weekly in the Lantern Centre, which was run by a Catholic group and managed by an accommodating Christian Brother named Michael. However, a Catholic-conservative change in management meant we were no longer welcome at this Christian-run center. So, we moved to the Harvest Moon Centre on Baggot Street in Dublin, where we stayed for over a year before it was sold to property developers. We were homeless for a few months then, until we began a rental at the Quakers Meeting House on Eustace Street, in Dublin city center, where we remained until the COVID pandemic meant the meeting house stopped all activities in the spring of 2020. In 2021, we signed a lease to open the Dublin Zen Centre at 11 Anglesea Street, in Dublin's Temple Bar area. Finally, we have an enduring home right in the center of Dublin city.

Accommodation is a real issue for minority religious groups in Ireland, especially in an expensive city like Dublin. Lacking the intergenerational wealth, numbers, and inheritance of the waning but long-established Christian churches, smaller faith communities endure a precarious existence here, and the bigger faith communities are not supportive in any meaningful way.

Three Rock Zen, by the way, was named after the mountain Three Rock, which overlooks Dublin city. The three rocks on its peak signify the triple gem of Buddhism: the Buddha, Dharma, and Sangha, on which all of Buddhism is based. The image informed a sonnet cycle I wrote back in 2014–15. But as the new sangha began to be called Zen Buddhism Ireland, I realized that that name made better sense, as it simply said, in plain terms, what we were all about. This was *Zen*, but not secular Zen or secular mindfulness. It was Zen *Buddhism*, as this was Buddhist practice that we were engaged in, belonging to that old spiritual and religious tradition. And it was Zen Buddhism *Ireland* because we were a uniquely Irish expression of the Zen school: we were practicing this ancient path right here and now, in this place and time, with all its specific character and flavor. Seeded in this description was the aspiration that I hoped to ordain a new generation of Zen teachers throughout the country, so that, hopefully, Sōtō Zen Buddhism could find some lasting expression here.

In any case, ten years after our first Midsummer's Day retreat, we continue. We have members in numerous counties throughout the country: Dublin, Wicklow, Kildare, Mayo, Donegal, Meath, Cork, Galway, and Sligo. I have ordained five priests, and three more are in preparation for ordination. We may soon have two priests in Donegal, one in Wicklow, one in Kildare, and three in Dublin. Some of these may become teachers in their own right and go on to set up Zen communities of their own. Also, as the pandemic has forced us online, we have attracted sangha members from other countries: Sweden, France, and the UK. In ten short years, Zen Buddhism Ireland has already grown much bigger than anything I might have expected on that first Midsummer's Day in 2014. It is amazing, as we have not once advertised an event. Whether we continue to grow in the years ahead is another question. In this transient world, we are here now. Little more can be said than that. We practice the Way together. That is all. Anything that flows from that is fine.

# Living and Dying as
# a Buddhist in Ireland

*It is not that religion should be banished from the
public sphere. Rather it's that the true richness of
our spiritual traditions should be honored for what
they can contribute to our society and shared life.*

WHEN BUDDHISM ENTERS THE public sphere in Ireland, it quickly
becomes apparent it is entering a sphere intolerant of faiths
other than Christianity. Lip service is paid to religious tolerance
here, but because of our history, every sphere of life in Ireland
is influenced by the Catholic Church. Christians in Ireland today
may feel that they are on the back foot, that secularity is eroding
their faith from every side. But when you come from a minority
faith position, you can see that the Christian mainstream is largely
unaware of the power it wields. If you are Jewish or Muslim or
Buddhist in Ireland, however, this Christian dominance is plain to
see, as it is your lived experience every day. As you attempt to live
a Buddhist life and die a Buddhist death in Ireland, you see that
many structures have evolved to exclude you. This would not be
the case in a genuinely pluralist and inclusive country.

In some respects, Ireland endures as a Catholic state. Children
today have a greater than 90 percent chance of being educated in
a Catholic ethos and at a Catholic school—regardless of whether
they are Catholic, Protestant, Muslim, Jewish, or Buddhist. The

Church still dominates education at every level. So, as you begin your Buddhist life in Ireland, you are shoehorned into a Catholic view of the world. There are some nondenominational schools, including some run by an organization called Educate Together, but they are not available in many areas—and where they are available, they rarely have openings for new students. This means that many non-Catholic children have to attend Catholic schools, where their identity is marginalized and where they are taught a religion that is not theirs, even a religion that their parents may have rejected. They may opt out of religion classes, but then they are the odd child out. And the inclusive elements of the curriculum are often ignored in these Catholic contexts. The culture of Holy Communion and confirmation is massive in these Catholic schools, and most children—even children from nonbelieving families—go through these rites of passage as coming-of-age rituals. Indeed, many non-Catholic children are hastily baptized just to get them into certain Catholic schools, which are seen as better or more prestigious than the Educate Together schools.

I remember once being at a Holy Communion party in Dublin, sitting in the garden having a glass of wine with a few other parents from a school where my friend's child went, in whose honor the party was being held. One of the mothers was complaining about the non-Catholic families in the school, who had opted out of the Holy Communion and some of whom instead had a humanist naming ceremony on the same day. "Who do they think they are?" she asked. "Why do they have to draw all this attention to themselves?" She felt that their humanist ceremony was a cranky attempt to draw attention away from the Holy Communion day. She could not countenance that maybe they simply were not Catholic and wished to offer their children some kind of special day, too, so that they would not feel so excluded. But whereas the Holy Communion preparation and ceremony had happened on school and Church property, the humanist ceremony was held without official approval in a nearby public park. In this instance, as in so many others, Catholic children are first-class citizens in many of our Irish schools, while non-Catholic children are second-class.

Even before they are born, the Catholic dominance of society overshadows children's lives. When my wife went for her pregnancy screening at Cork University Hospital, we encountered this firsthand. It was our first child, and my wife was nervous. Coming from France, she expected certain norms to be followed, including a test to detect Down syndrome or some other similar condition. When it became apparent that the nurse was not going to perform this test, my wife asked the nurse if she could do it. Friendly up until that point, the nurse became unpleasant and somewhat aggressive. One could only guess, but the subtext appeared to be that my wife wanted to know if her child had Down syndrome because she might consider termination if she heard unwelcome news from the scan. Such scans are the norm in most countries during pregnancy, but the nurse at this hospital only grudgingly performed the test, clearly against her wishes. "Why do you want to know this?" she asked. After the scan, I filed a complaint, but there was never any response.

In Ireland, this kind of experience is commonplace, although it is beginning to be tolerated less. Attitudes may have changed, but successive governments have shirked from fully separating church and state. Many hospitals and university chaplaincy services remain exclusively controlled by the Catholic Church. The Catholic Church has pride of place at state functions and ceremonies, with all other traditions in our diverse country excluded, or in a secondary position at best. Our media, while changing, still features just a Christian point of view—if they turn their attention to religion at all. The Angelus rings out daily on our national television and radio, like the call to prayer in Muslim countries. And almost all religious coverage in the media is Catholic only.

In my own life, I have encountered this reality many times. For example, I remember once needing a signature for a form to renew my passport. It was an urgent, last-minute situation. I went to the local garda station to see if the duty officer would sign my form.

He said that he could not, that he didn't have the authority. What I needed was a solicitor, bank manager, or member of the clergy. It being the weekend, and an urgent situation, my only option was to call into the church down the road from the garda station. It was ironic that as a priest myself, I had to go to a Catholic priest I didn't know to get my passport form signed. The priest kindly signed my form, which I appreciated, but not before grilling me about my Mass attendance. Maybe he signed in confusion, when I said that I was a Buddhist priest. Nevertheless, this satisfied the local policeman, who could then help me process my form.

I remember another time, going to vote on the Repeal the Eighth referendum to legalize limited abortion in Ireland for the first time. It had been a divisive question for as long as I could remember, and it was the flagship issue for the Church in public life. Having finally lost on divorce, they were determined to win on abortion. As I went to vote at my local polling station, I had to pass an imposing statue of the Virgin Mary holding the infant Jesus, looming outside. It was the Church's final chance to canvass me as I was about to cast my vote—at the polling station inside the local Catholic school, with all its Catholic paraphernalia.

It is remarkable that the Church lost this battle, considering everything that was stacked in their favor. Yet it is not just in the realm of the living that the Church has extended its dominance in Ireland. It also holds sovereignty over the realm of the dead.

In Irish hospitals and hospices, there is always a Catholic priest nearby to talk to you, and they have much of the same access and privileges as medical professionals. Sometimes the chaplain wears a hospital uniform as well, as though they were on the medical team. If you are dying in an Irish hospital or hospice, in most cases, no one has bothered to compile a list of whom to contact if you are a Hindu, Buddhist, or Muslim. They might ask what your religion is on the registration form, but if you're not Christian, then this is only a formality. They lack the structures to support you should you need spiritual advice or a relevant chaplain, as you go through your sickness, or even through your final hours of life.

During the COVID pandemic, my colleagues and I on the Dublin City Interfaith Forum tried to work with the national health service to remedy the lack of support for non-Christians, as so many people were falling seriously ill. We offered our services as volunteer chaplains during the crisis. But the health service was largely indifferent to our offer and didn't take it up. Indeed, I know from one chaplain in a Dublin hospital that extending the chaplaincy to a broader interfaith base was quashed by the Catholic nun leading this particular hospital's chaplaincy service.

People of minority faiths in Ireland often have only a Catholic chaplain available to them in their final hours. The Catholic Church largely controls chaplaincy in Ireland, and a degree in Christian theology is often required to become a chaplain. Minority faiths are thus locked out of the profession. Other countries such as Norway have devised multifaith pathways into chaplaincy—but not Ireland.

So, it is individuals rather than hospitals that find me when a Buddhist priest is needed. For example, one time a woman called me because her brother-in-law was dying in a Dublin hospital. They were Buddhists from Malaysia, and the hospital didn't offer any assistance in providing a Buddhist chaplain as the man approached death. They suggested their Catholic chaplain see them. Dissatisfied, the dying man's sister-in-law took it into her own hands to find a Buddhist priest. And so she found me. I changed into my robes in the hospital chapel, under a large crucifix on the wall, and offered the last rites at the deathbed. The nurses weren't quite sure what to do with me. Should I be allowed access or not? I had no official status. Was this OK? Ultimately, they were great and accommodating, but the hospital offered no help to this man on his deathbed.

I also did the funeral for this same man, first at the funeral home and then the day after at the crematorium in Glasnevin, in Dublin. Of the numerous funerals I've done, each time it's struck me how difficult it is to conduct a non-Christian funeral in a Christian context. First of all, many minority faiths in Ireland don't own any place in which to hold a proper funeral. For Christians, the funeral happens in their church, and only the lesser burial or cremation happens at the cemetery. But without a large church, for many minority faiths the whole service must happen at the cemetery, and that means fitting into a tight time slot. About thirty or forty minutes are allocated for each service, and services run back to back all day. That is fine if you have already held a proper funeral beforehand and are only finishing the rite of passage. But when the entire rite of passage is at the cemetery, it is a problem.

Then there are other constraints. The building where the service is held is designed as a Christian chapel, so you are sur-rounded by Christian symbolism for a non-Christian funeral. Burning incense is central to many traditions, but is usually for-bidden at cemetery facilities. Even candles are usually not allowed. And with the limited timeslot, only an abbreviated service is pos-sible. This lack of accommodation adds to the distress of the griev-ing. I know from speaking to Hindus, Muslims, and other friends that they have similar issues. Their rites around death are often discounted and not accommodated.

The world may have changed, but the societal structures remain the same. From maternity services to funeral rites, the keys are held by a Catholic cleric, or someone that understands spiri-tual services only in Christian terms. Any call for change is often seen as a threat, rather than simply a call for recognition and some semblance of equality. From schools to hospitals, universities to cemeteries, a concerted Church divestment needs to take place. It is not that religion should be banished from the public sphere. Rather, it's that the true richness of our spiritual traditions should be honored for what they can contribute to our society and shared life. But happily, things are moving in the right direction. Change may be slow and patience is needed. But the fundamental decency of most people means that our new diversity is something the majority welcomes, and are even kindly disposed to.

# Interfaith Ireland

*What I've learned is how much the public's view
of religious diversity diverges from reality. Ireland
seems to be a pluralist society from a distance,
but get close up and you see the old Church
powers hanging on to control for dear life.*

IN ORDER TO GAIN better accommodation for Ireland's diversity of religious traditions, I decided to become active in the Dublin City Interfaith Forum (DCIF), which aims to create awareness and dialogue through building relationships that nurture harmony and deepen understanding and respect. The DCIF is really the main interfaith body in Ireland; except for some interfaith groups in various cities, there is no national interfaith organization. Because of this, the DCIF is often engaged at a national level, by virtue of being located in the capital. We engage with a variety of governmental offices, including the national police service, government departments, the office of the Taoiseach (prime minister), national health organizations, the prison system, and the body that develops the national curriculum in schools. Because of my engagements in this way, I've witnessed firsthand the hidden realities of interfaith relations in Ireland.

One thing that is clear is how disengaged the majority, institutional Catholic tradition is from interfaith dialogue here. Publicly, respect is shown for interfaith work, but in reality, senior Catholic clergy rarely attend DCIF events or meetings, or even send a representative. (The same is not true of the Anglican archbishop, who is very active—or the lay or female Catholic clergy that are active in the Forum). In my experience, senior Catholic clergy may only show up at a DCIF event on the rare occasions that there is media present to cover the event. On one of these occasions, the clergyman in question distanced himself from the other faith leaders, and even made fun of my Buddhist robes, which Buddhists consider as sacred as Catholics consider the crucifix. I was wearing a Buddhist *rakusu* around my neck, and he asked if it was, in fact, a bulletproof vest. I let it go, and later wrote to him, politely explaining what the robe was and why his comment was inappropriate. My message received neither a reply nor an acknowledgment. Indeed, the next time he met me at an event, he made a similar remark.

What I've learned through working with the DCIF is how much the public's view of religious diversity diverges from reality. Ireland seems to be a pluralist society from a distance, but get close up and you see the old Church powers hanging on to control for dear life. Working to redesign the national curriculum on religious education in schools, it was staggering what resistance there was to change. After long negotiations and various drafts, we arrived at a religious curriculum that should be broadly acceptable to children and families of all faith traditions and none. But this curriculum is being taught mostly in Catholic Church controlled schools with a Catholic ethos. In light of this, the teachers delivering the program need not veer from the way they have always done things. Ultimately, I wonder if the only choice may be to remove religion from schools altogether.

As the Buddhist representative advising the Taoiseach, it is clear to me that no separation of church and state is imminent in Ireland. As a member of this body, I made the point to two prime ministers, Leo Varadkar and Micheál Martin, that there was great inequity in how the state was treating religious communities. Both men essentially said that it was not up to the state to ensure religious services for minority faiths in Irish society, even while that same state pours millions into schools, hospitals, and other services run by the Catholic Church. That the national police force and military only have Christian chaplains in Ireland illustrates the point.

Christianity enjoys preferential treatment at state occasions also. At national memorials usually there is a prominent Christian presence, even though the wider population is now much more diverse. The one exception is the National Day of Commemoration, which is for all Irish people that have died in past wars. At this event in recent years, there has been an effort to broaden the representation to a wider base of faith communities. It's a big, televised event, with the president and Taoiseach taking part, with leaders of the government and other prominent figures in Irish life attending. I've represented Buddhism a few times because of my involvement with the DCIF, and was the first Buddhist participant to offer a reading at the commemoration in 2019. It was fascinating to take part in the process, as it was clear that even while attempting to be inclusive, the state cannot help but default to offering Catholicism a special position of honor. For example, in preparation for the event, it was left to the Catholic representative to chair the meeting on behalf of the archbishop. It never occurred to the government representatives running the event that an independent chair would have been more appropriate. With the Catholics running the meeting, it felt that they were in charge again. Indeed, the Taoiseach's civil servants didn't know how to deal with non-Christian clergy. While the two Christian archbishops were addressed by their titles, the non-Christians were called by their first names—often mispronounced. These slights probably went unnoticed to the government officials involved, making it a perfect case of where unconscious bias training was needed.

As for the ceremony itself, the audience were invited to sit through the contributions of the Muslim, Jewish, Hindu, and Buddhist representatives, but they were told to stand when it came to the Catholic archbishop's contribution. The organizers were trying to be inclusive but seemed blind to the varying treatment of the different faiths throughout. And since they were so new to being inclusive, they deported themselves with awkwardness. And yet they had included us in the National Day of Commemoration, which was more than on most state occasions.

Progress comes slowly, one step at a time—but the time has come for a great leap when it comes to accommodating our diversity in Ireland. Through the DCIF, I argued that the way to change the culture was to work through the media. I surveyed the DCIF membership and found that the majority felt that their faith tradition was not represented in the Irish media—and when it was, it was misrepresented. Certainly, religious programming almost totally ignores non-Christian faith traditions, with a few notable exceptions. There are almost no hijabs to be seen anywhere on television, and very few people of color, if any. The national broadcaster's religious affairs correspondent didn't consider the formation of an Irish Buddhist union a story worth covering, even though the most minor pronouncement of an Irish bishop is always covered. As usual, the *Irish Times* did much better and understood that it was a story of note—but that was the exception to the rule. The national broadcaster airs Mass after Mass, the Angelus, and special religious programming for big Christian festivals—but as a public service broadcaster, it does much less for other faith communities. In the DCIF, we have decided to try and change that. But it was only really with the COVID pandemic of 2020 that things began to shift.

With so many people from so many different backgrounds dying, it suddenly became clear that the exclusively Christian approach to religious services was inadequate. Concerns around diversity had already entered the zeitgeist, and the pandemic created a moment of crisis that was also a moment of change. The television broadcaster RTÉ invited members of DCIF on air to offer a reflection. Zen Buddhism Ireland held the first ever Buddhist ceremony on Irish TV by performing the *segaki* ceremony in memory of all those thousands that had lost their lives to COVID. Later, for Saint Patrick's Day, DCIF members were invited back to offer another reflection, broadening the meaning of what had, since time immemorial, been a celebration of an exclusively Christian Irish identity. It is little compared to the airtime that the Catholic Church still receives, but it is a start.

At least the media is making efforts to change. The national health service is another matter. As the pandemic hit, DCIF tried to work with the health authorities to provide officially sanctioned, volunteer chaplaincy support from our members. Their almost exclusively Christian chaplaincy services were stretched to the breaking point, but despite our efforts, the health service did not take us up on our offer. They agreed in principle, but nothing really happened. We provided contact details and offered free support from Muslim, Jewish, Hindu, and Buddhist clergy, among others, but to no avail. There seems to be as much institutional resistance from the church as from individual decision makers.

And it is much the same with hospice services. Many religious traditions have particular requirements regarding what can and cannot occur as someone is dying or when they have recently died. Nevertheless, only Christian chaplains are available, while the dying and their families are not made aware that they have choices. In theory, they have the right to see a chaplain from their own tradition. Hospice staff also do not realize that other chaplaincy choices exist.

Through the DCIF, I have learned a lot about the direction we need to go. We need to introduce a non-Christian chaplaincy qualification and open up chaplaincy by making that qualification the national standard requirement. We need to see the state acknowledge with honesty its massive fiscal support for Catholic involvement in education and health, with a financial settlement being agreed on to sever that longstanding link. As various European countries have done, we need to see multi-belief spaces made available by the state for citizens to hold ceremonies around birth, marriage, death, and other life transitions. As things stand, humanists, atheists, and people from minority faith traditions lack spaces in Ireland in which to hold these important ceremonies.

But none of this is officially a problem, of course. The frame of public reference is set to ensure that this is a nonproblem. After all, we are an increasingly secular society, are we not? The influence of the Church is declining, is it not? We are a diverse country, isn't that so?

# Religion and
# National Identity

*Let it be clearly said: Buddhism is an Irish
religion. Why is that? Because people living in
Ireland are Buddhist and practice Buddhism.
The same can be said of Islam and Judaism,
Hinduism and Sikhism. These are all Irish faith
traditions now, as much as Irish Catholicism.*

B ECAUSE OF OUR HISTORY in Ireland, religion and identity were
fused together. The Irish were Catholics, and the English
were Protestants. When I was growing up, even Irish Protestants
were seen as somehow English. The nonreligious nature of Irish
Republican values was lost along the way. Religion became an
ethno-nationalist marker, similar to how it is in conflicts in the
Middle East and other places around the globe. It was not only a
betrayal of your faith to turn your back on the Church—it was a
betrayal of your country.

This attitude made sense in Ireland, as Catholicism had been
suppressed and discriminated against by the English occupy-
ing forces up until the 1830s. Then, in the succeeding decades,
as the country emerged from a devastating, genocidal famine—
caused mainly by British liberal and racist ideology—the Church
set about building its power base in the country. It educated and
nursed the poor and destitute, but also did with them as it pleased.

The Church became the de facto provider of state services, including health care and education. By the time the actual Irish state was set up, the Church had a controlling monopoly on these vital spheres of communal life.

Central to the invention of the Irish nation was the idea that Catholicism was native, and that all other religions were foreign. This plank of identity was so fundamental in the Irish conception of self that it persists today. People are not largely aware of it, as it is buried deep. But it is consistently evident in how we project our image in the public sphere. This Catholic identity is in our textbooks, media, art, advertising, literature—indeed, all forms of culture, including food and sport. It is an all-pervasive hologram that we put a lot of energy into sustaining, and it is required for deep reasons of personal and collective identity, stemming from the need to control resources and other economic factors. It also has a cultural and spiritual dimension. Mostly, however, it is related to the politics of culture, where one's self-definition comes about in opposition to another's.

Like all cultural projections, the images in the public sphere can be constantly reviewed and updated—or even returned to neutral, from where they can be reset. So, past enemies can become current friends, and former friends can be turned into demonic enemies. What was once a good thing can now be bad, and what once was true can now be false. Anything whatsoever can be projected in the public sphere. For example, the idea that Catholicism is native to Ireland is just such a projection.

Of course, Catholicism is no more native to Ireland than is Buddhism. It just has a longer history here, that is all. Catholicism, like all of Christianity, originated in the Middle East and came to us via Rome. The only truly native religion of Ireland is the pre-Christian religion of the druids—and even that was likely imported from the Continent. Ireland, a country never colonized by Rome, adopted the religion of Rome. It already had a religion but saw no issue in importing another. And why should it? The concept of *native* does not stand up to scrutiny. Everything is give-and-take.

Nations are recent and provisional imaginings. What's key is that this give-and-take happens in an exchange of mutual respect. Just as Buddhism is not natively Japanese, Catholicism is not natively Irish.

Let it be clearly said: Buddhism *is* an Irish religion. Why is that? Because people living in Ireland are Buddhist and practice Buddhism. The same can be said of Islam and Judaism, Hinduism and Sikhism. These are all Irish faith traditions now, as much as Irish Catholicism. And just as Catholicism has its origins in the Middle East and Rome, and put down roots here, so too have these faith traditions their own origins, and also put down their own roots in this place. With the invention of air travel and the internet, you cannot have it any other way. It is inevitable that the world will come home to you. So, best make yourself at home.

# The Invention
## of Tradition

*All this will disappear with time. But in inventing
a tradition, one hopes to transcend the boundaries
of one's own life. This is how the teachings came to
us, and this is how they will be carried forward.*

IN ZEN, THERE IS a long tradition of poetry. The teachings have
been expressed in China and Japan through various poetic
forms. And as Zen comes westward, poetry here is also finding
ways to articulate Zen truths. The Beats in 1950s America were
some of the first to do this, with Snyder, Ginsberg, and Kerouac
contributing to the tradition of Zen poetry. In some small way, I
found it important to do this too.

*Three Rock Sonnets* was my first collection of Zen poetry. Using
the European form of the sonnet, I wanted to use a form from
Western culture to express the universal teachings we find in the
Zen Buddhist tradition. Some of those poems were inspired by
poets and teachers I respected greatly, such as Allen Ginsberg,
who first taught me how to sit in meditation when I was showing him around Galway in the early 1990s. And Seamus Heaney,
whose widowed wife, Marie, wrote to me recently having read
the sonnets, saying "I found Sonnet XC dedicated to Seamus very
moving, very beautiful and very true to him." It is a postcard I
keep and treasure.

In Zen, the tradition includes enlightenment poems, teaching poems, and poems written as death approaches. In *Songs from the Denkoroku*, which is my second volume of Zen poetry, I was deliberately contributing to this tradition by writing a series of eight-line poems inspired by each of the ancestral masters' enlightenment experiences as detailed by Master Keizan in his *Record of Transmitting the Light*. The aim was to write into existence a tradition of Zen poetry here in Ireland, which is lacking, except for some wonderful practitioners of the haiku over the years. If each tradition has to spring into being with an act of invention, then that invention must occur. It is essentially the process of imagining a culture into being, of projecting new coordinates onto the map of reality. And that is exactly what poetry does. It invents a tradition. But it is not making things up from scratch. Rather, it draws from an ancient and deeply established tradition, allowing it to find new expression in new circumstances.

The same is true of the green *rakusu* and *okesa* that we sew in Zen Buddhism Ireland. The *rakusu* is the small, bib-like Buddhist robe worn around the neck, a miniature version of the big robe, the *okesa*, which is wrapped around the body. I inherited the sewing of the Buddha's robe from my teacher, Taïgu Rōshi, who is a master of the tradition. This is a tradition that began when the Buddha was walking through rice fields with his attendant, Ananda. Ananda observed that there were so many religious teachers and gurus around at the time, and wondered if some special clothing was needed to distinguish the followers of the Buddha from the others. Buddha suggested sewing a robe for Buddhists to wear, "like this," indicating the network of rectangular rice fields they were in—but really indicating the whole, vast body of reality. And so Ananda took it upon himself to sew the first *okesa* by joining pieces of cloth together in a pattern based on that of rice fields. Inspired by the land around them, the first Buddhist robe came into being.

Respecting this tradition, our sangha sews the green *rakusu* and *okesa*, which follows exactly the original *nyohō-e* tradition of sewing, using green material, to suggest the land around where we are. The finished robe reminds us of the fields and stone walls of the Irish landscape. It is the body of the reality around us that we wear. Even in our sewing of the Buddha's robe, we bring about a new interpretation of the tradition in a new context, but in no way diverging from the practice of millennia, which we respect as we inherit it while giving it new expression. My transmission *okesa* and *rakusu* followed this understanding. But now everyone that formally enters the Zen path in our sangha follows this way, by sewing a dark, forest-green *rakusu*. It brings to mind the muted light of the dark forests of Wicklow, fields under a gray sky, or the pine and larch that cling to our mountains.

In this spirit, my sangha presented to me a special *kotsu*, or Zen teacher's stick, a few years ago, which was made from yew. Yew (Irish: *iúr*) was one of the sacred trees in ancient Ireland, and the druids made their wands from it. The wood came from a tree over one thousand years old near Newtownmountkennedy in County Wicklow. A branch of the tree came down in a storm. The tree itself still stands to this day. After the branch was seasoned for a year, one of the sangha came across it and decided to make a *kotsu* from it. It is a beautiful object, with the wood having a rose and pink hue through it because of its age. It is something to pass down from teacher to teacher in our tradition, and I greatly value everything that it signifies for Zen in this country. May the yew *kotsu* find its way to many hands over many years, long after I am gone.

Still, all this will disappear with time. But in inventing a tradition, one hopes to transcend the boundaries of one's own life. This is how the teachings came to us, and this is how they will be carried forward. Unless it makes a home here, the Zen Way will remain foreign and imported, an exotic expression of an imagined Orient, rather than an ordinary and habitual, even natural, way of life.

So, we translate the Heart Sutra into Irish to chant. We sew the green robe and find myriad ways to express and manifest the arrival of Zen to this time and place. Everything has to start somewhere. And even the ancient ways have to be remade and maintained with every moment of expression. This is how time and eternity are intertwined. This is how the distant past and the fleeting present are one. It is in this dance, between the universal and the particular, that Zen truth shows its original face. It is the face you see on an East Asian Buddha statue in Dublin's Chester Beatty Library. And it is the face that looks back at you from your own mirror.

# The Bloodline
# of Irish Zen

*Western Zen has its own unique expression. While respecting the Japanese inheritance, we are in a new situation and cannot continue to look to a distant leadership in the East. We have to look to ourselves and grow new expressions of Zen right here.*

THE GREAT SCHOLAR OF Irish Buddhism Laurence Cox has written that the locus of power for Irish Buddhism has always remained overseas. Even when there were Buddhist communities in Ireland, they looked to a teacher living elsewhere, who came to visit once or twice a year to offer teachings. There were simply no Irish-based teachers of authentic Dharma for a long time. This remains largely the case in many instances, with Irish Buddhist groups usually being offshoots or affiliates of some headquarters in another country. There grew up, therefore, a relationship of dependence, where self-determination was not possible for many sanghas here. There was a glass ceiling in their growth, as training centers were not available and priests could not be ordained, since there was no one with the power to ordain them. Ironically, various Buddhist "Vaticans"—headquarters organizations in other countries—maintained control over Irish Buddhism, whose membership was made up largely of defectors from the actual Vatican and its power. Nothing could grow without permission from "Rome," and that was rarely forthcoming when it came to ordaining and empowering Irish people as Buddhist teachers. The growth of Irish Buddhism was stymied, as it always looked outward, away from its provincial status, toward a centrally controlling capital in another place.

This should be no surprise, as Buddhism was often like this in its long history. At first, China looked to India, and then Japan looked to China for validation and authenticity. To start with, there is the vital matter of lineage, or of bloodline. An authentic Buddhist teacher must be able to trace their authentic line back through their teacher and teacher's teacher, all the way through the successive generations of ancestors to the historical Buddha himself. In many Buddhist schools, Zen included, one cannot claim to be an authentic teacher without this ancestry. So, there was always the requirement to look toward a center of Buddhism located elsewhere. It is for this reason that the Japanese Zen master Dōgen idealized the Zen monasteries of China, where he trained, considering his own country a backwater in terms of the Dharma. But at some stage, once the lineage was handed on safely, self-reliance emerged in the new countries that Dharma found itself in. Beyond the matter of lineage, Japanese Buddhism did not remain institutionally reliant on China, just as Chinese Buddhism no longer looked to India for its authority. For similar reasons, the first generation of Zen teachers that came to North America and Europe did not seek to create an American or European Zen that relied institutionally on its Japanese masters. Shunryu Suzuki Rōshi, for example, was adamant that American Zen should go its own way, finding its own unique expression as it grew. Although Japanese himself, he had no desire to make American Zen dependent on the head temples of Eiheiji and Sōjiji back in Japan. American Zen would have to find its own way, he said. And this is exactly what had happened with Japanese Zen itself, as it broke away from China to find its own unique expression. The Zen traditions of Korea and Vietnam had a similar story. That is why there is no institutionally controlling body for Zen internationally. It does not have a center of power in the way that Catholicism does. Unique expressions of the true teaching emerged in various regions, with a common lineage of origin but with regional and national characteristics all of their own. With a self-reliant clergy in each region, Zen and Buddhism were in a position to grow and thrive wherever they found themselves, without the need to rely on a power center elsewhere for every move they made.

Still, the tendency to centralize control in religious institutions persists. This is usually justified with the argument that it prevents rogue elements engaging in abuse or heresy, as they need to be validated by an authoritative institution that ensures authenticity. However, the history of abuse in religious institutions well and truly buries that argument. Yet even in Japanese Zen there is this tendency toward centralization, with the two headquarters temples of Eiheiji and Sōjiji, which share a co-status as the two authoritative centers of Japanese Sōtō Zen. So, after its initial establishment by maverick teachers in the West, some later generations of Western Zen teachers sought authentication from these institutions of Japanese Zen. Often, those that had established Zen outside Asia never envisaged this happening. However, be it for reasons of anxiety or seeking supports from tradition, some Western teachers strained to reestablish the institutional links with Japan, seeking official registration in the Japanese institution, while other Western teachers saw no reason to do so. This has meant that there has been a somewhat unsuccessful attempt to ensure Zen of Japanese origin in the West is brought under Japanese institutional control. But this assertion of power has come after the fact of Zen's establishment here. The genie is already half in and half out of the bottle: some in Western Zen are forging those institutional links with Japan, while many others have sought to establish Zen's own way in the local cultural context. It remains an unresolved issue, with those officially registered with the Japanese institutions sometimes deporting themselves with superiority because of their Asian credentials. Some of those that seek a new way may see them as slavishly copying Japanese norms and power structures.

This dilemma has come up for me as a Zen priest as well. The root teacher in our lineage, Gudō Wafu Nishijima Rōshi, received his Dharma transmission, or authorization to teach, from Zuigaku Rempō Niwa Zenji, who was later in charge of the head Zen Japanese training monastery of Eiheiji—just about as institutionally orthodox as you can get. But as Nishijima was not a resident monk, and was working a normal job outside the monastery, the understanding in our lineage is that Rempō Niwa gave this transmission to recognize a new kind of expression of priesthood in society. Nishijima Rōshi went on to have many students in the West, who continued this in-the-world expression of the Zen priest's path. He also did much of this teaching outside the officially registered structures of Japanese Sōtō Zen, institutionally registering some ordinations, but not others. The rationale is an ancient one: only face-to-face Dharma transmission, from master to disciple, makes a teacher authentic in the lineage. Official registration has little or nothing to do with it, and is largely meaningless outside of Japan, where the Japan-centric institutional structures evolved in a national context that has meaning only within that national context. So, as Nishijima Rōshi's lineage has blossomed, it has done so mainly outside the official Sōtōshū, as institutional Japanese Sōtō Zen is called in Japan. To put it plainly: we practice Sōtō Zen, not Sōtōshū Zen. So, my teacher is not officially registered with the Sōtōshū, and neither am I. Neither, of course, are many of the leading Zen teachers in the West. Some years ago, there was an attempt by the Sōtōshū to bring some of these teachers into the Japanese structure. Some went for it, others did not.

In my own case, a delegate from the Sōtōshū office in Europe came on a retreat with our sangha, and in private suggested that I should register officially with the Sōtōshū. He said it was up to me, but that my transmission from my master, Taïgu Rōshi, would always be recognized, and that I could continue my activities as normal, leading my sangha as a teacher. I struggled with his suggestion for many months, but then decided to visit him in Paris to officially register. On that visit, I filled out the forms to officially register in Japan. But then he asserted that in public I must always wear the black robes of a trainee priest, and I could not present myself as a fully authorized Zen teacher anymore. This was contrary to what I had understood he had said when he visited us on retreat in Ireland. I had already ordained priests and lay people in our lineage, and I was already leading the sangha that I had set up. He had even assured me that my Dharma transmission would be recognized, as per ancient tradition. Was I meant to go back to my sangha now and say that the journey we had traveled together had been all meaningless? That I was again a trainee monk, with no right to ordain those that I had ordained, and with no right to give *jukai*? It simply would be an impossible betrayal, not only of my sangha but of my teacher, and of Nishijima Rōshi and Rempō Niwa Zenji, who had started our lineage to begin with. At the airport, before taking the flight home from Paris to Dublin, I phoned the Sōtōshū representative and said that it was all off. I didn't want to go through with official registration. My brush with institutional power had left me disenchanted with the whole experience. It made me realize the almost colonial dynamic of centrally located power structures in religion. This was not what the authentic Dharma was about. My teacher supported me totally in my decision to have nothing more to do with official registration. As Suzuki Rōshi had suggested all those years ago, Zen in the West has to find its own way. So I decided instead to register with the Soto Zen Buddhist Association (SZBA), a Western-based organization of recognized Sōtō Zen teachers, be they Sōtōshū registered or not. This was an emerging structure that made more sense to me. Although mostly North American, it stemmed from that original transmission of Zen to the West and was led by many of the disciples of those pioneering Zen teachers that went to America in the 1950s and afterward. It was related to, but independent from, the Sōtōshū, which required certain rituals to be performed in Japan at great expense in order to authorize teachers as "official." The

SZBA recognized that Western Zen was its own unique expression and, while respecting the Japanese inheritance, it understood that we were in a new situation and could not continue to look to a distant leadership in the East. We had to look to ourselves and grow new expressions of Zen and organizations for Zen right here.

These new expressions and organizations are still emerging. It is vital that they emerge if Zen is to have a future as a genuine religious tradition in the West. In this endeavor, Master Dōgen is our great teacher. He went about the same task we face now: establishing Zen in a new country. Dōgen, too, faced an established religious orthodoxy that actively blocked his efforts. His Zen Way was, in every sense, a minority religion operating on the fringes of society. Indeed, with translations of pivotal texts freely available, and with many places to practice, we in Ireland today may know more of Zen than was known in Dōgen's Japan.

In Ireland, there are forerunners to look to for inspiration—the skeletal structure of an Irish Zen lineage, albeit one comprised of people that studied under various teachers, all of whom can trace their Sōtō Zen lineage back to the school's founders:

Maura Soshin O'Halloran (1955–1982)
Ryushin Paul Haller (1947–)
Alain Tainan Liebmann (1945–)

Maura Soshin O'Halloran had planned to teach in Ireland, but before she had the opportunity, she died tragically in a road accident before she could return home from Japan. Ryushin Paul Haller is based overseas but is the guiding teacher at Black Mountain Zen Centre in Belfast, now supported by his Dharma heir, Djinn Gallagher. Alain Tainan Liebmann is a French teacher, based for twenty-five years in Ireland, who set up various Zen groups during that time, some of which have disbanded, and others have thankfully prospered. He returned to France a few years ago. But both Liebmann and Haller have ordained priests based in Ireland, so one would expect Zen to have much more secure roots in this country as the years pass and as more authorized teachers emerge. That, in turn, will make it possible for more priests to be ordained.

But, in truth, it is all of us involved in Irish Zen taken together that form the foundation for the establishment of Zen Buddhism in this country. All of us are the veins and capillaries of the ancestral bloodline. From the beginnings in the 1980s, which never happened but were imagined by Maura Soshin O'Halloran, to the true start of things in the 1990s, right up to the present: Zen is at its moment of nativity in Ireland. One can only hope that native lineages can begin here, and that these branches will grow out in every direction, in every corner of the land.

# A New Expression
of Zen

*We will aspire to be bodhisattvas moving invisibly
among the crowded streets, showing ourselves when
required, but otherwise no different than everyone
else. Manifesting the true spirit of the Mahayana,
there will be no aloofness to our Zen practice.*

I N ZEN BUDDHISM, THERE are various *shingi,* or training rules, for
governing the Zen community in practice. *Shingi* literally means
"pure standards," and they may apply to life in one monastery or
to regulations throughout the particular school or sect more generally. The earliest *shingi* developed in Chinese monasteries in the
seventh, eighth, and ninth centuries, and were later adopted in
Japanese Zen contexts. The famous set of rules that Dōgen wrote
in the thirteenth century, the *Eihei Shingi,* is still used in Sōtō Zen
contexts. The *shingi* are similar to the *Rule of Saint Benedict* for
Christian monks, and they govern the whole communal life of
Zen monks. There are instructions on how to take food, on how
to meet senior instructors, and how to cook, along with guidance
for the senior temple administrators. The *shingi* contain detailed
instructions on how to conduct oneself in communal life so that a
harmonious community can flourish.

On retreat, we follow these guidelines carefully. The day is
centered around meditation and highly structured, with every

minute accounted for. Everyone rises at the same time in the morning. They take meals in a specific way, beginning and ending all meals together. There is a lot of meditation and many chanting services, as well as periods of structured work, usually physical work. On retreat, we live like a monastic community: men and women practicing together, segregated only when it comes to sleeping arrangements. While the *shingi* we follow were designed for full-time monks living their entire lives in a monastery, the majority of us are lay people; we return to our secular lives after the period of retreat is over.

The question then arises, Are we monks at all? For the most part, we are not. While some Zen practitioners live celibate lives permanently in a monastic setting—and could legitimately be called monks—most leave the monastery. They spend most of their lives out in the world, running Zen temples or Dharma centers among a community, more like parish priests. They marry and have a family of their own. They offer daily services and perform funerals and blessings for the local people. They are more like clergy from the Protestant, Orthodox, Jewish, and Muslim faiths, who live the family life.

In much of the mostly Asian Buddhist world, clergy having families is seen as a serious break with tradition. The unique history that allowed Japanese Zen clergy to marry is an exception in wider Asian Buddhism. For the most part, Buddhist clergy are fully celibate, fully monastic, and in many Buddhist cultures, married clergy are simply not clergy at all.

Personally, I have seen what celibacy can mean. I grew up surrounded by celibate Catholic clergy. There were those that came naturally to celibacy and could make it work for them as a spiritual path. But many priests preached one thing and lived something else. Some had secret mistresses, while others went out cruising the gay areas at night, looking for sex. Many of them were decent and otherwise honest people, suffering from the burden of having no intimacy in their lives. But in addition, there were those many cases that emerged where children were abused by clergy—a situation enabled and exacerbated by the Church's approach toward celibacy and sexuality.

It is due to this experience that I am against enforced celibacy for clergy. It must be a path that is chosen freely, with another path available for those who could serve as priests in another capacity. This is how Japanese Zen Buddhist clergy is structured. Few in Japan stay in the monastery all of their lives. The majority go out into the world with their pastoral mission to serve.

My position is not ideological. It comes from lived experience and actual observation. I have seen far too much to think otherwise. But I do not wish to apply Western values to the great Buddhist cultures of Asia. As an outsider, I am in no position to preach to them. What I am talking about is Zen as it settles right here where I live, in the West. Already it has had to adapt to its new conditions, as it always has done. Not only have we a married clergy, but we have both men and women being ordained and training together in one place.

But it remains a fact that in the West we have a unique cultural moment, and that Buddhism must find a home within that. Quite apart from the matter of celibacy is the matter of practical support for the clergy. How does a Zen priesthood support itself? In Sri Lanka or Thailand, the general population is Buddhist and contributes to supporting full-time monks. But in increasingly secular Japan, Zen priests now often find it impossible to keep going and have to get other work. In the West, the absence of a wider Buddhist population means that many Zen centers struggle to get started and keep going. Those priests that do not complement their clerical activities with other work can become a burden on the small Buddhist communities that support them. I've seen this transpire more than once, where Zen students' *samu*, or work practice, becomes working for free for the full-time Zen teacher: moving furniture, making repairs, or driving them around on personal errands. Far better, I think, if Zen clergy do what many Catholic priests and nuns do: get a job as a teacher or caretaker, expressing their spiritual life by bringing their service into the lived world of the wider community. Not only does this bring bodhisattva practice out into the world, but it also provides financial support for the working priest, supporting their commitment to provide pastoral care and spiritual guidance. How many Catholic priests have you met that teach a class in lay clothes in the morning and put on robes to say Mass in the evening? It is a model that works, and one that should not be dismissed or looked down on by Zen clergy as Buddhism settles in the West. If you have the means to support yourself as a full-time priest without working, that's great—but without widespread adoption of Buddhism by the population at large, it will remain impossible for most. For most priests, it will be necessary to work in the world.

The great Japanese priest Shunryū Suzuki was keenly aware of all these questions when he came to teach Zen in the West.

> American students are not priests and yet not completely laymen. I understand it this way: that you are not priests is an easy matter, but that you are not exactly laymen is more difficult [. . .] You are on your way to discovering some appropriate way of life.[33]

I find these words inspiring. Suzuki Rōshi was well aware that the Japanese way could not be the American way. That would be nothing more than spiritual colonialism. We have had enough of that. He was adamant that this was still the undivided Zen of Master Dōgen but expressed in a new way. What is especially inspiring is that he says a new way must be found in this time and place. And yet I do not agree with him that "you are not priests" (he may, of course, have meant monks instead). Zen priests in the West very much are priests—but by necessity a new expression of the Zen priesthood.

As monks in the past were farmers and cooks, we will be teachers, IT staff, doctors, and bus drivers. We will have families and live just like the rest of the population, sharing their cares and concerns. But we will also be priests—just not a priestly class. We will offer spiritual guidance and correctly inherited ritual support when needed. Some of us may be full-time priests, but the majority will aspire to be bodhisattvas, moving invisibly among the crowded streets, showing ourselves when required, but otherwise no different than everyone else. Manifesting the true spirit of the Mahayana, there will be no aloofness to our Zen practice. It will be familiar, accessible, and ordinary. In the aesthetic of simplicity, it will find endless beauty.

In many ways, it will just be what Zen has always been, and what our great founders, Master Dōgen and Master Keizan, envisaged it to be. The line of our inheritance will continue. It will just be expressed in a new way.

# Catholic Zen

*It is important that we see the differences and*
*incompatibilities and be content that they are so.*
*Maybe given enough time to sit, the oil and the*
*water will become a new and dynamic liquid. But if*
*they sit together and maintain their distinctiveness,*
*that demonstrates the richness of their diversity.*

L IBERAL-LEFT CATHOLICS HAVE BEEN exploring Zen Buddhism
since the 1960s. Many, inspired by the writings of the American
Trappist monk Thomas Merton, have sought out spiritual renewal
in what Zen has to offer. Indeed, the earliest Zen practice group
in Ireland was founded in Tallaght in the 1970s by the Dominican
priest Philip McShane after a trip to Japan. The descendent of that
group still exists in the Dominican Retreat Centre in Tallaght, here
in Ireland, with many of the teachers and leaders there inspired by
the teachings of the Jesuit Robert Kennedy, who is also an empowered Zen priest based in America.

Research by Laurence Cox shows that many of those associated
with the original Tallaght group considered themselves Catholics.
Indeed, Kennedy's religious syncretism has proved attractive to
many in Ireland who grew up in the Catholic tradition but who
wanted something more. From experience, many Irish Zen practitioners still profess to be Christians. Echoing singer and Zen
monk Leonard Cohen's assertion that he was Jewish and did not
need a new religion, they say they do not see Zen as a replacement

religion. The rites and rituals of their Christian faith are perfectly fine, in their view. There is no need to make Zen into their new religious faith.

This position is perfectly coherent and sensible, even though I personally am unable to circle the square of remaining Catholic while also embracing the Zen Buddhist path. Maybe a distinction between Zen and Zen Buddhism is required? The former would be the practice of zazen almost solely, while the latter would involve zazen but also be grounded in the tradition, texts, philosophy, and practices of Zen, as inherited from the generations of ancestors. Having Catholic Mass on his retreats, as Robert Kennedy does, makes Zen a practice lived within the context of Christian Catholicism. But for me personally, there are too many tensions and divergences that need to be glossed over: the doctrines of an immortal personal soul, of an all-powerful and personal God, of the superiority of the spiritual realm over the material realm, of creation progressing toward resurrection and final judgment— these and many other doctrines are simply counter to the Zen Buddhist reading of reality. This is my view.

Zen teachers of the past, eager for followers, might have minimized these differences and incompatibilities when it came to teachings shared outside the central practice of zazen, but these differences cannot easily be ignored in any discussion of substance. Catholics practicing Zen remain Catholic. And they may find in Zen elements that conform to their preexisting faith. This "Catholic Zen" is possible also because it has been encouraged by Asian Zen teachers of the past. Students of Thomas Merton, including many Catholic Zen practitioners, will find well thought-out and articulated reasons why Zen practice is possible and available to Christians.

My one issue with this is that it sometimes feels like religious appropriation. Merton, for example, sees Christianity as "a religion of grace and divine gift," but says that Zen is not easily classified as "a religion" at all. For Merton, Zen is "easily separable from any religious matrix." Zazen can therefore be taken out of its well-established ground and transplanted to where the Christian wants to cultivate it. In reading Merton's *A Christian Looks at Zen*, I could not help but feel that it was engaging in a Christian attempt to take Zen for Christ; and that despite his deep respect for Zen Buddhism, he was involved in an act of appropriation. "It is quite possible for Zen to be adopted and used," he says, to "help us regain a healthy natural balance."[34] Maybe he does not see that there may be an issue worth investigating when asserting that Zen can be "adopted and used" by the Christian faith.

Merton's endeavor is only possible, of course, with a reductive reading of the First Ancestor of Zen's teaching that Zen is beyond doctrine, or "words and letters." But while Zen is beyond words and letters, it also includes them. This might be too fine a point. A zazen-only school might be what ancestors like Dōgen sometimes preached, but in practice they also valued and made use of Buddhist doctrine. Merton suggests that "All religions thus 'meet at the top', and their various theologies and philosophies become irrelevant."[35] And while he is rightly skeptical himself of his suggestion, he does proceed as though this were the case. I am not certain if it clearly struck Merton that he was offering a one-dimensional reading of Zen, dismissing another religion's "theology" while remaining faithful to his own.

In my many interfaith meetings over the years, I have certainly seen the recurring tendency to discount differences in favor of commonalities. Sometimes it is the first move in a strategy of "if we are all the same, then I can take as I wish from yours." The easiest way to co-opt what one wishes from Zen is to deny it the status of a religion. If Zen is a secular practice or philosophy, rather than a religion, then it can be dismantled, and pieces peeled off as desired. Indeed, I wrote to one Christian-oriented meditation center in Dublin querying why they said on their website that Zen is not a religion. I informed them that as a Zen Buddhist priest, I considered Zen to be my religion; that our Zen community was indeed a religious community. Just because Zen's rites and rituals are largely unknown in the West does not make Zen any less of a religion. The stripped-down, almost secular version of Zen that has largely been presented here has given an incorrect impression. I object to having my religion defined by Catholics as not being a religion at all. It is likely that they were entirely unaware of their project, which was in actuality to appropriate parts of the Zen tradition for Catholic practice. This was done by denying Zen Buddhism its status as a religion on par with Catholic Christianity.

In fairness, this Christian meditation center responded well to my point, consequently altering the wording on their website. But the incident illustrated how denying Zen the status of a religion is a double-edged sword. It allows Zen to flow into places it might otherwise be blocked from entering, but at the cost of jettisoning context, history, tradition, and philosophy along the way. The result is a lopsided Zen that rejects Zen's expression in this world, in a particular cultural context and in a particular time and place. It's not that Zen cannot be practiced by Catholics—or people of other religions or no religion—but one should keep in mind that the result will be something other than the teachings we have inherited from the Zen ancestors.

However, doesn't my position contradict itself? If Zen always finds new expressions in new contexts, why is this Christian or Catholic Zen any different? If Zen absorbs some Shinto in Japan and some of the native Bon religion in Tibet, why is it any different when Zen comes West? Is it not natural that it absorbs and coexists happily with Christianity?

Only time will tell. There are compatibilities and incompatibilities. Certainly, Japanese and Tibetan people did not simply expand their Bon and Shinto practices by taking pieces from Buddhist practice and absorbing them. Rather, they became Buddhist in their orientation and outlook. My fear for Catholic Zen is that it misses the radical potential of the Zen teachings and becomes nothing more than another instance of "spiritual colonialism." I am not arguing for some imagined purity and against religious syncretism. Rather, I am saying that the mix must be equitable and right. It must demonstrate compatibility and respect, representing a genuine union, albeit with equitable differences. It should not be a forced marriage or the plundering of one tradition by another, while denying that tradition its integrity to begin with.

It is important that we see the differences and incompatibilities and be content that they are so. Maybe given enough time to sit, the oil and the water will become a new and dynamic liquid. But if they sit together and maintain their distinctiveness, that demonstrates the richness of their diversity. The universalizing impulse can be offset by such peculiarity. Who knows? Maybe, ultimately, we will "meet at the top," in any case.

# Secular Meditation

*Mindfulness is the beginning of a journey that has
no end. If you can, why not take the next step?
If you cannot, then be content in having found
something precious. With its roots in Buddhism,
mindfulness has a great gift to offer. But there is
a whole treasure chest waiting for you to open.*

THE POPULARITY OF SECULAR mindfulness has been possible
because it is meditation stripped of all its religiosity and ritual. It can be practiced in schools and hospitals and workplaces
with no mention of its Buddhist origins. Like Christmas devoid
of Christianity, it can be served up as a value-free and neutral
practice for all. Piggybacking on the universalism of the secular,
it can present itself as innocuous. Its success is based on its very
lack of philosophical grounding or ethical demands. It is *samatha*
(calming meditation) without *vipassana* (meditation bearing an
insight into reality). It therefore lacks the radical potential for
transformation that can come from insight into reality's structure.
Mindfulness is a wonderful and valuable practice, but on its own,
it is not Buddhist practice. Unfortunately, there is the widespread
misconception that Buddhist practice and mindfulness are one
and the same.

Mindfulness is not religious, as it is more concerned with science than it is with religion. Mindfulness practitioners are encouraged by the research and data, which back up their understanding

that meditation changes the structure of the brain and reduces anxiety while improving brain function. The research is fascinating, but it is nothing new to the many generations of devotees who have practiced meditation for centuries. But there is more at play in meditation than the observable science of the brain, of the calming of the nervous system, or of meditation's use in treating various ailments of body and mind. Kōdō Sawaki's assertion that Zen meditation is useless has much to teach us in this regard, challenging the utilitarian drive to put everything into the service of the personal will. Mindfulness may address a variety of symptoms, but to root out the disease of suffering itself requires insight.

The noble eightfold path has eight parts, with mindfulness being one of them. The point of the Buddha Way is to live the entire path, rather than select one part and be done with it.

But please understand that I am in favor of mindfulness practice. It is a good thing to find equilibrium and balance through *samatha* meditation. If that is what you do, then very good. I hope it supports and helps you in your life. But on its own, it is not Buddhism. The beauty of mindfulness is that you do not have to be a Buddhist or practice Buddhism to benefit from it. But as a Buddhist, I believe a deeper, more radical transformation is possible—still waiting to be explored by those that content themselves with mindfulness practice only. If the self stops at the self—if there is no insight into the nature of the self—then awakening cannot take place. The vast boundless ocean still lies before you. The heart of compassion must still blossom. A step has been taken, but there are more ahead. As a Buddhist, this is how I think of mindfulness.

While mindfulness is a wonderful, albeit incomplete, practice, it is distressing how it has been commodified and sold in the marketplace. Mindfulness has become a course to take, a professional qualification to achieve. Mindfulness is taught to soldiers in order to make them more efficient killers; and it is a college course you can take for credit; it is even a smartphone app that you can buy. Mindfulness thus becomes merely a means to an end:

greater efficiency, a happier workforce, a more obedient citizen or employee.

In a multi-religious and multi-belief world, the secular public stage is vital to accommodate difference. It should be the sphere in which education and health care are offered. But the secular world is also the world where market value holds sway. It is the world of professionalism and commodity. It needs the wisdom and faith traditions to counterbalance its instrumentalizing tendencies. Secularism and scientism are arid without a capacity for *not knowing*. Mindfulness may center us where we are. But where are we? What is this?

This is where science ends and where religion and philosophy begin. This is a different kind of knowing. It is a knowing that includes not knowing. Also, it includes reality beyond both limited human knowing and not knowing. This is a reality in which no marketable value is put on anything because everything and everyone is invaluable and has no price. In having no applicable use, everything becomes precious in its own right. Its divinity is seen clearly. Self is transcended and insight is attained. Mindfulness is the beginning of a journey that has no end. If you can, why not take the next step? If you cannot, then be content in having found something precious. With its roots in Buddhism, mindfulness has a great gift to offer. But there is a whole treasure chest waiting for you to open.

# A Coherent Path

*It is best to follow a coherent path. Once you find*
*the right way, commit to it and stick to it. It will*
*have ups and downs, just like any relationship.*
*But if you stick with it, it will bear fruit.*

SOMEONE ONCE TOLD ME that it is important to dig in one place.
This is good advice for anyone interested in Buddhism. It
can be perplexing when faced with the vast variety of Buddhist
schools now teaching in the West: Theravada, Tibetan Buddhism,
Zen in its various forms. Then there are those that follow teachers like Thich Nhat Hanh, many of whom do not see themselves
as Buddhists at all. There are Christians practicing meditation
and practitioners of secular mindfulness. There are non-Buddhist
meditation approaches, from Hinduism and other traditions. And
then there are the new Buddhist movements, many of which con-
flate parts of these older traditions or make up new ones of their
own.

Even within authentic Buddhist meditation traditions, there
is a variety of practices: mantra meditation, visualization, koan
practice, and "just sitting," or objectless meditation. This whole
rich landscape must be confusing for those dipping their toes into
the water for the first time. The question is, where to begin?

Most important is to begin slowly. Do some research and
remain skeptical. There is a great cartoon I saw once of a man
dressed as a Buddhist monk, walking into a room where a woman

is sitting. The woman says, "Come on. You've been to *one* meditation class." And yet there he was, dressed as a monk. The eagerness to be excessive in commitment to practice is common to those starting out on the path. Often, all this enthusiasm is burned up quickly and they move on to the next obsession.

Other times, those I've given initial lay vows to want to throw themselves in even deeper. They begin to present themselves as fully authorized Zen teachers. In this, I need to correct them. Or then there are those that aspire to ordination, and they begin to wear the priest's robes before actually being ordained. In this case, they must be asked to desist until they have received the robes in the ancient rite of ordination itself.

It is important to begin practice slowly and modestly. There is no rush. Things take their own time, quite apart from our wants and desires to speed things up. Do not approach practice as a race that you wish to finish. Practice has no finish. It is endless. With this in mind, there is no need to rush.

To begin, I suggest doing your own research. Have a look online. You might find out that the free Buddhist class with the overly friendly monk is, in fact, offered by a new Buddhist movement with cult-like tendencies. Maybe that monk or nun really should not be wearing Buddhist robes at all. The first class might be free, but gradually you may find that you are being pulled in with an incremental approach that gradually demands more and more money from you, as more and more control is exerted over your life. Maybe there is a history of controversy or abuse connected with the organization you have chosen. How did they deal with that? Did they cooperate with the authorities and put in safeguards and reforms? Or did they try to cover it up and pretend that there was no issue to face up to at all?

This is where my third piece of advice comes in: remain skeptical. You can respect the etiquette and traditions of the Buddhist school you are practicing in, but never stop asking questions and having doubts. In Zen, to find awakening, the student is understood to need great faith, great doubt, and great resolve, in equal measure. Zen Master Boshan (1575–1630) expressed the Zen teaching of doubt like this:

> In Zen practice, the essential point is to rouse doubt. What is this doubt? When you are born, for example, where do you come from? You cannot help but remain in doubt about this. When you die, where do you go? Again, you cannot help but remain in doubt. Since you cannot pierce this barrier of life and death, suddenly doubt will coalesce right before your eyes. Try to put it down, you cannot; try to push it away, you cannot. Eventually you will break through this doubt block and realize what a worthless notion life and death is—ha! As the old worthies said: "Great doubt, great awakening; small doubt, small awakening; no doubt, no awakening."[36]

While I am speaking of conventional doubt, there is also this doubting in a very profound and essential way. One proceeds with faith and determination, because otherwise one cannot keep going with meditation at all. But it is essential to carry this doubt with you also. The Buddha advises us to examine the teachings, and to look for the following qualities: "These things are wholesome; these things are blameless; these things are praised by the wise; these things, if accepted and undertaken, lead to welfare and happiness."[37] On your journey, keep this teaching in mind. Keep an open and questioning mind. Be prepared to trust but be prepared to doubt as well. Doubt alone will lead nowhere. Trust alone will lead nowhere. Both are needed to complement and correct each other.

It is also important to spend many months or years visiting various teachers and trying various approaches to the Dharma. That is what I did. Sit with Theravada groups, Tibetan groups, Zen groups. Go away and come back again. Which path speaks to you? Which teacher appears to you to be teaching the true Dharma, and not just the Dharma that you like or dislike? Finding the right teacher is vital. This person will present themselves as a human being, just like you. If they require veneration or worship, look closely to see if it is ego or actually the conventions of the tradition. Remember that the teacher represents not only him- or herself, but also the Buddha and the entire lineage. That is why they are worthy of respect.

But you are worthy of respect, too. And the respect for the teacher is a respect with limits. Also, what can look like excessive respect may not be that at all. A teacher that appears strict and that is bowed to and held in high esteem may be the kindest and most gentle soul. On the contrary, a teacher that presents themselves as a casual and relaxed person may be nothing of the sort. Take your time. All is revealed with time. Do not jump to conclusions. Appearances can be deceiving. Wait and see.

Some Dharma groups lack a teacher. The problem with such groups is that the Dharma can be distorted in the conversational flow of contesting opinions. A fundamental teaching like *sunyata*, for example, can easily be misunderstood to be the same as nihilism. Or a teaching like Buddha nature can be misrepresented as some kind of immortal soul. In studying sutras and texts, the teacher is there on behalf of the tradition, to prevent free-for-all readings that move away from essential Dharma. Traditionally, it is best to practice with an authentic teacher in a recognized lineage of Buddhism—someone that has received the teachings, face to face, in an unbroken line that stretches back to the Buddha himself. Such a teacher has received Dharma transmission and been empowered to go out and represent the tradition, like their teacher before them, and their teacher's teacher, stretching back to the original teacher himself. That is why we show respect to the teacher even though the teacher remains nothing more than a human being, just like the rest of us. This is the Zen understanding.

Sometimes, other schools of Buddhism see the teacher as something more than human—or at least that is how it appears. It is important to realize that all these schools grew up over many centuries, in specific geographical and cultural contexts. In that slow growth, they developed coherence in their practice and approach.

Now that they have all arrived here in the West together, it can be confusing. It is easy to mix and match, taking a bit of one tradition and practicing it with a bit of another. But some traditions might not be compatible at the same time. That is why it is best to follow a coherent path. Once you find the right way, commit to it and stick to it. It will have ups and downs, just like any relationship. But if you stick with it, it will bear fruit. Do not flit in and out from one Buddhist approach to another. Practice wholeheartedly, with great faith. The coherence of the tradition and its sangha will carry you. Incoherence will only make practice muddled and confused.

The Buddhist teachings we have inherited have a coherence in the Zen tradition, even as they are expressed uniquely in each culture they find themselves in. The internal coherence of practice is what is most important, even as the externals of cultural specificity can vary. In China, Japan, Vietnam, Korea—and here in Ireland, in the West—authentic Zen is practiced in each context. Look less to the accent than to the words being spoken. And look to the silence between those words. This is where the truth is encountered. In its purity, it is unmistakable.

# Right Where You Are

*You don't need to live in the time of the Buddha or Dōgen to practice authentic Zen. You don't need to be in Kyoto or Tibet or someplace in the Himalayas. "The truth originally is all around." The ultimate awakening of Zen is available, right where you are.*

WHEREVER YOU ARE RIGHT now is the place of your awakening. It can be nowhere else, because here you are. This presence is the truth of your existence. We see, as Master Dōgen teaches, that the "immediate Universe exists; it is not awaiting realization."[38] We do not need to "abandon our own seat on the floor, to come and go without purpose through the dusty borders of foreign lands."[39]

The time has long since past when Zen can be seen as an exotic curiosity of the Orient. Yet the myth persists that the Western mind cannot encounter Zen truth. Zen truth is nothing more or less than ordinary truth—everyday experience seen clearly for the first time. You don't need to live in the time of the Buddha or Dōgen to practice authentic Zen. You don't need to be in Kyoto or Tibet or someplace in the Himalayas. "The truth originally is all around."[40] The ultimate awakening of Zen is available, right where you are.

All over Ireland there are sacred trees and holy wells. There are places associated with the spirit world and with the older religion of the land, as well as the many centuries of Christian devotion evident throughout the landscape, with its crumbling stone churches and ancient monastic sites. In isolated places, you can find roadside shrines and trees with strips of material tied to them as offerings. All these practices are more fundamental than any one faith tradition. Many of the holy wells and holy mountains were sacred long before Christianity came here. These are just sacred places: for pre-Christians and Christians, as well as for Buddhists and for everyone else.

In the years to come, there will be places in the landscape sacred to Irish Buddhism. There will be roadside shrines to Jizō Bodhisattva and trees with Buddhist prayers and sutras tied to them. We will sit zazen on top of Cruachán Aigle, as we have already done, and teach the Dharma to the generations to come.

When I see a cairn on an Irish mountain, I see an ancient stupa. And when I see a Saint Brigid's cross woven from reeds and hung above the door, I see the wheel of Dharma. We have inherited traditions, and we do not need to invent new ones. We already have everything we need to express the Dharma in this time and place. The ancient meaning that shines through is greater than any particular religion and is the common heritage of us all.

--------

I'm looking out now at Three Rock Mountain and I see that it is holy. The water that flows in the Dodder River is holy. Bees are humming in the garden and taking nectar from the sacred summer fuchsia. All about is a Pure Land that has never been far or distant. In the midst of our lives, we are in the midst of nirvana. The far distance has been close all along. Look about and see for yourself. Everything you need is here. It is free and priceless. It is your birthright. Use it with wisdom and compassion. See that you are blessed. Cherish this moment, which is your entire and endless life.

# Notes

1. From Uchiyama Kōshō Rōshi, "To you who has decided to become a Zen monk," trans. Muhō, accessed February 19, 2024, https://antaiji.org/archives/eng/kosho-uchiyama-monk.shtml.

2. From Eihei Dōgen, "Fukan-zagengi" in Gudo Nishijima and Chodo Cross, trans., *Master Dogen's Shobogenzo, Book 1* (Woods Hole, MA: Windbell Publications, 1994), 241.

3. From Shitou Xiqian, "Song of the Grass-Roof Hermitage," trans. Taigen Dan Leighton and Kazuaki Tanahashi, in Taigen Dan Leighton, *Cultivating the Empty Field* (Boston: Tuttle Publishing, 2000), 72–73.

4. From Shitou Xiqian, "Song of the Grass-Roof Hermitage."

5. Pierre Taïgu Turlur, *Apprivoiser l'éveil: A travers les dix images du buffles* (Paris: Éditions Albin Michel, 2018).

6. This and the other quotations here are from Kieran Kavanaugh and Otilio Rodriguez, trans., *The Collected Works of St. John of the Cross*, rev. ed. (Washington, DC: ICS Publications, 1991).

7. From Eihei Dōgen, "Genjōkōan," in Shohaku Okumura, trans., *Realizing Genjōkōan* (Somerville, MA: Wisdom Publications, 2010), 3.

8. Layman Ho-on appears throughout Master Dōgen's *Shobogenzo*. The quote here comes from "Jinzū."

9. From Red Pine, trans., *The Platform Sutra: The Zen Teaching of Hui-neng* (Berkeley, CA: Counterpoint, 2006), 37.

10. From Eihei Dōgen, "Fukan-zagengi," in Gudo Nishijima and Chodo Cross, trans., *Master Dogen's Shobogenzo, Book 1* (Woods Hole, MA: Windbell Publications, 1994), 241.

11. This is the same name as my own teacher, Pierre Taigu Turlur (b. 1964).

12. From John Stevens, trans., *One Robe, One Bowl: The Zen Poetry of Ryōkan* (Boston: Weatherhill, 2006).

13. This poem/teaching is my own. It was, however, read by Rev. Gengo Akiba Rōshi once to his sangha.

14. See Case 29 in Kōun Yamada, trans. and commentary, *The Gateless Gate* (Somerville, MA: Wisdom Publications, 2004), 143–47.

15. *Tendoku*, or ritual reading, involves shouting the title and volume number of the sutra, then quickly flipping through the sutra book itself.

16. From MN 63, in Bhikkhu Bodhi, ed. and trans., *In the Buddha's Words: An Anthology of Discourses from the Pāli Canon* (Somerville, MA: Wisdom Publications, 2005), 232.

17. *Shikantaza* is the style of objectless meditation we do when we say we are doing zazen. It is zazen as taught by Master Dōgen, in the context of the Sōtō Zen school.

18. From Juan Mascaro, trans., *The Dhammapada: The Path of Perfection* (New York: Penguin Books, 1973), verse 337.

19. From Eihei Dōgen, "Sansuigyo," in Gudo Nishijima and Chodo Cross, trans., *Master Dogen's Shobogenzo, Book 1* (Woods Hole, MA: Windbell Publications, 1994), 172–73.

20. *Shobogenzo, Book 1*, 176.

21. *Shobogenzo, Book 1*, 177–78.

22. From Eihei Dōgen, "Instructions for the Tenzo," in Taigen Daniel Leighton and Shohaku Okumura, trans., *Dōgen's Pure Standards for the Zen Community: A Translation of Eihei Shingi* (Albany, NY: State University of New York Press, 1996), 37.

23. From Gil Fronsdal, trans., *The Dhammapada: A New Translation of the Buddhist Classic with Annotations* (Boston: Shambhala Publications, 2006), 1.

24. Muiris Ó Súilleabháin, *Fiche Bliain ag Fás* (An Sagart Maynooth, 1933). Also available in English as Maurice O'Sullivan, *Twenty Years A-Growing* (New York: Oxford University Press, 1983).

25. From Keizan Zenji, *The Record of Transmitting the Light: Zen Master Keizan's Denkoroku*, trans. Francis Dojun Cook (Somerville, MA: Wisdom Publications, 2003), 29.

26. See note 15.

27. From Eihei Dōgen, "Genjōkōan," trans. Shohaku Okumura in *Realizing Genjokoan: The Key to Dogen's Shobogenzo* (Somerville, MA: Wisdom Publications, 2010), 2–3.

28. From Eihei Dōgen, "Uji," in Gudo Nishijima and Chodo Cross, trans., *Master Dogen's Shobogenzo, Book 1* (Woods Hole, MA: Windbell Publications, 1994), 111.

29. From "Awakening of Faith in the Mahayana," quoted in Thomas Berry, *Religions of India: Hinduism, Yoga, Buddhism* (New York: Columbia University Press, 1996), 170.

30. From Anzan Hoshin Roshi and Yasuda Joshu Dainen Roshi, trans., "Zenki: Complete Activity 全機," accessed January 23, 2024, https://wwzc.org/dharma-text/zenki-complete-activity-%E5%85%A8%E6%A9%9F.

31. From Eihei Dōgen, "One Bright Pearl," in Kazuaki Tanahashi, ed., *Treasury of the True Dharma Eye*, vol. 1 (Boston: Shambhala Publications, 2010), 37. In this essay, Dōgen explores Case 3 in the *Blue Cliff Record*, "Master Ma Is Unwell."

32. To receive Dharma transmission is to receive the power to ordain others and pass on the lineage in the Zen tradition. With Dharma transmission, you operate as an independent priest and teacher.

33. Shunryū Suzuki, *Zen Mind, Beginner's Mind: Informal Talks on Zen Meditation and Practice* (New York: Weatherhill, 1970), 133.

34. The quotes from Thomas Merton come from his essay "A Christian Looks at Zen," from his book *Zen and the Birds of Appetite* (New York: New Directions, 1968), 33–58.

35. "A Christian Looks at Zen," 43.

36. Jeff Shore, trans., *Great Doubt: Practicing Zen in the World*, by Boshan (Somerville, MA: Wisdom Publications, 2016), 3.

37. From AN 3:65, in Bhikkhu Bodhi, ed. and trans., *The Buddha's Teachings on Social and Communal Harmony* (Somerville, MA: Wisdom Publications, 2016), 22.

38. From Eihei Dōgen, "Mind Here and Now Is Buddha," in *Master Dogen's Shobogenzo, Book 1*, 52.

39. From "Fukan-zazengi," in *Master Dogen's Shobogenzo, Book 1*, 282.

40. From "Fukan-zazengi," in *Master Dogen's Shobogenzo, Book 1*, 279.

# Recommended Reading

Bancroft, Anne. *Zen: Direct Pointing to Reality*. London: Thames and Hudson, 1979.

Berry, Thomas. *Religions of India: Hinduism, Yoga, Buddhism*. New York: Columbia University Press, 1996.

Bodhi, Bhikkhu, trans. *The Buddha's Teachings on Social and Communal Harmony: An Anthology of Discourses from the Pāli Canon*. Somerville, MA: Wisdom Publications, 2016.

Bodhi, Bhikkhu, trans. *In the Buddha's Words: An Anthology of Discourses from the Pāli Canon*. Somerville, MA: Wisdom, 2005.

Cleary, Thomas, and J. C. Cleary, trans. *The Blue Cliff Record*. Boston: Shambhala Publications, 2005.

Connelly, Ben. *Inside the Grass Hut: Living Shitou's Classic Zen Poem*. Somerville, MA: Wisdom Publications, 2014.

Cook, Francis Dojun, trans. *The Record of Transmitting the Light: Zen Master Keizan's Denkoroku*. Somerville, MA: Wisdom Publications, 2003.

Cox, Laurence. *Buddhism in Ireland: From the Celts to the Counter-Culture and Beyond*. Sheffield, UK: Equinox Publishing, 2013.

Hanh, Thich Nhat. *The Heart of Understanding: Commentaries on the Prajnaparamita Heart Sutra*. Berkeley, CA: Parallax Press, 1988.

Kavanaugh, Kieran, and Otilio Rodriguez, trans. *The Collected Works of St. John of the Cross*, rev. ed. Washington, DC: ICS Publications, 1991.

Kodo, Myozan (AKA Ian Kilroy). *Three Rock Sonnets*. Dublin: Zen Buddhism Ireland, 2014.

Kodo, Myozan (AKA Ian Kilroy). *Songs from the Denkoruku*. Dublin: Zen Buddhism Ireland, 2014.

Leighton, Taigen Dan. *Cultivating the Empty Field: The Silent Illumination of Zen Buddhist Master Hongzhi*. Rutland, VT: Tuttle Publishing, 2000.

Leighton, Taigen Daniel, and Shohaku Okumura, trans. *Dōgen's Pure Standards for the Zen Community: A Translation of Eihei Shingi*. Albany, NY: State University of New York Press, 1996.

Mascaro, Juan, trans. *The Dhammapada: The Path of Perfection*. New York: Penguin Books, 1973.

Merton, Thomas. *Zen and the Birds of Appetite*. New York: New Directions, 1968.

Nishijima, Gudo, and Chodo Cross, trans. *Master Dogen's Shobogenzo*. 4 vols. Woods Hole, MA: Windbell Publications, 1994.

Okumura, Shohaku. *Realizing Genjōkōan: The Key to Dōgen's Shōbōgenzō*. Somerville, MA: Wisdom Publications, 2010.

Ó Súilleabháin, Muiris. *Fiche Bliain ag Fás*. Dublin: An Sagart Maynooth, 1933.

O'Sullivan, Maurice. *Twenty Years A-Growing*. New York: Oxford University Press, 1983.

Pine, Red, trans. *The Zen Teaching of Bodhidharma*. New York: North Point Press, 1989.

Shore, Jeff, trans. *Great Doubt: Practicing Zen in the World*. By Boshan. Somerville, MA: Wisdom Publications, 2016.

Stevens, John, trans. *One Robe, One Bowl: The Zen Poetry of Ryōkan*. Boston: Weatherhill, 2006.

Suzuki, Shunryū. *Zen Mind, Beginner's Mind: Informal Talks on Zen Meditation and Practice*. New York: Weatherhill, 1970.

Taïgu Turlur, Pierre. *Apprivoiser L'Éveil*. Paris: Editions Albin Michel, 2018.

Tanahashi, Kazuaki, ed. *Treasury of the True Dharma Eye: Zen Master Dogen's Shobo Genzo*. Boston: Shambhala Publications, 2010.

Uchiyama, Kosho, and Shohaku Okumura. *The Zen Teaching of Homeless Kodo*. Edited by Molly Delight Whitehead. Somerville, MA: Wisdom Publications, 2014.

Yamada, Kōun. *The Gateless Gate: The Classic Book of Zen Koans.* Somerville, MA: Wisdom Publications, 2004.

# Index

## M

Maha Maya, 186
Mahakashyapa, 170
Mahapajapati, 186
Mahaparinirvana Sutra, 172
Mahayana Buddhism, 90, 135, 171, 267
makyō, 62
Mary (mother of Jesus), 175
material realm, 19, 28, 110–11, 148, 150, 270. *See also* body; form
McShane, Philip, 269
meditation, 8–9, 15–16, 23, 77
  posture, 28–29, 73, 227
  samatha, 29
  secular, 91, 275–77
  shikantaza, 118–20, 288n17
  states of (*jhanas*), 60–61
  *See also* samatha; zazen
merit, 108, 184, 208
Merton, Thomas, 269
Middle Way, 71, 75, 152
Midsummer Eve, 182
mind, 9, 21, 28, 34, 43, 51, 62, 91, 94, 104, 110, 118, 124, 127
  body-, 15
  dualistic, 167, 182–83
  nondiscriminating, 148–50
  ordinary, 64–65, 79, 147, 180, 188
  parental, 67–70
  psychological treatment of, 276
  three attitudes of, 148–50
  unconscious, 128
  *See also* consciousness; ordinary mind
mindfulness, 28–29, 232, 275–77, 279
monasticism, 30, 52, 99, 104, 115, 144, 148, 152, 185, 264–65, 266–67

offering to, 208
unsui (novice monks), 191–92
"warrior monks," 131
*See also* ordination; Vinaya
mono no aware, 37
Mount Brandon (Cnoc Bréanainn), 45–47
*Mumonkan*, 64
Myōzen, 5

## N

Nagarjuna, 102, 134–35
*Navigatio Sancti Brendani Abbatis (Voyage of Saint Brendan the Abbot)*, 45–46
Nepal, 173–74
Newton, Isaac, 138
nihilism, 103, 171, 282
nirvana, 133, 135, 150, 171–72, 286
Nishijima Rōshi, 186, 258
noble eightfold path, 91, 114, 116, 276
nonthought, 60
no-self, 20–21, 54–56, 131, 133, 134, 277

## O

offerings, 3, 51, 105–8, 125, 128, 170, 175, 201, 207–10. *See also* generosity (*dana*)
O'Halloran, Maura, 64, 260–61
opinions, 97–100, 141, 282
Opus Dei, 71
ordination, 187, 188–89, 211–14, 216–17, 229, 258, 280, 289n32. *See also* monasticism
Orientalism, 63–64

# About the Author

 Myozan Ian Kilroy is a Sōtō Zen Buddhist priest and a Dharma heir of Taïgu Turlur Rōshi, in the lineage of Nishijima Rōshi and Rempō Niwa Zenji. Based in Ireland, he leads the Zen Buddhism Ireland sangha, where he is the founding teacher and abbot at Dublin Zen Centre. Myozan is the founding president of the Irish Buddhist Union and represents Buddhism on the Dublin City Interfaith Forum. He is also a registered teacher with the Soto Zen Buddhist Association.

Myozan works in the school of media at the Technological University Dublin. Before that, he was a journalist for many years, working with the *Sunday Tribune*, *Magill Magazine*, the *Irish Times*, and the *Irish Examiner*, where he was arts editor. He still contributes regularly to the *Irish Times* and has contributed to the *Ecumenical Review* on religious matters.

Active in campaigning for greater religious diversity in Ireland, Myozan advocates for reforming religious education curricula and extending chaplaincy services to other faiths. He has represented Buddhism on national radio and television, in advisory panels for the Taoiseach (Ireland's prime minister), and in the National Day of Commemoration in Ireland, which remembers all Irish people that have died in past wars.

Originally from Galway, Myozan now lives in Dublin with his wife, Isabelle, their sons, Arthur and Éamonn, and their cat, Rocky Road. Visit zenbuddhism.ie to find out more.

# What to Read Next from Wisdom Publications

**Inside the Grass Hut**
*Living Shitou's Classic Poem*
Ben Connelly

Shitou Xiqian's "Song of the Grass Roof Hermitage" is a remarkably accessible work of profound depth; in thirty-two lines Shitou expresses the breadth of the entire Buddhist tradition with simple, vivid imagery. Ben Connelly's *Inside the Grass Hut* unpacks the timeless poem and applies it to contemporary life.

**The Complete Illustrated Guide to Zen**
Seigaku Amato

"I loved this book and smiled the whole way through. But don't be fooled by its whimsy! There's a wealth of experience, knowledge, and devotion behind these illustrations. This book is a perfect guide for a beginning Zen student and makes a delicious snack for the more advanced practitioner."—Gesshin Greenwood, author of *Bow First, Ask Questions Later*

**Pure Heart, Enlightened Mind**
*The Life and Letters of an Irish Zen Saint*
Maura O'Halloran

"A grand adventure."—*New York Times* Book Review

**Mind Sky**
*Zen Teaching on Living and Dying*
Jakusho Kwong
Foreword by Shohaku Okumura

"This is a wise and beautiful book of heart teachings by a great
Soto Zen teacher, Jakusho Kwong-roshi, who shows the way to open
infinite Dharma doors through Zen practice."—Roshi Joan Halifax,
abbot, Upaya Zen Center, author of *Standing at the Edge* and *Being
with Dying*

**Bow First, Ask Questions Later**
*Ordination, Love, and Monastic Zen in Japan*
Gesshin Claire Greenwood

What happens when a free-spirited, modern American girl goes on
a spiritual quest into structured, traditional Japanese Zen life?

# About Wisdom Publications

Wisdom Publications is the leading publisher of classic and contemporary Buddhist books and practical works on mindfulness. To learn more about us or to explore our other books, please visit our website at wisdom.org or contact us at the address below.

Wisdom Publications
132 Perry Street
New York, NY 10014 USA

We are a 501(c)(3) organization, and donations in support of our mission are tax deductible.

Wisdom Publications is affiliated with the Foundation for the Preservation of the Mahayana Tradition (FPMT).